Twelve Powers in You

Twelve Powers in You

David Williamson, D.Min.

Gay Lynn Williamson, M.A. Psy.

Robert H. Knapp, M.D.

Health Communications, Inc.
Deerfield Beach, Florida

www.hci-online.com

The teachings in this book should not be interpreted as a substitute for proper medical treatment. See a physician when you have questions about any aspect of your health or when you need medical care. Use this book's information about the Twelve Powers in conjunction with the most effective methods that modern medicine and all professional health-care providers have to offer.

Library of Congress Cataloging-in-Publication Data
Williamson, David
    Twelve powers in you / David Williamson, Gay Lynn Williamson, Robert H. Knapp.
        p.   cm.
    Includes bibliographical references.
    ISBN 1-55874-746-X (trade pbk.)
    1. Unity School of Christianity—Doctrines. I. Williamson, Gay, 1955-II. Knapp, Robert H.; 1946-III. Title.

BX9890.U55 W55 2000
289.9'7—dc21
                                                        99-057245

Publisher: Health Communications, Inc.
                3201 S.W. 15th Street
                Deerfield Beach, FL 33442-8190

Cover design by Larissa Hise
Inside book design by Dawn Grove
Anatomical illustrations by Robert Knapp
Author photo credit by David Hall

CONTENTS

ACKNOWLEDGMENTS

We'd like to express our appreciation to the following people:

Charles Fillmore, pioneer of the Twelve Powers insights and system, who always taught that we should be open to change and further insights. We deeply appreciate his passionate exploration as we have joined him on the quest for wholeness. We believe Mr. Fillmore would wholeheartedly approve of ongoing research and development of his original ideas in the light of modern science, as he had such an investigative and open mind himself.

Unity of Hollywood, Florida and the Mark-Age organization for supporting the three of us in the research and writing of this book, and also creating the companion video series by the same title.

Irv Rudley, for the love and passion he poured into professionally creating the companion video. Many of the graphics in this book were supplied by the video, courtesy of Creative Films and Amnesia Video. With the dynamic help and assistance of Bruce Solomon, he helped to design the book, video and audiotape covers. David Hall also shared his talents as a professional photographer to add a number of pictures in this book.

Peter Vegso, Christine Belleris, Matthew Diener, Allison Janse and Susan Tobias of Health Communications, Inc., for believing in this book and seeing it through to publication. Thanks also to Larissa Hise and Dawn Grove in HCI's art department for their marvelous design work.

From David:

Gay Lynn, for holding the vision of a book and video series that would bring the Twelve Powers to a world audience.

Vera Dawson Tait, Carol Marie Guental and Ed Rabel—teachers at Unity School—who originally presented the Twelve Powers to me.

Robert Knapp, for inspiring me to think in new ways about the Twelve Powers as a holistic—spirit, mind and body—system after hearing him talk at a Unity retreat in Boca Raton, Florida in 1981.

Ed Rabel, for his fine tape series of talks on the Twelve Powers and the use of some of Ed's affirmations, collected by James Sherman.

The congregation of Detroit Unity Temple, where I was Senior Minister for eighteen years and where I first taught "The Year of Power" for twelve months in 1991. That formed the basis for this book.

My son, Keith Williamson, graphic designer for the drawings in the Understanding chapter. These drawings are adapted from ideas in the book, *Human Be-ing*, by William Pietsch.

Sandra du Monde, Julie Johnson, Mamie Rader, Kay C. Adams and all those who help with the work of The Transformative Center, an alternative Unity ministry that produced the companion videos and the "52 Weekly Lessons" for "The Year of Power."

Dr. Tom and Esther Hopper for reading this book and making valuable suggestions.

Judy Trutwin, librarian at Broward County Library, for her research assistance.

William Earle Cameron, for his Twelve Powers research help.

From David and Gay Lynn:

The spiritual family at Unity of Hollywood, for the love and generous support countless people have given from the depths of their souls to make this project a success. They rightfully feel a sense of ownership in what has been created. Special love and gratitude to our magnificent staff: Cindie Campbell (who administers with love and care, and who keeps all the details in divine order), Julie Johnson, Kay C. Adams, Mamie Rador, Maran Banta and Jennifer Stella.

The Board of Directors of Unity of Hollywood for their unstinting care and support of turning a year-long program in 1998 into resources that will reach around the world from their church.

Team ministry of Unity of Hollywood and all those who have volunteered to make this book and companion video series come to life. Many volunteered to work on the sets, act in the mini-dramas and prepare food for the video crews.

The Prosperity for Life group of Unity of Hollywood who called David, Gay Lynn and Robert for months with an affirmative prayer for success with the *Twelve Powers in You* book and videos.

From Gay Lynn:

David and Robert, for all the joy in working with two brilliant and heartfelt men. You are God's gift to me.

All of my friends and colleagues in ministry, psychotherapy and publishing, who have believed in and encouraged me.

All the counselors and friends who granted permission for the use of their stories of overcoming in this book.

The two great spiritual families who are my dear friends and go with me on the quest: Unity of Hollywood and Detroit Unity. Your love and support are a part of the greatest treasures in my life.

My family and children who have been a continuous source of love and inspiration.

From Robert:

Nada-Yolanda, my beloved spiritual teacher and dearest friend, whose inspiration, guidance, perseverance and faith have been the sustaining power behind all my Twelve Powers projects. And El Morya/Mark, the cofounder of Mark-Age, also my beloved teacher.

Mark-Age staff and associates around the world, for their love, unflagging support and friendship.

Deborah Jacobs and Janet Thiemermann, for their uplifting songs and music, as well as being dear friends.

David and Gay Lynn, who amaze me with their knowledge, compassion, insight, energy, wisdom, optimism and special talents in creating all parts of our Twelve Powers in You program. They are dear friends and spiritual family.

All the people at Unity of Hollywood, who have embraced me and made me feel such a special part of their loving community throughout 1999.

INTRODUCTION

There is a story of a man who sells all that he owns to buy a field where he has found a pearl of great price. Perhaps you are like that person: searching, maybe in trouble, having challenges, wanting to feel more empowered, wise and guided. Are you looking in many different fields, relationships and jobs, or to other people, to find the pearl? Although you may have looked "out there" for a long time—searching for someone or something for your answers, your pearl, your power—the pearl is not "out there."

The fertile field and the pearl of great price are not outside of you. You are the field. The pearl is within you. The pearl is your true Self, your spiritual Self, that inner core of you that knows and has the pearls of wisdom. As you read this book and look within yourself, you will find the pearl of great price and with it Twelve Powers that will totally transform your life. The pearl is you. The Twelve Powers are within you.

You will also discover that each of your Twelve Powers externalizes and expresses in your physical body as a particular organ or system. In other words, your physical body has a cosmic blueprint. Your Twelve Powers and your physical body are not separate, disconnected aspects of your whole being. Rather, they are like two sides of one coin. For example, your power of love flows through and expresses as your heart and circulatory system.

POWER	PHYSICAL CENTER
Faith	Cerebrum of brain
Love	Heart & circulatory system
Strength	Spinal cord & nerves
Wisdom	Endocrine system
Power	Larynx, muscles & limbs
Imagination	Thalamus of brain
Understanding	Five physical senses
Will	Respiratory system
Order	Digestive system, skin & bones
Enthusiasm	Hypothalamus & medulla oblongata
Release	Colon & urinary system
Life	Reproductive system

How do you lay hold of these twelve innate powers? How do you utilize them to heal your mind, soul and body? Follow our lead. As a minister, psychotherapist and medical doctor, we have spent most of our lives exploring the field and terrain of our whole beings. We bring a comprehensive and unique blend of skills to help you explore and develop the Twelve Powers that are within you and every person. We have helped thousands of people to access these dynamic powers, and to use them in a balanced and harmonious way, bringing them healing, love and success.

In a whole-brain learning approach, we present a wide array of stories, visualizations, affirmations, graphics, self-examination exercises, medical illustrations and descriptions of your Twelve Powers. These learning methods stimulate and engage both sides of the brain, helping you to easily make these Powers a vital part of your life. Your rightful heritage is to live empowered. Live consciously from that place of power every day. Take the first step with us as a team of experts, and know you are a person of great power!

WHY TWELVE POWERS?

You may ask, "Why are there Twelve Powers?" The number twelve is often associated with fulfillment or wholeness. Following are a few examples of twelve being a number of completion:

- Twelve months of the year
- Twelve inches to a foot
- Twelve days of Christmas
- Twelve grades in school
- Twelve signs of the zodiac
- Twelve steps in Alcoholics Anonymous

In the Judeo/Christian tradition, the number twelve has played a prominent role. In the biblical Book of Genesis, Jacob had twelve sons whose descendants became the twelve tribes of Israel. Jesus had twelve major disciples, each of whom represented one of the Twelve Powers. (See Appendix A.) In the Book of Revelation, the tree of life has twelve fruits and the New Jerusalem has twelve gates.

In the East, Chinese acupuncture speaks of twelve major meridians that carry vital energy or chi to the whole body. Each meridian is said to carry a different type of energy or power. These meridians encircle and encompass the entire physical form.

Throughout the world, twelve is not the only number that symbolizes fulfillment, but it certainly is one of the most used to represent completion and wholeness.

SEVEN CHAKRAS

The concept that each of our Twelve Powers expresses in specific parts of our body also is found in Eastern religions such as Hinduism and Buddhism. However, rather than talking about physical organs, these Eastern teachings describe seven chakras or energy centers. Each center is said to radiate a particular power or aspect of consciousness. So, love flows through the heart chakra, power expresses via the throat center, and creative life force manifests via the regenerative chakra. In the West, the Hopi Indians speak of comparable energy centers. In the chart on page xviii, you can see how the Twelve Powers express via the seven chakras as particular organs and systems in the physical body.

AS ABOVE, SO BELOW

When you use any of your Twelve Powers in a balanced, healthy and harmonious way, the corresponding physical organ reflects and manifests this balance and harmony. This is an expression of the principle, "As above, so below. As within, so without." If you are loving, caring and compassionate—if you express your power of love in a masterful way—then your heart and circulatory system are vibrantly healthy. Here, then, is the key to the health, well-being and balance of your whole body. Develop all of your Powers. Express them in loving, wise, balanced and masterful ways. Then your Twelve Powers will energize, vitalize and harmonize all of your body organs.

What happens if you do get sick? You can use your understanding of the Twelve Powers to go to the source of your disorder—to focus on the corresponding Power whose imbalance may be causing, or contributing to, your physical disease. For example, when people develop coronary heart disease, they can concentrate on their power of love, on "opening their heart." Indeed, scientific studies have shown that individuals who are hostile, critical, suspicious, lonely or isolated have a greatly increased incidence of coronary artery disease. However, when they open their heart, become more loving and feel more connected with others, their hearts often are healed and restored to normal functioning.

This does not mean we are to ignore physical causes and treatments of a disease. To the contrary, always take a holistic approach, using the best of all effective physical, psychological and spiritual therapies. If symptoms persist or are serious, always consult with a professional health-care provider. However, in treating our imbalances, we are most powerful when we heal from the inside out—when we use our Twelve Powers to harmonize our mind, soul and body.

HISTORY OF TWELVE POWERS

The concept of the Twelve Powers was first made popular by Charles Fillmore. He and his wife Myrtle were cofounders of Unity School in the late 1800s. The Fillmores initially learned about the Twelve Powers from Emma Curtis Hopkins, the teacher of teachers in the so-called New Thought movement at the turn of the century. Mr. Fillmore correlated the Twelve Powers with corresponding locations or centers in the physical body. He often called our powers "mind faculties." They are presented in all his books, particularly in *Christian Healing* (1909) and *The Twelve Powers of Man* (1930), which was reprinted in 1999 as *The Twelve Powers*.

Building on the solid foundation and framework that Fillmore developed, we have added our own insights and descriptions based on our long, in-depth study of the Twelve Powers. We have updated and adapted some of Fillmore's correlations of the Twelve Powers with particular body organs and systems, based on Dr. Knapp's extensive medical research since 1974. (See Appendix B.)

TOOLS OF TRANSFORMATION

To help you develop your Twelve Powers, we have devoted one chapter to each of them. Within each chapter are three sections called Spirit, Soul and Body.

Under the Spirit heading, David Williamson draws upon his experience as a Unity minister since 1960 to describe each Power, to show how to improve your expression of each Power, and to help you avoid common pitfalls and misuses of the Power.

In the Soul section, David's wife, Gay Lynn Williamson, shares powerful stories of personal change and healing transformation. She is a Unity minister and psychotherapist. The word "soul" is derived from the Greek word "psyche," which is the root word of psychology. So our soul carries the stories of our lives, the happiness and the tears, the overcomings and the downfalls. Gay Lynn's true stories will touch your soul and invite changes to emerge from within you.

In the Body section, Robert Knapp, M.D., reveals how each Power externalizes as a particular organ or system in the body. Case histories show how others have used their Powers to heal their mind and body, and how you can do the same. In the Body sections, you will come to a new realization of how your entire body functions, and how it truly has a cosmic design. You will see a blending of science and spirituality, of medicine and mysticism.

Throughout this book, names of people in stories and case histories have been changed to protect the privacy of these individuals.

Each chapter has a unique, guided visualization written by

Dr. Robert that you can use to anchor and refine each Power. Self-examination exercises are included as another tool. Each chapter ends with approximately thirty affirmations that will help you to build in that Power. If you wish, you can concentrate on one Power each month, using one affirmation for each day of the month. Or, you can use one or more of these affirmations at any time that you choose.

STEP INTO YOUR FIELD OF POWER!

You are the pearl and the field is fertile within you. Each of your Twelve Powers is waiting to be more fully expressed to heal your mind, soul and body. Begin today to fill your life with love and wisdom, and to reveal more of your true Self. Follow these pages and take a magnificent journey to a new level of vitality, joy, peace, prosperity and happiness that await you.

You are a person of great power! Accept and step into your field of power today!

TWELVE POWERS IN YOU

POWER	CHAKRA	ORGAN/SYSTEM
Faith	Crown	Cerebrum of the brain: central computer
Love	Heart	Circulatory system: heart, liver, spleen, blood
Strength	Spine as conduit	Spinal cord & nerves: communication system
Wisdom	Third eye	Pituitary gland & all other endocrine glands
Power	Throat	Larynx, muscular system & limbs
Imagination	Third eye	Thalamus of brain & psychic senses (ESP)
Understanding	Five minor centers	Five physical senses & conscious analysis
Will	Throat	Respiratory system: nose, bronchi, lungs, trachea
Order	Solar plexus	Digestive system, skeletal system & bones
Enthusiasm	Third eye	Hypothalamus & medulla oblongata
Release	Sacral	Colon & urinary system: kidneys, ureters, bladder
Life	Regenerative	Male or female reproductive system

1
The Power of FAITH

FAITH

FAITH is my perceiving power of mind, my insight. Faith is a spiritual power, but it is not confined to religion. I use my faith faculty all the time when I give mental attention to something. Jesus said, "Have faith in God." That is, I focus my mental attention on the good, on the limitless flow of renewing energy. Faith externalizes in my physical body as the cerebrum of my brain.

Spirit

FAITH IS THE FOUNDATION

David. Faith is a power that we all have. Charles Fillmore, the American mystic and cofounder of Unity School, said, "Faith is the perceiving power of our mind." Faith is insight. It is the ability to see with our thoughts. We often think of faith only in relation to our religious experience. We talk about the "Catholic faith" or the "Islamic faith." These are religions, but faith is a power we all have, whether we are part of an organized religion or not.

We can clearly see that if we have faith in ourselves, we will accomplish more than if we don't believe in ourselves and our abilities. If we have self-doubt, we look on ourselves as being inferior. If our faith in ourselves is strong, we then perceive our true worth, our value.

Faith often has been called the rock or the foundation on which we stand. There is a wonderful dialogue in the Bible between Jesus and Simon, whom Jesus called Peter which means "rock." Jesus asked his disciples who they thought he was. Simon replied, "You are the Son of the living God." (Matthew 16:16) That is, he recognized and perceived Jesus' true Self, his inner essence. Jesus realized that Simon had this insight, so he said to him, "You are Peter and upon this rock I will build."

In like manner, we ask ourselves the core question, "Who am I?" In response, via insight and faith, we perceive that we are a Son or Daughter of our Father-Mother Parent. We are a child of the living God. We have the spark of divinity within us. We may call this eternal part of ourselves the Christ, the I Am, the Buddha nature, the Atman, the transpersonal Self, the Spirit within us.

Here then is the foundation of life: To see the truth about ourselves, to perceive that we are the expression of the Creative Life Force. This is the rock on which we build, the truth on which we stand. We are to have rock-solid faith that we are good because we are of God, that in this presence and power we live and move and have our being.

FOCUS YOUR FAITH ON THE GOOD

Fear often is perceived as the opposite of faith. However, there is no opposite; there is only how we use our faith faculty. Thus, we may put our faith in fear, but that does not mean that fear is the opposite of faith. Worry, dread, apprehension, expecting the worst—all are uses of our faith. That is, we are "looking" or "asking" for trouble, rejection, a bad outcome. Then we may say, "I knew it! I could see it coming." This is fear—faith in fear.

When we focus our faith power on expectations of health, success and finding solutions, we are more likely to bring these about. Our positive use of faith empowers us to express greater peace, love, abundance and harmony. Faith is the ability we have to perceive the reality of God's kingdom of good, despite seeming evidence to the contrary. "Faith is the assurance of things hoped for, the conviction of things not seen." (Hebrews 11:1) Our positive use of faith assures us that we have the power to do the seemingly impossible. This use of faith draws to us our heart's desire, right out of the invisible spiritual potential of all possibilities of good.

We activate our faith power in the highest and greatest way by saying "Yes" to God. We have positive faith that unlimited good is being manifested in our life and all life. As Jesus taught, "If you have faith as a grain of a mustard seed . . . nothing will be impossible to you." (Matthew 17:20) Faith is our ability to draw our good from the invisible realm. That is why we say, "You will see it when you believe it."

Mahatma Gandhi said, "It is faith that steers us through stormy seas, faith that moves mountains and faith that jumps across the ocean. That faith is nothing but a living, wide-awake consciousness of God within." When Gautama Buddha was asked to describe himself, he said simply, "I am awake." Via faith, he had awakened to and perceived the light within him and all life. By insight, he had become enlightened. And he believed and taught that everyone like-wise could wake up and see the light of their being.

Faith is the measure of our capacity to receive Spirit's good light and love. "According to your faith let it be done to you." (Matthew 9:29) Our faith can be likened unto a measuring cup that we hold out to be filled. We can hold out a cup, a bucket, a barrel, a tank truck, a tanker ship. God-the-Good is unlimited, willing to abundantly pour forth through us.

WHAT AM I ASKING FOR?

"Whatever you ask in prayer, you will receive, if you have faith." (Matthew 21:22 NRSV) Jesus says: "Ask and it shall be given you." (Matthew 7:7)

How, then, do we "ask"? Do we plead? Beg? Bargain? Make formal petitions? Use the right "religious" language? Pray using the correct names for God and the right formulas that please God? What understanding can we have of the "asking" process that is based on a fulfillment of a mental law, which brings our thoughts into harmony with the energy flow that is God's will of absolute good for us and for all? Let's look at how we often use the word "ask" and this will give us an important insight into how we place ourselves in the position to receive or exclude our good. We receive according to what we are "asking for." Have you ever had someone say to you, "Well, you asked for it and you got it"? If you are going fifty mph in a twenty-five-mph zone and a police officer stops you, he or she might say to you, "I'm going to give you a ticket." You might protest that you didn't know the speed limit or didn't see any signs or had your thoughts on other things. But the officer says, "You were just asking to get a ticket, going that fast on this street!"

Now, you were not driving along saying, "Oh, I hope I get a ticket. Are there any police around to issue a ticket? A ticket is just what I want most." We "ask" by our thoughts, feelings, actions, reactions and behavior patterns. And we "receive" according to what we are "asking for."

We ask by how we think and act, not by "asking" God for this or that. God expresses in our life according to the law of mind action. Now we "see," "perceive," "have faith" in God, not as a supplicant to a magistrate, but as a receptive soul becoming more conscious of the marvelous Powers that are ours to use constructively and productively.

I use my faith, love, imagination, will, wisdom and all my other Powers to express the positive Power of my mind to the glory of the good and the upliftment of all humanity.

HOW DO I SEE MYSELF?

Our perception of ourselves is so important. In the late 1800s, Myrtle Fillmore, wife of Charles Fillmore, was told that she was going to die because she had inherited tuberculosis, which ran in her family. So, she took on that view—that image, that perception of herself—and held on to it and she was dying. Then she went to a metaphysical lecture and she heard a phrase, an affirmation, a statement of truth: "I am a child of God, and therefore I do not inherit disease."

She took that new image of herself, that affirmation, that prayer thought, and she held on to it. She centered her faith in the affirmation, "I am a child of God, and I am filled with

Myrtle Fillmore

health and healing power." She started to get well. Others, including her husband, started to notice this and to realize that something was happening. So, from a perception of herself as dying, she shifted her view of herself to a person who was expressing healing power. She redefined, rethought and recreated herself, and she was healed. Even more important, she lived forty more years and influenced millions of people, because she had changed her thoughts about herself and had developed a new perception of who she really was and of the power that is within all of us. One person changed her perception of herself and helped change the world!

Seeing ourselves as an expression of the One Source: This is the foundation. This is the basis of our faith, our perception, our insight, our ability to see ourselves, to conceive ourselves. See who you really are. Know your value. Realize your marvelous power. "I am a child of God," said Myrtle Fillmore.

I am empowered from within to live my life in great ways and to make a great contribution to life.

THE FAITH CONNECTION

This picture of a statue of an angel represents our "angelic" or higher Self. There is a mental law that says, "What we put our attention on, what we have faith in, we connect with or we are tied to." So, we can see in the picture that there are threads that attach the angel to various objects. "Where your attention goes, energy flows." So, our energy flows into the things we are connected to, like along the strings into the different objects.

Let's say my attention is centered on, and my energy is flowing into, the newspaper. I get intensely involved with all the "news" of the day that the paper sees fit to publish. However, there may be all kinds of dire predictions and fearsome things in there. So, I may need to detach from that sometimes and to attach myself to meditation books or to the Bible. I may need to shift my concentration as intensely into material that calms and inspires me, such as biographies of people who have demonstrated a resilient faith in their lives.

Let's say that I am doing a lot of outer communication on the telephone. I may need to detach from that sometimes and to emphasize inner communication, to put my attention within and to have inner communion as well as outer conversation. Each day, I need time for quiet reflection, contemplation and entering into the stillness where I commune with the Higher Power.

Let's say I work very hard, and I may be in danger of becoming a workaholic. I may need to shift out of the work mode or drive and to focus on nature, recreation or renewal.

I may be spending a lot of time with the television, giving a lot of attention and energy to watching TV. Therefore, I may need to detach from that sometimes and to spend quality time with others in positive, creative and constructive ways.

Some people put their faith in alcohol or drugs to solve their problems and alleviate their pain. So, they need to detach themselves from these substances, let them go, get into and stay in recovery, and get attached in a creative and positive way to Alcoholics Anonymous or to other Twelve Step groups.

It is important to realize that we can't just detach. We make the choice to do this, but we also have to reattach to something else. We disconnect and we reconnect. Jesus said, "Have faith in God." (Mark 11:22) This indicates that we can have faith in, or we can give our attention to, all kinds of things. He said to give it to God, to give your attention and faith to the good. Put your faith in that which is healthy and positive, nourishing and creative. Express your spiritual Self by directing your energy flow into that which is productive, helpful and life-enhancing.

We have to practice our faith. We don't necessarily always get what we want in life. More often we get what we expect. What do you expect to get? How do you focus your attention? Where are you putting your faith?

You can evaluate this in a rather existential way by looking at your date book and checkbook. Where are you spending your time and money? This will give valuable information and clues as to where you are investing your life. What really is claiming your attention? Remember, where your attention goes, your energy flows.

THE POWER OF PERCEPTION

Gay Lynn. Have you ever tried looking through someone else's glasses? It's a strange feeling to try to adjust your eyes to someone else's way of seeing. Putting on someone else's glasses can be painful and disorienting, so we take them off quickly. No matter how good the glasses are, or how much was paid for them, they were created for someone else's eyes.

Just as we may put on someone else's glasses, we also may put on someone else's perception of us. Many times, we are trying to see ourselves and our world  through Mom or Dad's glasses. We take on their hopes and fears about us. Their beliefs become our beliefs, often without us really knowing that this has happened. Their perceptions may become the limiting way in which we see ourselves, and it causes pain or discomfort, just like wearing someone else's glasses! Remember, faith is the perceiving power of the mind, and the perceptions we have about ourselves really mold and shape our lives. Perhaps our parents' perception was that we were a "failure," and consciously or unconsciously we still perceive or see ourselves through their eyes.

One man I knew had one bad relationship after another. Part of this was related to early perceptions of himself as being unworthy and unlovable. His perception of himself from well-meaning but critical parents was that he was not good enough. He could not live up to their need for him to be "perfect," and so he felt that no one truly cared for him. Moreover, his parents rarely touched or hugged him. He was kidded or put down for any emotion or sentiment that he shared. These gradually grew into self-perceptions that needed to be "taken off." He lacked confidence in himself, faith in his own self-worth, in his ability to love and to be loved for who and what he was.

Then, he started "seeing" himself differently. He began perceiving himself as being lovable and capable of giving and receiving love. He gained enough confidence to participate in a class on love and healing relationships. He read how families sometimes withhold love as a form of punishment or as a means to control one another, and he recognized this pattern in himself. He learned to receive love and appreciation from other classmates, and his confidence in sharing his feelings grew stronger. He developed greater faith in his own goodness. He opened up physically to share more hugs and to receive more support from loved ones and friends in the class. He risked sharing more of the pain and isolation that he felt at times.

Slowly, gradually, as he changed, the quality of the relationships he attracted into his life changed. Eventually, he welcomed a beautiful love relationship in which he perceived himself as desiring and deserving. He now had a renewed and deeper faith in himself. His new relationship was the most fulfilling experience he had ever had with another human being.

So, ask yourself, "What old perceptions of myself am I still carrying around inside my head?" "Am I seeing myself for who I really am, or am I seeing myself through the eyes of others?" Maybe you are seeing yourself through your mother's eyes, your father's eyes, or the eyes of a significant other. If so, take off the limiting views that constrain you and cause you pain and discomfort. Take off those old glasses! See yourself through fresh eyes and perceive yourself in new ways. Have more faith in yourself as a child of God.

If you are looking through someone else's glasses or perceptions, you can think "positive" with all your might but your "inner vision" will still be blurred. You need to take off the antiquated perceptions and then the positive thoughts and affirmations can really be most effective.

How you perceive yourself is the rock or foundation of your life. Whether you see yourself as incapable, unlovable and a failure at relationships, or as capable, lovable and a success at relationships, is a choice. Choose to perceive yourself kindly—through the eyes of love and acceptance—even as you are growing and changing.

SEEING THE GOOD IN OURSELVES AND OTHERS

Often we are able to make positive shifts and changes because someone has seen something in us that we are unable to see in ourselves. I remember two English teachers who encouraged me to write, and I am sure they would be beaming with pride today to know that I am a published author. Perhaps you have had a teacher, parent, sister or brother, aunt or uncle, coach, minister, counselor or friend who has seen more in you and encouraged you and helped you to have a larger vision of yourself. These wonderful people had faith in you, helped your confidence and boosted your self-esteem. They trusted you to be all that you could be.

How can you now do this for others? All of us have had times when we felt afraid, when we put our faith in our fears, and when we have given our fears undue attention and power. For example, sometimes we have worries, fears and anxieties about what will happen to our children or other family members. When they are having problems in their lives—divorce, unemployment, illness, legal problems, financial difficulties, or making poor choices—our fearful thoughts surface. We ask ourselves, "How will they ever get through this?"

Our own doubts, irrational fears and imagining the worst can consume us mentally and emotionally. What can we do? This is the time when our faith power is so important. We need to release our faith in our fears and securely place the power of our faith in the Spirit within them to lead them through their challenges. This is not telling our families what to do or trying to get them to live their lives the way that we think they need to live them. We can help, love and support, but that does not mean telling them what to do. Rather, we hold the vision with them and for them that they will find a way through—a way that is truly right for them. We prayerfully perceive the Higher Power working through them.

Following is a wonderful prayer of faith to help you do this:

CHILD OF LIGHT

Child of light, I bless you!
I think of you, I pray for you,
Not in terms of what I think you need,
Or what I think you should do or be or express.
I lift up my thoughts about you.
I catch a new vision of you.

I see you as a child of light.
I see you guided and directed by an
inward Spirit that leads you unerringly
into the path that is right for you.
I see you strong and whole;
I see you courageous and confident;
I see you capable and successful.
I see you free from limitation or bondage of any kind.
I see you as the spiritually perfect being you truly are.
Child of light, I bless you!

May Rowland
Silent Unity Director 1916–1971

Body

CEREBRUM OF BRAIN

Dr. Robert. "On this rock I will build." (Matthew 16:18) This is what Jesus said to Peter, who represents our own power of faith. Where do you think this rock is in our physical body? What is the most rock-like part of our body? It's the hard, rock-like, bony skull. More accurately, the "rock of faith" is the cerebrum of the brain within the protective confines of the skull. (See Figure 1.) The cerebrum serves as the body's central computer that monitors, regulates and controls all the other body organs.

Faith is our perceiving power, and in our body all perception takes place within the cerebrum. All of our thoughts and feelings, memories and dreams, psychic impressions and physical activities are programmed in and through our incredible cerebral computer.

The cerebrum is the largest and uppermost section of the whole brain. The cerebrum consists of two cerebral hemispheres. In general, the left cerebral hemisphere controls the activities of the right side of the body, whereas the right cerebral hemisphere controls the activities of the left side of the body. The left cerebral hemisphere also is the principal physical site for conscious mind functions such as analysis, logic and decision-making. Subconscious mind functions such as intuition, symbolic thinking and image formation are programmed primarily in and through the right cerebral hemisphere. Within both hemispheres, numerous centers exist where specific functions occur, such as hearing, vision, touch, speech and muscular control.

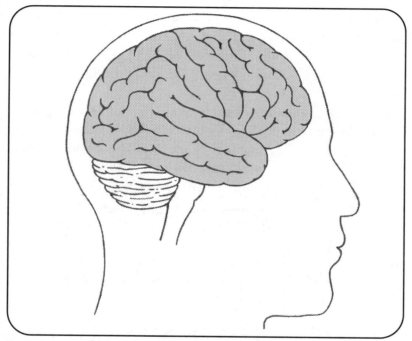

Figure 1. Lateral view of cerebrum of the brain (shaded)

Jesus also said to Peter, "I will give you the keys to the kingdom." (Matthew 16:19) So, what are these keys? Where are they found in the "kingdom" of the physical body? The keys are the key cells, centers and neural networks in our cerebrum. Our brain contains an estimated 100 billion neurons or nerve cells. Each of these brain cells has tiny nerve fibers called axons and dendrites that connect them with hundreds of thousands of other neurons. This makes up the vast, complex circuitry of our brain.

In computer parlance, we would say that this circuitry is the "hardware" of our computer brain. And that hardware is just sitting there waiting to be programmed. The key is to program it with faith in the Higher Power, faith that we are created in the image and likeness of our Creator, faith in our own innate healing power and talents. Then we enter into what Jesus called the kingdom of heaven, which simply means spiritual consciousness. Like the Buddha, we are awake.

In Eastern teachings, the area at the top of the head is called the crown chakra. Commonly, it is depicted as a thousand-petalled lotus, to indicate it is the highest center whereby we perceive and know without a doubt that we are a child of God, that we are one with the Creative Energy that flows throughout the universe, in and through us and all life. Via faith, our perceiving power, we commune with this transcendent reality. Then we program this divine perception right into the cells and circuitry of our cerebrum, which transmits this information to the rest of our body.

CONFIDENCE IN HEALING POWER

"By your faith you are healed." In essence, this is what Jesus said on many occasions when he performed healings. So, how does this work? How is it that faith restores health to your brain and the rest of your body?

Think back to a time when you were feeling confident, positive, hopeful. How did your mind and brain work at that time? Well, they worked wonderfully. Your mind was clear, open and ready to respond in a creative way to any challenge or difficulty. You trusted the flow of ideas that easily came to you, knowing that you were being guided by the still small voice within you. You felt good about yourself and others. Your memory was sharp and accurate. And your head was free of pain and discomfort, as was the rest of your body.

Now, remember a time when you were plagued with fears, doubts, lack of confidence; when you were afraid that you might make a mistake or fail; perhaps when you felt alone, even separate from the One Source. How well did your brain function then? How clear was your mind?

You may have felt like you were in a fog. You probably had trouble thinking things through, difficulty believing in yourself. Dark thoughts and feelings may have tormented you. It may have felt like your brain had shut down and along with it your memory. Other people may have sensed this and said things such as, "You have a dark cloud around you." Psychic sensitives and healers may have reported a darkening or lowering of the "energy" in and around your head. You may have felt this yourself.

This constriction or lowering or blockage of energy may have led to a series of biochemical and neurological changes in your brain, which caused symptoms such as headaches. The most common type of headache is called a tension or muscle-contraction headache, which is one of the most prevalent disorders known to humankind. This may be felt as a tight band around the head or as pain in the temples, the back of the head, or anywhere in the head and down the neck. The other most common headache is a migraine, which typically affects only one side of the head, and may be accompanied by visual changes, nausea, vomiting and sensitivity to light and sound. About twenty percent of Americans experience migraines at some time during their lives, with women being affected more often than men.

Thus, if you have difficulties with your faith faculty, you

may develop headaches. But does this mean that all headaches are caused by a fractured faith? No. A headache may simply be the result of a stressful day, or may have a physical cause such as noxious fumes, chemicals in foods, sensitivity to certain foods, low blood sugar, reactions to medications or weather changes. Headaches also may stem from other physical disorders such as high blood pressure, constipation, eye problems or sinusitis. Moreover, the headache may be relieved by a neck massage, a short nap or meditation, or taking an analgesic like aspirin or Tylenol.

However, if the headaches have no physical cause, occur frequently and are not relieved by common treatments, it is essential to focus on your faith faculty. Remember, *faith and the cerebrum are like two sides of one coin.* So, when your faith falters, you may develop headaches. If so, see a physician—this is essential if your head pain is intense or accompanied by fever, mental disturbances or loss of consciousness. For treatment, use the best of all physical remedies, including medication, relaxation exercises, nutrients, herbs, chiropractic and biofeedback.

At the same time, examine how your doubts, fears of failure, insecurities, lack of confidence or other difficulties with faith may be the principal cause of your headaches. Talk about this with a friend, teacher, doctor, minister or counselor to help you see and transform the underlying pattern. When you fortify your faith in yourself as a child of God, when your confidence becomes rock solid, when you truly trust in the Higher Power that is all around and within you, then your headaches will be relieved. By your faith, you will be healed.

Blockages in faith also may be the primary or a contributing cause of more serious cerebral disorders, such as epilepsy and benign and malignant tumors. These diseases always require prompt medical attention and treatment, including appropriate medication and surgery. But if full healing is to occur, attention also must be given to the power of faith, since it directly and specifically influences the health of the cerebrum.

No matter how minor or major the cerebral illness, regardless of its cause (physical, genetic or psychological), whether it takes moments or months or years or a whole lifetime, via faith in your own inherent wholeness as a child of God, your cerebrum is healed.

THE FAITH FACTOR AND THE PLACEBO EFFECT

Medical researchers have verified the faith factor as a key in healing all kinds of disorders. They call this faith healing the "placebo effect." So, what is a placebo? And how does it work?

Let's say you have a severe headache and you come to see me as your physician. I take your history, do a thorough examination, and make sure that you do not have a physical disorder that requires antibiotics, surgery or other conventional treatments. Then, in a confident and assured manner, I give you some pills and say that they will relieve your headache. Sure enough, when you take them your headache disappears. However, the pills actually are filled with an inert, non-therapeutic substance like starch—they are a placebo. So, why are your symptoms relieved? Obviously, it's because of your belief, your faith in the pills and my talents as a physician.

Numerous double-blind studies have proven that from 30 to 70 percent of people taking a placebo have partial or total relief of their symptoms. Moreover, this includes nearly all types of disorders such as heart disease, kidney problems, ulcers and even some cases of cancer. What these studies prove is our enormous, often untapped power to heal ourselves. In taking a placebo, we place our faith in the supposed healing power of a remedy. But our faith is misplaced. We get well because our faith activates our own internal healing mechanisms.

Our faith directly affects and reprograms our cerebrum, which in turn controls and regulates all the rest of our body. The brain sends signals via the nerves to bring about the healing that we perceive is possible. The brain also directs a rebalancing of our hormones and immune system. Faith in our healing power stimulates the brain to release chemicals like endorphins—the body's own morphine-like substance— to eliminate pain and to generate feelings of joy and well-being. Throughout our body, our belief becomes physical fact and reality.

MIGRAINE HEADACHES

I was twenty years old when I had my first migraine, with excruciating, throbbing pain on the right side of my head, nausea and vomiting—a totally frightening and disturbing experience. The day before, I had learned that my older brother had been hospitalized with depression. I did not understand it at that time, but his hospitalization had activated deep emotional scars from my childhood. When I was seven years old, my baby sister had died suddenly of unexplained causes. Shortly thereafter, my mother had been hospitalized for depression and my father took my brother and me to stay with an aunt and uncle. Shaken, feeling abandoned by my parents, not feeling loved by my new "family,"

I had bonded emotionally with my brother to deal with our catastrophe. Now, fifteen years later, I felt like I had lost my brother. All over again, I felt alone, disconnected, hopeless, and afraid of the seeming fragility and unfairness of life.

At age seven, to deal with the painful loss of my mother, I had put a shell around myself, closing down my feelings, because I had concluded that it was too painful to love someone who might be taken away from me. In my teenage years, I had become an atheist. In my Protestant upbringing, I could not find comfort or reason as to why my sister had died or my family had been fractured. Underneath an apparently happy and healthy exterior, I was depressed, even suicidal at times, as I thought that life had no purpose or meaning.

Following the first migraine, I got prompt medical attention, had all the proper medical tests that found no physical abnormality, and took the prescribed medication that helped with the pain but did not prevent the migraines that recurred a couple times each month. My doctor pointed out that my migraines might have a genetic basis, since my mother also suffered from headaches.

As with so many illnesses, the migraines were a blessing in disguise, for they inspired me to seek out other forms of treatment and to look for answers to my deepest doubts and fears. Within weeks, I was exposed to yoga, Zen Buddhism, biofeedback and the Edgar Cayce readings. Practicing yoga exercises and meditation, I learned how to relax my mind and body and to release the chronic tension that my insecurity, lack of confidence and fear of emotional losses had caused. In the stillness of meditation, I rediscovered a faith in the Divine that I long ago had abandoned. I also got rid of the junk food in my diet, began taking nutritional supplements and became a vegetarian.

In my budding spiritual studies, I was struck by reading

about the law of karma and reincarnation. Here was the answer that I had looked for since age seven, the principle that helped me begin to understand the bigger picture and the underlying causes of my family's tragedy. Life took on a whole new meaning.

With a more expansive perception of myself, with renewed faith in myself as a child of God, with renewed faith in the sanctity and purposefulness and beauty of life, over a period of one year my migraines diminished in frequency and then stopped altogether, never to return. By my faith, I had been healed.

Sit in a comfortable chair, with your hands resting in your lap. Take a few slow, deep breaths, letting go of any tension as you breathe out. Let your mind become calm and still.

Then visualize yourself sitting under a majestic waterfall. The waterfall represents the pouring out of Spirit upon you. The water is a liquid light that flows down into the top of your head, into your crown chakra and cerebrum. This is the inflow of the healing waters of faith.

Imagine this fluid light flowing into both sides of your brain, bathing it with the power of faith. You may not see this flow of light so much as you "sense" or "feel" it, as it activates and stimulates your cerebrum. You may just know without a doubt that this is happening.

Think of the waters of faith flowing into all of the key centers in your brain, into each of its billions of neurons. As you imagine this, the top of your head may feel more open, energized, aglow with light. As you sense this, affirm:

- I have faith in God-the-Good.
- The light of faith now lights up my brain.
- I am a being of faith.

When your crown chakra/cerebrum feels filled to overflowing, then visualize the fluid light spilling down from your head into every other part of your body and all around your body. Especially see and feel the faith power entering into your heart, which is your love center. With faith and love combined, all things are possible.

Continue to visualize and to experience this infilling of the fluid light of faith until you sense that your whole being and body have been charged with renewed faith, that you now are full of faith or "faith-ful." Then, gradually come out of your meditation and radiate this new faith into all that you think, feel and do.

1. I am full of faith.
2. My faith is established in God's unfailing goodness.
3. I see the Divine in everything, visible and invisible, and my faith grows and increases hour by hour, day by day.
4. My life is founded on the rock of faith.
5. I say "Yes" to my good.
6. I have faith that Spirit opens new doors of good for me at all times.
7. I take the next step in my life with faith and confidence, for Thou art with me.
8. I see myself clearly, I know who I am—a spark of divinity.
9. My faith lifts me above all fears and concerns, into the light of my Self.
10. I have faith that I am whole and holy, healthy and harmonious.
11. The light of faith enlightens my mind and brain.
12. I have faith in my God-given healing power.
13. I have faith in my power to do seemingly impossible things.
14. By faith, I now call forth the healing of all parts of my cerebrum and the rest of my body.
15. I place my faith in "I can" rather than "I can't." I can because I know I Am.

16. I have faith in the magnificent power and performance of my cerebral computer.
17. My faith is large enough to receive an infinite flow of good.
18. My mind and brain are awake, alive, alert and filled with faith.
19. I see myself as capable, lovable and a success in relationships.
20. When my life is swept by storms, I stand on the rock of faith in the Good.
21. I program my cerebral computer with the faith that I have as a child of God.
22. I have faith in my own goodness.
23. My head is filled with light and is full of faith, so I am free from head pain.
24. My positive faith is the key that unlocks the treasure house of riches.
25. Faith activates my brain and my memory is sharp and clear.
26. I have faith that my loved ones are being guided and directed in positive ways.
27. My mind is clear, open and ready to respond in creative ways to any challenge.
28. I believe in myself as God believes in me.
29. Faith now flows through all the cells and circuits of my cerebrum.
30. I am faith filled, secure and confident.
31. By my faith, I am healed and made whole.

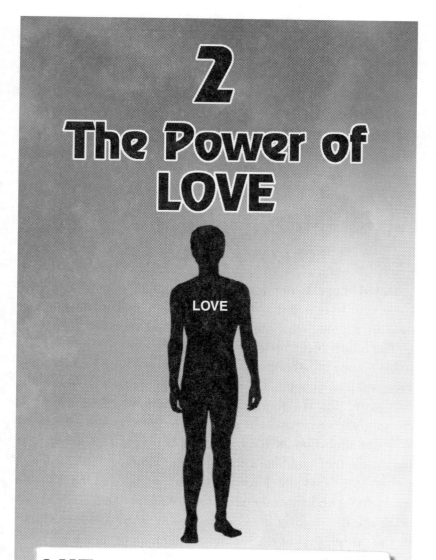

2
The Power of LOVE

LOVE

LOVE is my ability to know oneness with all and to desire that good comes to all. Love is my ability to share, to draw together. Love heals, harmonizes, renews, prospers and unites. I know: "God is love, and I am that love power expressing as me." The power of love casts out fear, loneliness and selfishness. Love externalizes as my circulatory system: heart, liver, spleen, blood vessels, blood and lymphatic system.

TO LOVE IS TO LIVE

David. Love is not just an emotion. It's a real power we have. Our lives are shaped by the way we use our love power or ability, along with our other powers. To love is to live!

The Scottish scientist and minister, Henry Drummond, said in his classic little book *Love: The Greatest Thing in the World,* "You will find as you look back upon your life that the moments that stand out, the moments when you have really lived, are the moments when you have done things in a spirit of love."

A dynamic flow of life expresses through us. We call this life force by religious and scientific names: God, energy, prana, chi. This life force seeks to express itself fully and freely in us and through us—actually as us. We free or maximize the life flow by love. To love is to be in the flow of life, in the circulation of life, in the abundance of life.

The Dalai Lama has said that his religion is summed up in one word: kindness. He is following in the footsteps of Gautama Buddha, whose teachings and example centered on compassion. Love, kindness, compassion: are not these just different words to describe the very same power, the power of love?

A lawyer asked Jesus, "Master, what must I do to inherit eternal life?" Jesus then told the parable of the Good Samaritan, which has love and kindness at the heart of its philosophy and way of life. The story tells of someone who is mugged on a lonely road, and how a priest and Levite (an expert in the law) avoid him.

A "priestly" attitude in us might be: "I will pray for him, but I don't want to get involved." Or, "I want to maintain my high consciousness and see everything as perfect so I don't want to behold his troubles."

The Levite represents our tendency to judge by the letter rather than the spirit of the law. We may show the "Levite" tendency when we encounter someone who is confused, afraid, having trouble, ill or upset, and we think, "Well, if something has happened, he is just reaping the result of his own negative thinking! So, why should I help him?"

The Samaritan in the story doesn't avoid the painful, messy situation but rather takes personal responsibility for giving practical help. He doesn't blame, shame or avoid himself or the "other" (who is really a part of himself). He represents our power of love—our ability to be fully alive through expressing kindness.

A haunting question of this parable is why Jesus has a Samaritan be the helper. The Samaritan would be the shunned, the rejected, the outcast in that Jewish society. Why doesn't Jesus have a Jew helping a person that a Jewish person would ordinarily not go out of his way to help at all, no matter how dire the need? Could it be that the storyteller wanted to say that the Samaritan had the empathy the others lacked because he had been hurt and ignored himself, and he knew what it felt like? This is the power of acceptance and the ability to be of help, which is found in Alcoholics Anonymous and other Twelve Step groups.

George Bernard Shaw has said, "The opposite of love is not hate, it is indifference." The priest and the Levite (remember these people represent parts of us) did not dislike the man.

They were simply indifferent to his pain and need. He didn't look good and was a mess. It was easier to just avoid him.

Jesus answered the question about inheriting eternal life by putting before us the case of a person who is hurt and how we might respond to this situation as the measure of our aliveness. We are hurting or life places before us someone who is hurting. So, here is a "living moment" that we often encounter. It is "eternal" in that we encounter the need to use our love power over and over again, eternally. Eternal has nothing to do with the hereafter or how long we live, but only the quality of aliveness we find through loving one another.

Smiley Blanton, M.D., wrote: "Love is the immortal flow of energy that nourishes, extends and preserves. Its eternal goal is life."

LET YOUR LOVE FLOW

We can compare the restrictions we place on ourselves to a rubber band I put around my finger. If the rubber band represents my prejudices, grudges, holier-than-thou attitudes, wanting to get revenge, feeling superior or inferior to others, then it's like winding a band around my life circulation process. What happens to my finger? I'm cutting myself off from the life flow. I'm hurting myself! Soon my finger starts to swell, redden, hurt, and then turn blue from lack of circulation. This can get serious!

However, if I let go of those old prejudices, hatreds, negative hard feelings, if I forgive, release, desire good to come to all, then as the saying goes, "I let go and let God." The flow is taking place. The cells in my finger are blessed by the healing, vital flow of fresh blood that nourishes, restores, renews, cleanses and invigorates my finger.

So what condition do I want? The life force in me wants to be free to circulate, and I need to cooperate with it, to open myself, to unrestrict myself, to be more loving and forgiving and friendly, to be "care-ful" towards myself and people, and to give and receive in positive ways. Then I get into the flow of greater life. I value myself, others, life. Truly, to love is to live!

RELEASE YOUR BLOCKS

We've heard it said that in order to be forgiven, we have to forgive. As it is stated in The Lord's Prayer, "Forgive us our debts as we forgive our debtors." What does this mean? Does it mean that if I don't forgive someone, God won't forgive me? If I forgive, then God will also decide to forgive? That's what it sounds like, but that would require a mean, change-able God who stubbornly withholds and punishes us if we try to hurt or punish others. If we believe in a principle rather than a fickle personality, then there is a constant Divine Love.

I realize that I can block my own good by holding onto resentment, blame, hard feelings and revenge. It's like pick-ing up a heavy block of wood in each hand and holding onto them. I get "blocked." I'm not free!

I tell myself, "But I have every right to hold onto my resentment. . . . Jane really pulled a dirty trick on me. I'm not going to just let it go. She knew she was doing it. I'm going to keep cursing her the rest of my life!"

Am I upsetting Jane? Who am I blocking? Who am I hurting?

The Buddha said: "Holding onto anger is like grasping a

hot coal with the intent of throwing it at someone else—you are the one who gets burned."

So, here I am holding onto these blocks, and my wife tries to hug me. What happens? Or my friend tries to give me a gift. Am I able to receive the good? And how do my arms feel? I'm using all this energy to grasp the blocks—it takes a lot to keep them in my hands. Now eventually I see (perceive) the good sense of releasing the blocks. So I put them down. Now I'm free. It's basically not for Jane's benefit. It's for mine! I help myself to be free. I forgive. I give forth. I give and receive. I enjoy life. I am unburdened. I "lighten up"—

my burden is light.

Then I run into someone and he asks about Jane. And I respond, "Yeah, I hope she suffers as much as I have. She's no good. I can't stand her!"

So, I probably have to release the blocks more than once, to do it over and over—"seventy times seven" as the wise saying from Jesus goes. To forgive means to desire only good to come to all concerned—myself, others and all people.

I take this "love principle" and "process" it scientifically in the laboratory of my life. I apply loving actions and see the positive, life-producing results demonstrated in my life, workplace, neighborhood, nation and planet.

Let there be love on Earth and let it begin with me.

MODERN-DAY SAMARITAN

Gay Lynn. I received the following letter from Deryl Fisher, whom I like to call a modern-day Good Samaritan:

It was a hot South Florida day and I was headed north on I-95 to visit one of my construction jobs, when I saw an old beat-up van with a flat tire pulled over on the shoulder. Now I know what it means to be stranded and I help when I can. I got out of my van and walked back and fell in love. Here was this beautiful young lady about thirty-five years old, blond hair, sweet smile, sundress and lovely blue eyes. There was a pair of kids in the back seat making a perfectly matched set.

"Do you have a spare tire?" I asked. "It's flat, too," she told me as her blue eyes flooded with tears.

Her name was Patty. Timmy was about ten and Tammy appeared to be about eight. They had left their home on the south side of Miami and were headed to her mother's house in northern Georgia. Patty's husband Larry had beaten her up for the last time and she was making her escape. Timmy piped up from the back seat, "He hit Mama again last night." Then I saw the bruise on her thigh where it extended out of her dress and another bruise on the side of her face.

I had left a disastrous relationship a few months before and felt that I was ready to give love another try. Here was not only a lady in need, but also a wonderful pair of kids. I didn't ever intend to be a father again, but I have a lot of daddy love that I am willing to lavish on all children that come into my life.

Talking with them further, I found that she not only didn't have a good spare tire, but she didn't have any money or food, the kids were hungry and the gas gauge was low. Thoughts began to race through my mind. "They can come home with me. I've got room. I can take care of them." I jacked up the car and removed the flat tire. But then I began realizing how much healing work it takes after a difficult love relationship, and how jumping from one relationship to the next is not always a good idea. No, I thought, I definitely would not interfere in Patty's life.

We went to Burger King where I intended to leave them to eat something, while I took the two tires to be fixed. But eight-year-old Tammy took my hand and asked if she could have a Kid's Meal and my heart melted. I looked at the young mother and I was sure that if I tried to gather her in my arms, there would be no resistance. I sat down to eat with them and Timmy told me how much he liked fishing. My eyes misted up with fantasies of taking the tyke out fishing and of reeling in our catch rapidly to keep it out of the jaws of alligators.

I ended up buying a total of three used tires, filling her tank with gas, and buying some munchies to eat on the road to Grandma's. I gave the sweet lady two twenty-dollar bills. "I can't accept that, you have already done too much for us," she said. "It's not for you, it's for the kids," I told her, as I hugged them all good-bye. Patty asked, "You're married, aren't you?" "Yes," I lied. "I hope she appreciates what she's got," is the last thing she said as they drove out of my life with the kids leaning out the side window waving.

I had to grit my teeth to keep from yelling, "Hey, come back, I can't let you go." But I did. I let them go with love.

The test of love is sometimes shown in our greatest moments of being able to let go. It would not have been healthy for Deryl to take Patty and the kids home. The greatest gift was to help them and to let them go, with love.

HEART TO HEART

Listening is one of the greatest gifts of love that we can give to each other. Many times when we are having trouble in our relationships, it is because we are not listening. The art of listening is a skill that can be learned and developed, but it requires practice. Keeping the love in circulation in our families can be a challenge. How can we help the family to keep communicating the love that each one feels for the others?

We started early in our family by having a Heart-to-Heart ritual. (See *Transformative Rituals: Celebrations for Personal Growth* by Gay Lynn and David Williamson.) In our home, there was a little red stuffed heart that we kept available. Whenever anyone in the family wanted to get together, they would simply get out the heart. This was the signal that we all needed to come together. The main rule with the Heart-to-Heart ritual was that only the person with the heart got to talk. This little heart was valuable in helping us to keep quiet and to listen with love. When the heart was passed and we were holding it, we then could speak.

We entered into an agreement before we began the Heart-to-Heart ritual, and we would share it out loud to remind us of what our agreements were in listening with love.

HEART-TO-HEART COMMITMENT

I commit myself to speak from my heart all during this time of sharing. I agree to be honest with myself and others. I also will make every effort to listen intently, looking directly at the person with the heart who is speaking. I will help to create an atmosphere of trust, safety and peace where we can feel secure in reaching our own hearts and communicating Heart-to-Heart. I will honor and keep in confidence all that is shared and never use it against the person or as gossip later.

I make this commitment in the belief that love is the greatest thing in the world, that love can heal, uplift, harmonize, prosper and bring peace. I claim all of these good qualities and results for myself and others having a Heart-to-Heart with me.

We modified the commitment for our children when they were young, so that it was simple and they knew the most valuable thing to do was to listen to the person with the heart.

When our daughter Kyleigh was about five years old, she would go over to stand next to her older brother Joshua when he was lined up with his buddies at his classroom. Well, you know what happens when little sister goes over to stand with big brother—he shooed her off and told her to go over by her own class. A few days later, Kyleigh asked to have a Heart-to-Heart. We all sat around the dining-room table. Kyleigh had the heart so she started. She looked at her brother and said, "When I don't see you during the day Josh, I miss you, and I just wanted to let you know that I love you." All of us welled up with tears, and Josh really heard for the first time the love his sister had for him, and it changed his heart.

Now our children are grown, and they are young adults. They have kept close to one another and continue to share the ability to listen and to be a loving support to one another. Perhaps a small part was learning to really tune in and to honor what the

other had to say. They simply listened with love.

The ritual of passing an object to aid communication also

is found in the Native American culture. The "talking stick" is a sacred object that is handed from person to person. Only the person with the talking stick gets to talk, and he or she receives the full respect, reverence and attention from all the others in the group. I have seen many beautiful talking sticks that have been created with objects from nature.

I have used the Heart-to-Heart ritual in many different places. In one college classroom, students at first tossed the heart around like a football, but after a while they began sharing the stress and strain of college life—trying to work, to get papers turned in, and to maintain other family and home obligations. For the first time, they learned they were not alone—that other students were having similar challenges.

I remember using the Heart-to-Heart ritual in a recovery hospital where I was leading a therapy group. All these big, burly guys started filling in the circle, and I was getting nervous thinking how silly I was going to come across with this red stuffed heart I was about to pass around. How would they respond? Again, I was pleasantly surprised as they began sharing how difficult it was to maintain their sobriety, and how alone and isolated they felt most of the time. I truly witnessed some amazing transformations as one by one they really listened to one another and moved beyond the usual banter they were accustomed to throwing around, often a cover for their pain. Many of the other therapists approached me later and asked what I had been doing with their clients, and they wanted to borrow my little red heart.

I have sat with countless couples in counseling and one of the most common problems is communication. Usually it is related to listening rather than to talking. Perhaps that is why God gave us two ears and one mouth. We need to lovingly give twice as much attention to listening as we do to speaking!

Give the gift of love today and listen to someone whom you care about. Many couples whose marriages break up because one or both of the pair is having an affair often say that they felt that the one they were attracted to really listened to them, understood them, heard what their needs were. Isn't that interesting? What a greater chance we give to the success of our marriages when we *listen*!

Begin now to listen more closely to those around you. Repeat back to them what you hear them saying. Give that special listening attention to your children, friends and co-workers. Watch them relax and flow more easily with loving feelings because you have listened to them with love from the heart.

HEART AND CIRCULATORY SYSTEM

Dr. Robert. What part of the body do you think of when you think of love? Probably the heart. This is because the power of love externalizes in the body as the heart and the rest of the circulatory system, which includes the liver, spleen, blood vessels, blood and lymphatic system. (See Figure 2.)

We intuitively recognize the direct correlation of love with the heart. From our inner wisdom, we speak of love welling up in our heart, of opening our heart to others. We say that a kind, compassionate, loving person has a good heart or a heart of gold. Someone who is mean or hostile is called heart-less, hard-hearted or cold-hearted; he may be said to have ice in his veins. When someone speaks angrily or spews forth venom, it used to be commonly said that she was venting her spleen. These are more than just figures of speech, because scores of scientific studies have documented the intercon-nection of love and the heart.

The physical heart is the very essence of love in action. As a muscular pump that is about the size of a fist, the heart is always beating, always pumping, always giving of itself and serving the rest of the body. With each beat of the heart, blood is pumped through the arteries and the arterioles to the capillaries. These tiny vessels have small openings that allow the blood's contents to diffuse into the fluid bathing the cells of all parts of the body, bringing water, oxygen, nutrients, minerals, hormones, antibodies and numerous other vital substances. The veins then carry blood from the capillaries back to the heart.

Blood is the elixir of life. No blood, no life. After only a few minutes, for example, brain cells begin to die unless they are supplied with new circulating blood. In like manner, our inner spirit dies a little bit each time we restrict and block the flow of love in our life.

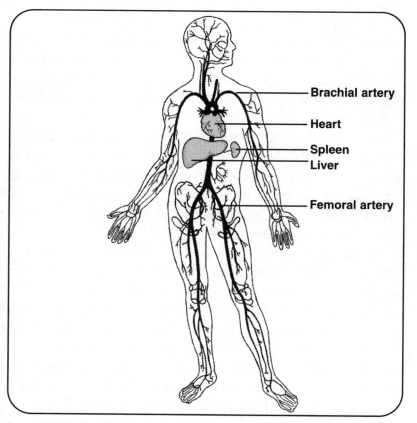

Figure 2. Heart, liver, spleen and arteries

Blood consists of two components: cells and fluid (plasma). The cells are divided into three major types: red blood cells, white blood cells and platelets. Red blood cells contain hemoglobin, which combines with oxygen. White blood cells protect the body from infection—they are the major component of the immune system. Platelets are part of the blood-clotting system.

The liver is located on the right side of the body, below the right lung and the diaphragm. It carries out hundreds of chemical reactions, most of which prepare substances for entry into the blood or remove other substances from the blood, keeping the blood chemistry in right harmony and balance. The liver also serves as a blood purifier, removing toxic items and converting them into harmless compounds that can be removed from the body. The liver further plays a role in digestion, producing bile that helps the body to digest and absorb fats.

Just as the liver daily performs hundreds of chemical reactions to maintain the right balance and health of the circulating blood, you have hundreds of opportunities each day to demonstrate and circulate your love. Each time you feel and give love, it helps to heal, harmonize and transform all life around and within you.

The spleen is located on the left side of the body, below the left lung and the diaphragm. It serves primarily to remove old, worn-out red blood cells from the blood, retaining the iron from the hemoglobin and storing it for future use. The spleen also removes and destroys harmful microorganisms.

In addition, the spleen is a major part of the lymphatic system, which also consists of lymph nodes and lymphatic vessels. These vessels carry fluid, proteins and other compounds away from the cells back to veins near the heart. Thus, the lymphatic system is a vital part of the overall circulatory system.

The spleen and lymph nodes produce and contain lymphocytes, a type of white blood cell that is a key component of the immune system. B lymphocytes produce antibodies that attack bacteria and viruses. T lymphocytes—commonly called T cells—help the body to destroy parasites, cancer cells, fungi and transplants of foreign tissue.

HEALING POWER OF LOVE

How do we keep our immune system healthy and thereby stay free from disease? More and more, scientists are discovering that, in large measure, we do this with love. That is why love is a major key to healing—love of God, love of one another, love of our enemies, love of our body, love of all that we have attracted into our life.

Love protects us from infectious diseases, since it strengthens our immune system. In one study, Harvard students watched a film of Mother Teresa demonstrating selfless love in serving the sick and dying in Calcutta. Afterwards, their saliva showed a significant increase in protective antibodies, which help the body to destroy viruses. In another study, researchers placed rhinovirus (which causes the common cold) in volunteers' noses. Those who had the most friends and the greatest diversity of relationships—in other words, who had the greatest flow of love in their lives—had the least chance of actually developing a cold.

As reported in *Love & Survival* by the famed cardiologist Dean Ornish, M.D., multiple large-scale studies have shown that people who are socially isolated, who feel alone and unloved, have at least two to five times the risk of premature death and disease from all causes. Another study revealed that people who had loving parents or who perceived them to be loving were one-third as likely to develop disease in mid-life versus those individuals who rated their parents as low in parental caring. A different study of 1,100 men indicated that the best predictor of which men would get cancer decades later was the closeness of the father-son relationship earlier in life.

In the 1950s, Drs. Friedman and Rosenman performed studies indicating that individuals with Type A personalities—who are hostile, self-involved, impatient and always in a hurry—had significantly more coronary heart disease than those with Type B personalities. (In coronary artery disease, the coronary arteries, which supply blood to heart muscle, may be narrowed or closed off by atherosclerotic plaque.) Later studies did not confirm these findings but, in more recent research, investigators clearly documented that the component of hostility in the Type A behavior increased the incidence of coronary heart disease. In a review of forty-five studies, the harmful effects of hostility were found to be equal to or greater than physical risk factors like high cholesterol levels and elevated blood pressure. People who are hostile generally feel alone, alienated, isolated and suspicious. They feel unloved and are unloving. Researchers have discovered that individuals who feel the most loved and supported have substantially less blockage in the arteries of their hearts.

Blockage of the coronary arteries may cause damage or death to some of the heart muscle, in what commonly is called a "heart attack." What is it that "attacks" the heart? In part it is the sustained and suppressed anger, hostility, hatred, rage, and profound feelings of isolation, separation and loneliness. All of these emotions block and shut down the flow of love through the heart, which in turn leads to physical heart disease.

A high-fat diet, smoking, obesity and lack of exercise also

increase the risk of developing cardiovascular disease. Therefore, these physical components require appropriate treatment, including medication, nutritional supplements, dietary changes and exercise programs. A procedure called angioplasty may open narrowed coronary arteries, or open-heart surgery may bypass these vessels.

But the heart also must be opened on an emotional and psychological level, or the coronary arteries may get blocked again, as they commonly do after angioplasty or bypass surgery. The deepest healing occurs when we open up spiritually, when we open our hearts to the inflow of God's love, when we realize that our true nature is love, when we forgive and we feel forgiven.

Blockages in love also may cause or contribute to numerous other circulatory disorders. These include high blood pressure, congestive heart failure, heart valve disease, irregular heartbeats (arrhythmia), hepatitis, cirrhosis, anemia, cancer of the white blood cells (leukemia), cancer of the lymph glands (lymphoma), AIDS (wherein a virus destroys T cell lymphocytes) and autoimmune disorders (wherein the body makes antibodies against its own cells).

Whatever the disorder of any part of the circulatory system, the key to healing it is love. Therefore, let love be at the center of your holistic healing program that utilizes the best of all remedies and therapeutic approaches. In love, for love, with love, giving and receiving love, you will be made whole.

Relax, breathe slowly and deeply, and let go of any worries or concerns. Then, as you did when focusing on faith, visualize yourself under a waterfall of wondrous, fluid light that first flows into your brain and then down into your heart.

As this inflow occurs, you may feel it as warmth in the center of your chest or you may just sense a welling up of love within you. As you visualize and experience this inflow of love, affirm: My Father-Mother Creator loves me; I am a being of love; my heart is now open and is filled with love. I forgive and I am forgiven.

Then, just as the physical heart pumps blood through the blood vessels to all parts of the body, imagine love flowing from your heart to all parts of your body. Begin by visualizing love and light radiating into your liver that is to the right and below your heart. Then imagine and experience love circulating to your spleen to the left and below the heart. Envision the flow of love to your head, neck and abdomen, down to your arms and legs, until love circulates through your whole body.

Next, think of someone that you want to love more deeply and purely, perhaps someone you need to forgive. Picture this person sitting right in front of you, only a few feet away, as if you were having a close, intimate, heart-to-heart sharing with this individual. Open your heart and let love flow through you to this person. See the good, focus on the good, and love the good within this soul. Feel the fluid light of love flowing from your heart into his or her heart, and from there into his or her whole body and whole being. Forgive this individual and ask to be forgiven.

As you are guided from within, gradually come out of your meditation and give thanks for all the love that has been shared and exchanged.

1. I am loving and I am loved.
2. My heart is filled with pure love; I am made whole and free.
3. I love to see good come to all—myself and all others.
4. I release hard feelings by forgiving others for what they have said and done.
5. I overcome the tendency to bypass people in trouble, and I reach out to help them with compassion and wisdom.
6. I express love in all the "little" things I say and do today.
7. I give others the freedom to make their own choices and to live their own lives as they choose. I do this because I love them.
8. Lord, make me an instrument of your peace and love by showing me the opportunities I have to help people today and every day.
9. I live in "eternal life" as I love in the eternal moment of now.
10. I deserve love and I accept love.
11. I am not afraid to ask for help.
12. I admit to myself and others when I feel hurt, scared or sad.
13. I avoid the tendency to call myself and others negative names.

14. I overcome indifference, so I can see the hurts and help heal them.
15. I have within me the power to be kind and compassionate.
16. I have the love, strength and wisdom to set healthy boundaries when others try to take advantage of or manipulate me.
17. I honor the unity and diversity of all people.
18. All people are sacred, including myself. My life and your life are both part of the One Life.
19. I love people and let them go with love.
20. Love is a magnet that draws to me riches and good without end.
21. I have a good heart.
22. My heart, liver, spleen and blood vessels are filled with health and harmony.
23. I do not isolate myself. I involve myself with people in creative, constructive and enjoyable ways.
24. I strengthen my immune system by joining with others in loving, serving community.
25. I care for my heart, liver, spleen and blood by expressing the healing power of love.
26. I overcome loneliness by reaching out to others with friendliness. I make a friend by being a friend.
27. I open my heart and love flows throughout my whole being.
28. The power of love is mighty to heal my life and my world.

3
The Power of
STRENGTH

STRENGTH is my ability to hold fast, endure, stand firm and stay in integrity. Strength often is seen as physical force (Samson type), but inner strength (Jesus-the-Christ type) is found in quietness, confidence, peacefulness, love of enemies, giving good for evil. Strength is balance between thinking and feeling, logic and emotion, intellect and intuition. Strength externalizes as my spinal cord and nerves—the body's communication system.

STRENGTH IS BALANCE

David. A well-balanced person is truly strong. If someone pushes you but you have both your feet firmly planted on the

floor, you are strong. You are able to stand the pressure and stress because you are strongly balanced. But what happens if you stand on only one leg? Then you can be pushed over with one finger by anyone. You have all the same body parts, but you are not balanced and therefore you can be a "pushover."

Balance is strength. What are some of the ways we need to be well-balanced?

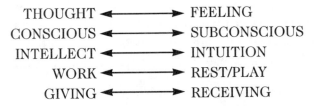

THOUGHT	⟷	FEELING
CONSCIOUS	⟷	SUBCONSCIOUS
INTELLECT	⟷	INTUITION
WORK	⟷	REST/PLAY
GIVING	⟷	RECEIVING

This goes for men and women, because we are looking at ourselves as *whole* persons.

Carl Jung, psychiatrist and well-known explorer of the human spirit and psyche, called the two aspects:

ANIMUS ◄————► ANIMA
MALE ◄————► FEMALE

The male and female principles are in every human being. We need to have a strong center, so that we can incorporate both sides of our nature. Then we are well-integrated and well-balanced, like an airplane with two wings. We can be steady and stable when we are pulled to one side or the other of our whole being.

Ancient Chinese philosophy refers to two interacting energy modes: yang and yin.

YANG ◄————► YIN
ACTIVE ◄————► PASSIVE
OUTER ◄————► INNER
DAY ◄————► NIGHT
BRIGHT ◄————► DARK
SUN ◄————► MOON
DRY ◄————► WET
POSITIVE ◄————► NEGATIVE

Today, we conceive of electricity as requiring positive and negative polarities in order to work.

To be energized and strong, we need to be well-balanced. If I am all thought and intellect, I will be a cold fish analyzing everything and everyone. If I am all feeling and intuition, I will be "off in the clouds," dreamy and oblivious to what's going on. Sometimes, we attribute thought to men and feeling to women. But we all need to have thought and feeling, intellect and intuition. We each need to be a whole person— to use all of our capacities in order to be a strong, well-balanced person.

INNER STRENGTH

Where do we find our strength? The Hebrew prophet Isaiah said: "In quietness and confidence shall be your strength." (Isaiah 30:15) How do we develop real strength? By being still. By centering ourselves. By listening to the still, small voice within.

We often have associated strength with lots of noise, horsepower, force. Bigger guns. Bigger bombs. Bigger cars. Bigger muscles. The hero is "strong" if he says things like:
"Step outside."
"Draw."
"Make my day."
Folk heroes displaying this type of strength are Dirty Harry, Rambo and James Bond. In the Bible, the strong man in this outer way was probably Samson.

There is another facet of strength. It is inner strength, quiet strength, stillness. Like a deep lake waiting to go through the hydroelectric generators to produce millions of watts of electricity, it is calm and still. And yet tremendous energy is there. Quiet strength. Inner confidence. Poise. The ability to be peaceful, not to retaliate when provoked, nonviolent strength. Here the folk heroes are people like Mahatma Gandhi, a little man with great strength of character; Dr. Martin Luther King Jr.; Mother Teresa; Rosa Parks. The strong person of inner strength in the Bible is Jesus. People of inner strength say "step inside" rather than "step outside."

Gandhi took the strategy of nonviolent activism and changed India. He called his strategy of strength *Satyagraha,* meaning "truth force." Gandhi called his autobiography, *The Story of My Experiments with Truth.* He said his aim was to transform conflict rather than to suppress it or explode it into violence.

There are all kinds of strength. The cartoon character Superman performed amazing feats of physical strength. The actor best known for portraying Superman in the movies is Christopher Reeve. It was such a popular role that Reeve was thought of by many people as being Superman—able to "leap tall buildings at a single bound."

Then one fateful day, Reeve fell from his horse and was left paralyzed from the neck down from a spinal cord injury. Since then, he has been a tower of strength, of a different kind than the Superman character. He has found and demonstrated great courage, tenacity and inner strength. He has turned a tragedy around and become more of an inspiring hero to millions by his comeback and activism for people with spinal cord injuries. He is a survivor—a man of great strength, who has looked inside to find a power found not just in muscles and bones, but in spirit, mind and heart.

Strength is our ability to:

- endure, hold fast, stand firm, keep the faith
- "hang in there" and keep our balance
- stay in integrity and not compromise our principles
- ride out the storm
- "keep on keeping on"
- make positive contributions in spite of disappointments, rejections and injuries

On the mental and emotional levels we need strength:

- so people cannot sway us from our positive convictions
- to stand firm when everyone else may be rattled
- to know we are up to the job—that we can do it

Real strength is not being rigid or inflexible. Strength is being able to bend with pressure and stress. The willow is stronger than the oak in a high wind.

Bull-headedness is not strength. Stubbornness is not strength. Strength is being able to look at new ideas, admit we made a mistake, change our way of thinking, and do things in better ways.

Remember: "In quietness and confidence shall be your strength." We can be still, become more aware, meditate, get centered and affirm: I am poised and centered in infinite strength.

God, you are my core strength and stability.

OVERCOMING REJECTION AND THE STRENGTH TO KEEP GOING

Gay Lynn. Have you ever thought about writing a book? Perhaps you know someone who has. My husband and I had this seed of an idea that grew inside of us, and so we put a book together. I chose to "agent" the book myself, which means that I sent a lot of proposals to publishers. I hoped that I would get a positive response from one of them.

Well, I did get responses, but they were not what I had hoped they would be. Rejection letters came in droves saying, "Thanks, but no thanks." It's said that you're not an author until you can wallpaper a room with rejection letters. Well, I really felt that I was on my way to becoming an author because I received a lot of those rejection letters. Finally, we received a letter from a good publisher that said, "Yes, we're interested."

We were thrilled. We just knew this was the one. It was a fine publisher, very cutting edge. We celebrated, already in that mode of feeling our success.

Then I had a dream. In the dream, I was told that the proposal was going to be sent back. I actually saw the proposal being returned in the dream. David and I often share our dreams in the morning, but I didn't want to talk about this one. I avoided talking about this dream because it wasn't what I really wanted to happen.

David went to the office before me that day and he called to say, "Gay Lynn, I have some bad news for you—the proposal has been returned." And I said, "Oh, just like the dream had foretold!"

I felt so discouraged, devastated and disappointed. I cried and cried. My dog came over to me. (Our pets can be so comforting to us. They pick up on our emotions and our feelings.) She stayed beside me as I cried and felt completely devastated. I doubted myself, wondering why I'd ever gotten into this project in the first place. It was a dumb idea. Who was I to think

that I could get a book published? So I had these doubts, and the fears and tears just kept coming.

Suddenly, I heard a voice inside of me, often called "the still, small voice within." The voice said, "Make another call." I replied, "No, no, I couldn't possibly do that. I feel too raw right now. I hurt too much. I feel too vulnerable. I can't take any more rejection right now. No, there's no way."

But the voice persisted and said, *"Make another call!"*

So, finally, I blew my nose. I looked at the list of publishers that I hadn't heard from yet (and believe me, the list was getting pretty small). I went over to the phone and made another call. Actually, I made a few calls. Finally, on one of those calls, I was able to speak to the Senior Editor, who was very encouraging and interested in the book. She asked if I could send the proposal to her right away. I said, "Absolutely!" So I did and *Transformative Rituals* became a reality, published in 1994 by Health Communications, Inc.

Looking back on that moment of feeling so down, it would have been so easy to give up. It would have been so simple to just let the whole thing go in that moment. But I persisted. I was stronger than my fears, I moved past my doubts, and I made the next call.

So, whatever it is that you have in your life right now, that dream that you'd like to see made a reality, take the next step. *Make the next call.* Rise above and beyond your feelings of rejection or despair. You have the strength within you to do great things. Do it now.

STRENGTH IN THE FACE OF CHALLENGES

When things aren't going well in our lives, how can we stay strong? I've had to explore this many times in my own life.

Many years ago, we came to a wonderful church in Hollywood, Florida. We began working there, helping this spiritual community to grow. When we arrived, we realized that the church had many challenges before it. It had a very large mortgage to pay, but not enough people to make the payment or pay us a decent salary. So, I was scared, fearful and anxious. Perhaps you've felt that way at times in your life, especially around money issues.

Again I had a dream.

Dreams are the language of the soul. Our soul is that part of us that recognizes the larger perspective, the big picture, the grand scheme, the greater wisdom. From our soul, we can draw strength and wisdom to tune into unconscious prompting and guidance.

The Swiss psychiatrist, Carl Jung, discovered in his work that the guidance we need to find our way through problems can come from both our inner and outer lives. He wrote, "Indeed, many of our dreams are concerned with details of our outer life and our surroundings. Such things as the tree in front of the window, one's bicycle or car, or a stone picked up during a walk may be raised to the level of symbolism through our dream life and become meaningful. If we pay attention to our dreams, instead of living in a cold, impersonal world of meaningless chance, we may begin to emerge into a world of our own, full of important and secretly ordered events." (*Man and His Symbols*, p. 208)

Our dreams can provide us with a wonderful resource of strength. I journal my dreams every single night, and in my dream during this period of feeling fearful and anxious, I heard a voice. The voice said to me, "*If anything can possibly go right, it will!*"

Isn't that interesting? Just the opposite of what we usually call Murphy's Law. But this was a higher law, a stronger law that I could really focus on and depend upon. I knew the dream was indicating that things were going to be all right in our church home. We were going to grow. So I shared that with our spiritual community. I said, "Let's hold this affirmation of truth together: *If anything can possibly go right, it will!*" We did that and the church grew, people came and prosperity flowed.

So, my friend, if you're dealing with a challenge in your life right now, know that within you is the strength that you need to deal with anything that is before you. You have a resilient spirit, a spirit that is able to overcome any challenge. I ask you to hold this affirmation for yourself:

If anything can possibly go right, it will!

SPINE AND NERVES
ARE TREE OF LIFE

Dr. Robert. As a medical doctor, I have worked with many people who needed great strength and lots of "backbone" in order to bring about their healing. What do you think about when you think of strength? One of the images that comes to my mind is of a huge, majestic, strong tree. Just think—this tree grew from a tiny seed. It took strength just to push out its first shoots above the ground to become a small seedling, and to sink its roots down into the earth to form a strong foundation. Then, each year the tree grew—its trunk got bigger and stronger, it put out more branches and leaves, and its roots grew deeper.

In its lifetime, the tree encountered storms and high winds, floods and droughts. However, it was strong enough to weather the storms, flexible enough to bend but not to break, and resilient enough to always come back to its center and keep on growing. Sound familiar? Is this how you have weathered the storms and challenges in your life? How have you demonstrated strength, stability and steadfastness on your life's journey?

Eventually, after many years, the tree reaches its full height and potential, and then it bears its own fruits and seeds.

As many others have done, I like to compare this tree to one of the major systems in our physical body: our spinal cord and nerves that serve as the body's communication system. (See Figure 3.) The trunk of a tree is like the central spinal cord, whereas the branches and roots of the tree are like the many nerves that go to every part of our bodies. In this sense, we have a "tree" right within our physical form, made up of our spine and nerves: our tree of life.

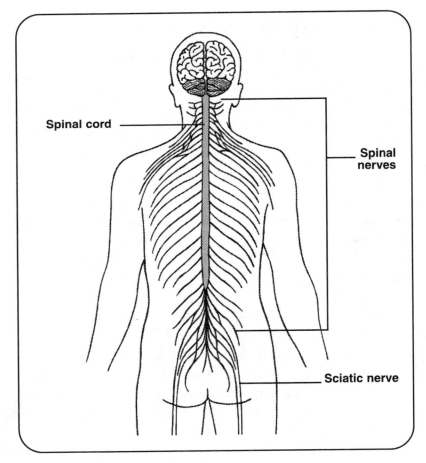

Figure 3. Spinal cord and nerves

Like an actual tree, the very nature of our spinal cord and nerves is to be strong, steady and resilient. Therefore, as we are growing and evolving, we don't have to be weak and indecisive, to be "spineless." Rather, we have the power of strength right within us, which expresses itself through our spinal cord and nerves. So whatever the challenge, we can strengthen our spine and steady our nerves, to reach our full potential as a human being. Then, our tree of life will bring forth plentiful and nourishing fruits.

COMMUNICATION SYSTEM

The spinal cord and nerves serve as a communication system that connects the brain with the rest of the body. As explained previously in the chapter on Faith, the cerebrum of the brain is the central computer for our whole body. All of our thoughts and seed ideas, all of our feelings and memories, anchor in and through our brain cells and circuits. Then these ideas and directives have to be communicated to the rest of the body, because the brain regulates and monitors all other body organs.

Thoughts, feelings and memories get converted into bioelectrical impulses in the cells and circuitry of the brain. From there, these nerve impulses travel down nerve tracts to the base of the brain and out of the skull by way of the spinal cord. The spinal cord, which continues down to the low region of the back, is housed within the protective confines of the spinal column or backbone, which is made up of bony vertebrae. The backbone protects the delicate spinal cord just as the skull protects the brain.

Along the spinal cord, at regular intervals, spinal nerves exit between the vertebrae and carry nerve impulses to all parts of the body. At the base of the spine, numerous spinal nerves join together on either side of the body to form the sciatic nerves, which carries nerve messages to the legs.

In addition to the central spinal cord, there are also twelve pairs of other nerves called cranial nerves that exit from other openings in the skull. These carry bioelectrical nerve impulses to and from the head, neck, chest and abdomen.

There are many types of nerves. Motor nerves carry signals from the brain to the muscles, causing the muscles to contract. (Commonly, when most people speak about strength in the body, they are talking about the strength of the muscles. However, when we use the word "strength" in this chapter, we are referring primarily to the strength, stability and steady functioning of the nerves, without which the muscles could not contract nor be coordinated in their many movements. We correlate the muscles with the quality of power, because muscles move our body and thereby give us power and dominion. See chapter 5.)

Autonomic nerves include the sympathetic and parasympathetic divisions, which innervate all of the body's internal organs. In general, the sympathetic nerves are more active during periods of excitement, activity, stress, fear and anxiety. They send nerve signals that cause the heart to beat stronger and more quickly, the lungs to breathe faster, and blood to be directed to the muscles. They also direct the adrenal glands to pour out adrenalin which accounts for the great strength that we may demonstrate during periods of intense activity or crisis. The parasympathetic nerves predominate during periods of rest, relaxation and meditation. They cause the heart and breathing to slow down, blood pressure to drop, and blood to flow to the digestive tract after meals.

The balanced expression of the sympathetic and parasympathetic nerves brings balance to the whole body. Equating them to the positive (yang) and negative (yin) polarities discussed previously, the sympathetic nerves come under the yang or active polarity, whereas parasympathetic nerves reflect the yin or passive polarity. We can demonstrate great strength both in times of tremendous activity and stress, as well as in periods of outer inactivity, rest and reflection.

Yet another type of nerve is the sensory nerve, which carries nerve impulses from the sense receptors to the spinal cord and up to the brain. For example, when we touch something with our finger, our touch receptor sends a signal from the finger along a sensory nerve up the arm to the spinal cord, which then relays the signal up the spinal cord to the brain.

So, you can see that thousands of nerve signals travel every day from the brain, down the spinal cord, and out the nerves to the body's organs; and thousands of other impulses travel via the sensory nerves back up the spinal cord to the brain. Indeed, the spinal cord is our body's communications superhighway. To function properly, there can be no short circuits, no blockages, no impairments in the nerves. The nerves must be resilient, strong, finely tuned and steady in order to convey the vast amount of information that flows to and from the brain.

STRENGTHENING THE SPINE AND NERVES

When you are feeling strong and stable, when you are in a good steady flow in your life, how do your spinal cord and nerves function? Unless there is some major structural defect or nutritional deficiency, they work wonderfully in expressing your power of strength and stability.

How about when you feel weak and indecisive, when you waver or vacillate, when you feel overwhelmed or agitated—now what happens with your nerves? In these instances, they may become irritated and inflamed.

Have you ever sensed that your nerves were "on edge," "frayed" or "shot"? Have you ever felt that you were stretched to the limit, burnt out or overextended? At these times, you may have said, "I'm so upset and edgy, I just can't seem to settle down." Or, "I'm trembling inside."

Maybe your difficulties with strength showed up in your dreams. One patient of mine dreamt that the electrical wiring in his house was not insulated properly, so the wires overheated and caused a fire. What did this mean? The house represented his consciousness—his mind, emotions, memories and physical body. The wiring symbolized his nerves, which had become on fire or "inflamed" because he had not taken sufficient quiet time to strengthen his inner resolve, and to insulate himself from the stress and strain in his life.

If you have any such problems with your nerves, concentrate on your power of strength. Pull back, take a deep breath, get recentered and then affirm, "I am strong and stable. My nerves are steady and resilient. I am in full alignment with the good within me, which strengthens and stabilizes my spinal cord and nerves."

One of my favorite affirmations comes from the Book of Proverbs in the Bible: "The Lord is a tower of strength." (Proverbs 18:10-11) What is this "tower" in the body? Of course, it's the spine. So, when your nerves are jangled, when you are shaken or agitated, when you feel like giving up, confidently affirm, "I am a tower of strength. My spine is a column of solid light. All is well and in divine harmony." And then visualize or think of your spine as being a magnificent column or tower of light.

At other times of difficulty with the power of strength, people may have inflammation and discomfort in the nerves in their neck, sometimes with pain, numbness or a tingling sensation that radiates down the nerves into the shoulder and arm. In some cases, the pain and inflammation may be in the nerves of the mid-back region or all along the spine. (People who lack courage or the strength of their convictions are sometimes said to have a "yellow streak" down their backs.) Perhaps most commonly, people have pain or discomfort in their lower back, which often involves the many nerves in that region. This can include so-called sciatica, which is inflammation of the sciatic nerve that travels down the leg.

All spinal and back pain, however, is not due to nerve inflammation (neuritis). Consider other causes like muscle and ligament strains, muscle spasms, poor posture, trauma to the spine, arthritis, misalignment of the vertebrae or spinal tumors. A slipped or prolapsed disc in the lower back may press on the sciatic nerve and cause sciatica. If the pain persists or is severe, see a physician, get the necessary diagnostic tests and begin appropriate treatment. In addition, you may benefit from chiropractic adjustments, massage, acupuncture, pressure-point therapies, nutritional supplements such as the B vitamins, exercise, relaxation exercises, counseling and many other therapies.

No matter what else you do, however, always remember that the power of strength externalizes as the spine and nerves. Therefore, if you are having difficulty with your nerves, always focus on your indwelling strength faculty. You already have the strength and steadfastness that you need to bring about your rebalancing. Think about being strong. Affirm that you are flexible, resilient, persistent and courageous. In the silence, draw upon the vast pool of inner strength that resides within you. Be a tower of strength.

Sit quietly and begin to relax. Take a few slow breaths, breathing deeply from your diaphragm. Each time you breathe out, let go of any tension, worry or anxiety that you may have. As you breathe slowly and deeply, you become calm and at peace.

Then visualize yourself being outdoors or actually go outside. Focus on the sun above you, which is the source of energy for all physical life and is symbolic of the One Source. Imagine yourself basking in the golden-yellow light of the sun, in the light of Spirit, which streams down upon you. Visualize and feel this light entering into the top of your head and your brain, which become highly energized and illumined.

Then see the golden-yellow light starting to flow from your brain down your spinal cord. It moves first into your spine in the region of your neck. As it does, sense and feel your spine and nerves being strengthened and stabilized. Then the light slowly descends along your spine to the mid-back region, which it also energizes, reinforces and strengthens. Finally, the light flows all the way down to the base of your spine.

Now visualize the light flowing from the spine along the nerves to every part of your body: your arms and hands, your chest and abdomen, your legs and feet. Wherever you may feel a weakness, inflammation or discomfort in any of your nerves, see the sunlight invigorating, strengthening, revitalizing and healing them.

Visualize your whole spine as being a solid, steady, stable column of golden-yellow light, which now radiates along all the nerves to every part of your body. Affirm: I am a tower of strength; my spine and nerves are steady and stable; I am illumined and strengthened in the light of God.

As you are guided from within, slowly come out of your meditation and think of some new way to be strong in your life.

1. I am strong, steady and stable.
2. I am a tower of strength.
3. God's spirit in me makes me steadfast.
4. I transform conflict, and act with confidence and strength.
5. I have the strength to meet and handle successfully all that comes to me.
6. I persist through obstacles and rejections; I go to meet my good.
7. Doubts and fears have no power over me, for I am strengthened from within.
8. I use my strength to benefit others, not to dominate them.
9. I have the strength to "keep on keeping on."
10. I am strengthened by my dreams, which give me guidance and direction.
11. If anything can possibly go right, it will.
12. I am a strong, well-balanced person.
13. I have the inner strength to hold fast, stand firm and endure.
14. I weather the storms of life by being flexible and strong.
15. My spine communicates strength to my entire body.
16. I stay steady and balanced in the midst of my busy life.
17. My nerves are calm, steady and resilient.

18. I bend but I do not break; I always return to my center.
19. In quietness I listen; my being is filled with newfound strength.
20. I am committed to bringing light and healing to the world.
21. I make my life count for something; I can be counted on.
22. My strength is not in being stubborn but in being persistent.
23. I am poised and centered in infinite strength.
24. I have verve in my nerves.
25. I use my strength to move beyond rejection or put-downs.
26. I have a resilient spirit.
27. I have a strong "backbone"; I stand up for my convictions.
28. My spine is a column of light.
29. It is the storm, not me, that is going to blow away.
30. I have a lot of nerve to do all the good that I am guided to do.
31. My tree of life is strong, firmly rooted and fruitful.

4
The Power of WISDOM

WISDOM

WISDOM/GOOD JUDGMENT is my ability to discern, evaluate and make decisions. Every day is judgment day. Heaven and hell are not places I go after I die; they are states of mind that I create by the decisions I make in the courtroom of my mind. Wisdom expresses in my body via the pituitary gland and the rest of the endocrine system.

JUDGMENT DAY IS NOW

David. Every day is judgment day. It's important to use wisdom and good judgment. Our wisdom or judgment ability

is our power to evaluate and to choose. We sit on the bench in the courtroom of our mind. We make rulings. We make judgments and choices. We hand down decrees. We decree a thing and it becomes so for us. It becomes our reality. We may say, as we get up in the morning, "I dread today. I know it is going to be a mess." Or, we may say, "I look forward to this day and I go to meet my good today." The difference is not the day. The difference is our judgment and choice.

Is the glass half full or half empty? Do rose bushes have thorns or do thorn bushes have roses? Do we focus on the roses or the thorns? It's our choice, isn't it? Do we make choices that lead us to a fuller, better, healthier, more fulfilling life?

There's a story of a reporter at a baseball umpires' convention. The reporter is interviewing various umpires about how they make split-second decisions in hotly contested games. What pressure they are under to make the call! The reporter was especially interested in how these umpires call balls and strikes when the baseball travels at nearly 100 miles an hour and just cuts the corner of the plate. He asked one umpire how he could make such a snap decision. The umpire replied, "Well, son, there's balls and there's strikes, and I calls them the way *I sees them.*"

The reporter thanked him and caught up with another famous umpire. He asked him the same question. This umpire said, "There's balls and there's strikes, and I calls them the *way they are.*"

Pursuing another old-time umpire, the reporter received this answer: "There's balls and there's strikes, but *they ain't nothing till I call them!*"

Till I call them: Our choices determine our lives. What kind of an "umpire" am I? How do I make the calls? What kind of self-talk do I use? What do I call myself? Failure? Stupid? Weak? Growing? Forgiving? Overcomer? What do I call other people? Situations? Work? My family? The day of judgment is every day of our lives, because we must choose the quality and nature of our thoughts—every single day and minute therein.

We need to use our best wisdom and good judgment to choose what is worthwhile, helpful, healthy, healing, positive, peace-making, and for the highest good of all concerned. Sure, we often have tough, difficult decisions to make, which involve complex factors. Moreover, everybody may not like or agree with every decision we make. We still need to rely on our power of wisdom and good judgment to choose wisely and compassionately. This is our day of judgment.

CHOOSE CONTINUOUS IMPROVEMENT

There is an old Chinese wisdom that says, "The road turns with your feet." That means, I can't really make a fatal mistake or error, from which there is no recovery or way to proceed in life. There is no dead end. I may think I made a terrible mistake or a horrible decision, but life goes on. The road turns with my feet, as long as I keep moving forward. I can learn from that decision and weave that into my wisdom.

It is like jazz musicians playing a wrong note, which they do all the time. They weave the note into the melody and keep right on going. The wrong note creates a dissonance that the musician skillfully uses to modulate to a new key. The musician makes it appear as if the whole progression was intended that way, as if it was the only way it could have been.

In like manner, we can hear or recognize our misjudgment, and then transcend the mistake and incorporate the lesson we have learned. Rather than stop, beat ourselves up, lament or call ourselves negative names, we can change key, change perspective, stay in the flow and keep going.

THE KINGDOM OF HEAVEN IS IN THE STATE OF MIND

John Milton said in *Paradise Lost*, "The mind is its own place, and in itself can make a Heav'n of Hell, a Hell of Heav'n." Heaven and hell are not places we go after we die. They are states of mind that we create by the decisions we make in the courtroom of our mind. We can make a hell of a life or a heaven of a life. It is largely up to us. We always have a choice. We are creating our life choice by choice, action by action.

Again, we are the judge in the courtroom of our mind. Life does not judge or punish us or have a "last judgment" to condemn us. The stories we all have heard of being brought up before a throne and being sent to heaven or hell are allegories. As the famous teacher and author of *The Power of Myth*, Joseph Campbell points out, these stories are really powerful, mythological ways of portraying the ability all of us have to send ourselves toward freedom and peace, or punishment and misery.

According to reports on July 28, 1999, in newspapers and on television, Pope John Paul, a week after telling Roman Catholics that heaven is not a place up in the clouds, declared that hell was not a physical place either. It exists, he said, but it is more a state of mind. "Hell is not a punishment imposed externally by God, but the condition resulting from attitudes and actions which people adopt in this life," he said. The Pope explained that artists pictured heaven and hell as literal places, but he said it is not Catholic teaching.

USE JUDGMENT WITH EXTREME CARE

We are warned about using this particular power of ours: "Do not judge, so that you may not be judged." (Matthew 7:12) We have all heard that. Does that mean we are never to make judgments? That would be like telling a judge in a courtroom not to make decisions, not to decide right from wrong, not to decide the case before the court. We have to make good decisions, choices and judgments. We have to use our wisdom faculty every day.

The caution really is about being judgmental. Be careful about condemning yourself or others—that is, being "damning." "You are no good." "There's no good at all in me—in you!" That's condemning—a negative decree that has no compassion or love, not looking beyond what has been done to the inner spirit of the person.

The power that most needs to be combined with judgment is love. We can see the harshness, vindictiveness and witch-hunts that take place when we highlight errors, point fingers or cast stones. The tempering, compassionate power of love is needed to balance our power of judgment. We often find that we can get ourselves into a "hell of a life" by having lots of love, but failing to use good judgment in picking the people with whom we fall in love. We can be very "loving" but fail to set healthy boundaries as we try to "help" others, thereby allowing them to "use" us for their own selfish purposes. I once knew a woman who complained about her unemployed alcoholic husband. As I talked with her one day, I found out that this was her third alcoholic husband. She had made that choice for the third time in her life.

Love and wisdom combined create a powerful synthesis. In biblical accounts of Jesus and his disciples, James and John are portrayed as brothers. James is often understood to represent wisdom, whereas John represents love. Their brotherhood indicates that love and wisdom are closely related. Jesus almost always took Peter (who portrays faith), James and John with him when he went to pray or make a major decision, or when he faced a life crisis. In like manner, we take with us faith, wisdom and love as our primary helpers in meeting the challenges of our life.

READER/CUSTOMER CARE SURVEY

If you are enjoying this book, please help us serve you better and meet your changing needs by taking a few minutes to complete this survey. Please fold it and drop it in the mail.

As a special **"Thank You"** we'll send you news about new books and a valuable **Gift Certificate!**

PLEASE PRINT   C8C

NAME:_____

ADDRESS:_____

_____

TELEPHONE NUMBER:_____

FAX NUMBER:_____

E-MAIL:_____

WEBSITE:_____

(1) Gender: 1)_____Female 2)_____Male

(2) Age:
1)_____12 or under   5)_____30-39
2)_____13-15   6)_____40-49
3)_____16-19   7)_____50-59
4)_____20-29   8)_____60+

(3) Your Children's Age(s):
Check all that apply.
1)_____6 or Under   3)_____11-14
2)_____7-10   4)_____15-18

(7) Marital Status:
1)_____Married
2)_____Single
3)_____Divorced/Wid.

(8) Was this book
1)_____Purchased for yourself?
2)_____Received as a gift?

(9) How many books do you read a month?
1)_____1   3)_____3
2)_____2   4)_____4+

(10) How did you find out about this book?
Please check ONE.
1)_____Personal Recommendation
2)_____Store Display
3)_____TV/Radio Program
4)_____Bestseller List
5)_____Website
6)_____Advertisement/Article or Book Review
7)_____Catalog or mailing
8)_____Other_____

(11) What FIVE subject areas do you enjoy reading about most?
Rank: 1 (favorite) through 5 (least favorite)
A)_____ Self Development
B)_____ New Age/Alternative Healing
C)_____ Storytelling
D)_____Spirituality/Inspiration
E)_____ Family and Relationships
F)_____ Health and Nutrition
G)_____Recovery
H)_____Business/Professional
I)_____ Entertainment
J)_____ Teen Issues
K)_____ Pets

(16) Where do you purchase most of your books?
Check the top TWO locations.
A)_____ General Bookstore
B)_____ Religious Bookstore
C)_____ Warehouse/Price Club
D)_____ Discount or Other Retail Store
E)_____ Website
F)_____ Book Club/Mail Order

(18) Did you enjoy the stories in this book?
1)_____Almost All
2)_____Few
3)_____Some

(19) What type of magazine do you SUBSCRIBE to?
Check up to FIVE subscription categories.
A)_____ General Inspiration
B)_____ Religious/Devotional
C)_____ Business/Professional
D)_____ World News/Current Events
E)_____ Entertainment
F)_____ Homemaking, Cooking, Crafts
G)_____ Women's Issues
H)_____ Other (please specify)_____

(24) Please indicate your income level
1)_____Student/Retired-fixed income
2)_____Under $25,000
3)_____$25,000-$50,000
4)_____$50,001-$75,000
5)_____$75,001-$100,000
6)_____Over $100,000

NO POSTAGE
NECESSARY
IF MAILED
IN THE
UNITED STATES

BUSINESS REPLY MAIL

FIRST-CLASS MAIL PERMIT NO 45 DEERFIELD BEACH, FL

POSTAGE WILL BE PAID BY ADDRESSEE

HEALTH COMMUNICATIONS, INC.
3201 SW 15TH STREET
DEERFIELD BEACH FL 33442-9875

((25) Do you attend seminars?
1)_____Yes   2)_____No

(26) If you answered yes, what type?
Check all that apply.
1)_____Business/Financial
2)_____Motivational
3)_____Religious/Spiritual
4)_____Job-related
5)_____Family/Relationship issues

(31) Are you:
1) A Parent?_____
2) A Grandparent?_____

Additional comments you would like to make:

_____

_____

_____

_____

N-CS

MAKE BALANCED JUDGMENTS

The most creative and balanced decisions in our lives come from a combination of our rational and intuitive capacities. We arrive at our best judgments when we honor our head and heart, our thoughts and feelings, our logic and intuition. Most of us are better in one mode of thinking than the other. We may tend to be logical and analytical, but not utilize or value our intuitive side. Or, we may just go with our heart and whatever feels right, without using common sense or logical analysis in arriving at our judgments.

Following are some of the "left brain" or rational, logical approaches:

- Gather facts. Get comparisons. Look at probabilities and consequences.
- List priorities. What is most important? What comes first, second, third?
- What is the timetable? Schedule? Plan? Flow chart?
- Who will do it? Who will assist? Who is responsible?
- Consult experts and knowledgeable authorities. Check reference books, articles and reports to gather and verify facts. Go to the library. Look on the Internet.
- Go for counseling. Sort out your thoughts and feelings. Consider various consequences. Look at options and alternatives. Set priorities and goals.

How about our intuitive ability? Our intuition is sometimes called our inner tutor or teacher. We may have flashes of insight that just come to us. At times, we see or feel something that "tells" us what to do or not do.

In the past, our educational system, religious training and business procedures often were rationally centered. The realm of our intuition was commonly relegated to poets, mystics and "women's intuition." However, that is changing now. "Medical intuitives" work with and train some doctors. Nurses scan a patient's energy field and body with "therapeutic touch." Businesses give their employees seminars that focus on intuition, following one's heart and honoring one's "gut feelings."

The president of Sony Corporation says he likes to "swallow" a deal before he signs it, to see how it feels to him, if it is digestible or indigestible. Ray Kroc once had a feeling that he should buy some small hamburger stands in Chicago, which later became the giant McDonald's chain. Winston Churchill once had a sense of danger and avoided a trip where he probably would have been assassinated.

Here are some of the intuitive, "right brain" approaches:

- Meditate quietly and be open to ideas and feelings.
- Pay attention to and work with your dreams. Value and befriend them.
- Have a prayer life, where you commune silently with God. Listen to the "still, small voice" within you.
- Spend time in nature. Work in your garden. Feel oneness with all life.
- Read good poetry. Listen to quality music, especially meditative music.
- Do drumming, chanting, dancing, yoga, tai chi.
- Put your hands over your heart when you lie down or meditate. Bless your heart and let your heart "speak" to you.
- Keep a life journal in which you write your innermost feelings.
- Do artwork: drawing, painting, sculpting.

This is much different from racking our brain, trying to get others to tell us what to do, allowing ourselves to be emotionally swayed or "sold," or just spontaneously jumping into something. Postponing the decision indefinitely, just living with the pain or trouble, doesn't work very well either.

Go beyond just making a quick judgment; discover the right and best way for you and all concerned. You always have a choice. You may feel sometimes like you just have to live with things the way they are. But you always have a choice. Make a good and wise judgment!

THE STARFISH BY THE SEA

Gay Lynn. In 1994, my husband David and I were traveling across the country on an extensive book tour. We found ourselves in a beautiful coastal city and decided to spend a warm summer's day at the beach. I love the seashore and I

joined a little girl who was very friendly and playing by the surf. Her parents were an average-looking, white, middle-class couple who waved to me in a friendly way as they sat on their beach blanket. As the little five-year-old and I played together, an African-American couple came by. They had found a beautiful starfish and graciously shared their beach treasure with us. The little girl was thrilled when they gently placed the starfish in her hand. We all delighted in the moment, sharing her joy of holding a starfish for the first time.

As the couple walked away, the little girl leaned over and said to me in a loud whisper, "Those are the bad people. You have to be careful of them." Why, I asked? "Because they will rob you and hurt you." I thought how tragic it was that this child's viewpoint was already formed and developed at such a young age. Her power of judgment had already been patterned in a prejudiced and biased way. I said, "Who told you that these were the bad people?" And she said, "Mommy and Daddy." I replied, "These people did not hurt you. In fact they were very nice to you and let you have their starfish." She only looked at me in confusion because her mental image was programmed to have a negative view. Even though her experience was different, her "family tape" of prejudice and bias based solely on the color of a person's skin was still running.

We, too, must look at our own "family tapes" and do some deleting and editing. Our family fears and judgments may have unconsciously taken root in us and, like the little girl, we automatically judge something or someone even though our actual experience might be very different. Some families have judged that only "crazy" people go for counseling and they don't see themselves as being "crazy." This prejudice can block our ability to seek the help and support we need.

What are some of your family's prejudices and negative judgments that you have absorbed and now need to change or release?

DIVORCE: THE MOST DIFFICULT DECISION

Over half of the marriages in the United States end in divorce. I have met with numerous couples over the years and struggled to help them make the most agonizing, gut-wrenching decision of their lives. Making this judgment affects children, grandparents, aunts, uncles, cousins, neighbors and friends. Everyone in that family is emotionally affected in some way. My advice to people is to work things out, to stay and grow together whenever possible. Many couples are able to do this. They get counseling, learn new communication skills, become less judgmental, and work more cooperatively with the whole family. Many of the ideas in this chapter can assist you in making good decisions for your entire family, which requires looking at the big picture and weighing all the thoughts and feelings in the scales of balance.

Some families do go through the divorce process. Often they are left with emotional wounds and scars that affect the rest of their lives. To stay in a marriage that is dysfunctional, abusive, or lacks love or warmth is also damaging. So the decision to divorce has to be evaluated and judged by each person and family. Many things must be considered, especially the well-being of the children.

I found myself wrestling with this decision in 1984 with my former husband. We had two lovely children, a nice suburban home and a supportive family, but our love and companionship were eroding almost daily. I questioned myself about what part I was playing in the erosion. I wrote in my journal regularly, to sort out my thoughts and feelings about myself, my husband, my children, and other family members who were influencing our lives. I paid close attention to my dreams, talked to a counselor and received support from my minister.

During this time, one of the most vivid dreams that I had involved my grandmother. She was standing at the top of a staircase and had her hand extended to me. She motioned for me to come to her. My grandmother had been dead for many years, and her loving presence gave me comfort. She could see that I was sad and distraught, and told me that I did not have to keep going on this way. I could be with her. I realized in a flash that if I took her hand, I, too, would die and be with her. In that moment, I made a conscious decision to live and withdrew my hand. She smiled with love and I woke up knowing that no matter what I had to go through in the next weeks, months or years, I would survive.

It seemed to me that on a deep feeling level I was making a decision. I needed to be out of the marriage. How would I make that change? It is like a death experience. Something dies, but something new also arises out of the ashes of what has been. Now, my soul was saying, "How are you going to move out? You choose." Some people literally move out of failing family situations by getting sick or dying. I did not want to give myself this message. I wanted to live. I wanted to start a new life. This was the wisdom that I held onto, and my mind and body responded.

The ensuing months were painful. I made the most difficult decision of my life and decided to let the children's father have physical custody, while we both shared joint custody. They lived with him during the week and with me on the weekends. More women today are making this decision, but many years ago this was unusual and I felt judged by many people. To be judged in this way was hurtful, which made the decision even more difficult for me. I felt myself collapsing into fears that had me paralyzed. I prayed for strength. I asked for love to lift me out of this harsh judgment I was making on myself and getting from those around me. How could I go on? A part of me just wanted to run back into the marriage and make do.

In the midst of this turmoil I had a vision. I was sleeping and was awakened by the feeling that I wasn't alone. I sat straight up in terror with adrenalin pumping and heart racing, as the figure of a man appeared at the foot of my bed. "Oh Jesus!" were the first words of shock out of my mouth.

As my eyes focused I repeated the words, but this time they were words of recognition. It was Jesus! No words were spoken, only a profound feeling of peace and strength flooded my whole being. I laid back down and all my paralyzed fears and anxiety melted away in the glow of his loving presence. I knew that I would be able to walk through whatever was before me. I felt at the deepest level of my being that I was loved, that I was not being judged, that I could serve a higher calling in my life and in my work, which I have been privileged to do for many years.

My decision to get a divorce is not one that is right for everyone. Each of us needs to follow our own best guidance and the wise counsel of others. Here is an exercise to help you in using your power of wisdom and good judgment effectively:

Sit quietly and breathe deeply following each of these statements:

- I am capable of making good and wise decisions.
- I am loved and supported by my wise heart that guides my every decision.
- I am gentle with myself and release harsh and critical judgments that I have made about others and myself.
- I listen to my heart and my head, my thoughts and my feelings, my intuition and my intellect, my dreams and the counsel of others.
- I am a wise woman (or man) and true to myself.

Body

PITUITARY GLAND AND ENDOCRINE SYSTEM

Dr. Robert. The entire physical body has its own innate wisdom and good judgment. The body always seeks balance and harmony, wholeness and health.

In particular, our power of judgment-justice-wisdom expresses by way of our seven major endocrine glands: pineal, pituitary, thyroid, thymus, pancreas, gonad and adrenal glands. (See Figure 4.) Each of these glands serves as a wise judge that oversees the functioning of a particular organ or activity of the body. Endocrine glands release hormones into the bloodstream, which carries them to the organs that they regulate. In general, the more there is of a hormone, the more active its target organ becomes.

The pituitary gland is the master gland of the entire endocrine system. This peanut-sized organ found at the base of the brain in the middle of the head is the principal seat of judgment in our body. Think of the pituitary as being the chief justice of the seven judges or endocrine glands.

Just like a wise judge in a courtroom, we make good judgments by carefully gathering and evaluating all relevant information about a given situation, and then by choosing that which engenders health, balance and harmony. This is

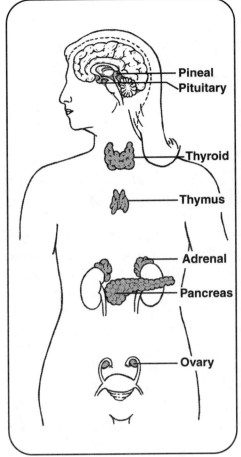

Figure 4. Endocrine glands (female)

precisely what the pituitary does. All of the hormones secreted in the bloodstream by the other endocrine glands pass through the pituitary gland, which also receives information from the hypothalamus that is located just above it. Carefully weighing and evaluating all this input, the pituitary sends out more or less of its nine major hormones, which regulate the other endocrine glands, determine the growth and repair of the body, and regulate the excretion of urine.

Focus on a period in your life when you felt good about yourself, when you were wise and just in your evaluations. How did your body feel then? No doubt, it felt at ease, full of energy, without any imbalance or dysfunction. That's because the pituitary gland reflects and enacts our good judgments. It secretes the right amount of its hormones to harmonize the other endocrine glands, which in turn secrete the right amount of hormones to bring balance to all the body's organs. We make a judgment and it manifests in our body. As we sow, so do we reap.

Consider a time when you were confused or conflicted about someone or some situation you were judging, when you made harsh, unloving or shortsighted judgments about yourself or others. During this period, did you feel tension, discomfort or pain in your temples and forehead area? Did it feel like a vise or clamp exerted pressure on the front and center of your head, in the area of your pituitary gland? Maybe your brow was knitted as you struggled to see the light, as you sought the wisdom of Solomon in solving the dilemma that weighed heavily on your mind. Your difficulties with judging wisely also may have caused an actual imbalance in your pituitary and other endocrine glands.

Perhaps you had trouble sleeping, which is regulated by the secretion of melatonin by the pineal gland. Some people take small doses of melatonin to help them sleep. Melatonin is the only hormone that can be purchased without a prescription.

As you wrestled with making a wise judgment, maybe your energy level diminished. You may have felt like you had no choice but to give up or to give in to the decisions that others were making for you. Perhaps you considered yourself to be weak, inadequate, unable to make tough choices, lacking in power and vitality, unable to make it on your own. You may even have lost the will to live. Responding to these judgments, your thyroid gland in the throat region may have secreted less of its hormone, thyroxine, thereby lowering your metabolic rate and energy level.

Have you ever felt that it was too painful to love, that you were unlovable, that it was safer and easier to be alone and isolated rather than intimately connected with others? The gland this judgment probably influenced the most was your thymus, since it is located in the center of your chest, in your love center. The thymus secretes thymosin and other hormones that regulate the functioning of the lymphocytes, a type of white blood cell that is an integral part of the immune system (see chapter 2). Unloving judgments lead to lowered immunity. Making wise decisions to open your heart and to be close to others, to care for friends and let them care for you, invigorates your thymus and enhances your immune system.

How about the judgments we make about the food we eat? In countries where the diet is high in refined sugar, processed food and fat, the incidence of diabetes or high blood sugar is high. Such a diet affects primarily the development of Type 2 or adult-onset diabetes. (In Type 1 or juvenile-onset diabetes, the body makes antibodies that destroy the cells in the pancreas that produce insulin, which is needed to transport sugar from the blood to the cells. Type 1 diabetics always need to take insulin.)

In Type 2 diabetes, the pancreas produces insufficient insulin or the body cannot use the insulin that is made. Most Type 2 diabetics are overweight. Treatment usually begins by changing the diet to include lots of fruits, vegetables, grains and other whole foods that are high in fiber, minerals and trace elements. Weight loss is essential. Nutritional supplements also may help.

If you have Type 1 or 2 diabetes, always consult with your physician to find the best treatment for you. At the same time, focus on the power of wisdom and good judgment as a way to help balance your blood sugar. It is well known that stress alters the amount of insulin or other medications that a Type 1 or 2 diabetic needs to maintain proper blood-sugar levels. The judgments we make about ourselves have a direct influence on our pancreas and other endocrine glands. Therefore, make wise judgments that bring order and harmony into your thoughts, feelings and physical form.

Stress also may cause the lowering of sexual hormones (progesterone in females and testosterone in males). Depression, likewise, may lower these hormones, causing a lowered libido. A woman's adverse reaction to stress may lead to infertility, irregular menstrual periods or having no menstrual periods at all.

What happens when we decide we are in harm's way, when we feel threatened, or when we need greater strength to deal with a crisis? Our adrenal glands sitting atop our kidneys, being the wise judges that they are, respond immediately by pumping out more adrenalin (epinephrine). As a result, our brain and mind become more alert, our muscles have more strength, our heart beats faster and our lungs breathe more quickly. At the same time, our adrenals also secrete more corticosteroid hormones, including cortisone and cortisol to help our body respond to the perceived or actual stress.

High levels of adrenalin and cortisol for short periods of time promote health and well-being. They are our body's wise response to a stressful event or condition. Sometimes, however, we feel fearful, upset, shaken or threatened long after an actual challenge or difficulty ends. Or, we may live in a family or work someplace for years where we are not loved or treated with respect. As a result, our adrenaline and cortisol levels remain elevated, which may lead to diseases like heart attacks, ulcers, strokes or lowered immune functioning. In these instances, we must use good judgment and wisdom in letting go of the past and in removing ourselves from an unhealthy or dysfunctional environment. Then our adrenal hormones return to normal levels.

If you suspect you have an imbalance of your endocrine glands, use your good judgment and go see a physician. Be careful not to jump to any conclusions until you get all the necessary tests. Sometimes, we fear the worst and let our anxieties run rampant. "Oh my God," we say, "it could be cancer or some other horrible disease." Then it turns out to be nothing. Other times, we deny that anything is wrong with us and delay seeing a doctor. This is not wise, either. Here's another caution: If your physician does find that one of your glands is overactive or underactive, or that you have some other kind of endocrine disease, be careful not to feel guilty about "creating" this disorder. It may have a strictly physical cause. Genetics may have played a major role. Despite all your introspection and self-analysis, you may never determine what brought about the disorder. You may not need to know this. You are wise to ask your Higher Power to show you how your lack of wisdom or your mis-judgment may have caused or contributed to your disease. But be careful about making simplistic, snap judgments about the origin of your disorder. It may take many years before the right answer finally dawns on you.

In the meantime, use the best of all physical remedies to treat any endocrine imbalance. In addition, always focus on your power of wisdom-judgment-justice. Remember the guiding universal principle: As we judge, so are we judged. This means we enact and play out our judgments right in our own body, particularly in our endocrine glands. As we judge, so do these judgments influence our hormones. Therefore, to bring about healing, be wise and discerning, loving and just in your ongoing evaluations. In due time, when you have judged right and used healthy judgment, the result will be vibrant health of your endocrine system.

The power of wisdom and good judgment also includes the aspect of justice, which has been portrayed as a woman whose eyes are blindfolded. This indicates she does not judge only by outer facts and appearances, but she also intuitively and psychically senses what is right and just. (Intuition commonly is described as being part of the feminine nature or polarity within every man or woman.) In her hand, she holds a balance scale in order to wisely judge what is required to bring a condition into proper balance, harmony and equilibrium.

Envision yourself as a balance scale. Visualize a vertical pole of light that goes from the base of your spine up to and above the top of your head. Then, visualize a horizontal pole that travels through the temples of your head, which intersects the vertical pole in the area of the pituitary gland. Here is the primary seat of judgment in the courtroom of your mind. The horizontal pole extends a couple feet to both sides of your head. Hanging down from each end of it are three chains that hold a pan or balancing station.

Consider a major decision or evaluation you need to make now. It may involve a relationship with a loved one, a possible move or change of jobs, or a health challenge. As you ponder this situation, place all of the facts and figures involved in making your judgment in the right balance station. Consider all the pros and cons of whatever you might decide and how it would affect you and all those close to you. Carefully analyze and think through all of the many levels, ramifications and possibilities involved.

Next, in the left balance station, place all of your "gut" feelings, dreams, visions, heart's desires and inner promptings that help you to make a wise judgment. These dreams and intuitive impressions may be contrary to your conscious analysis or may add a facet or dimension that you have not considered or given enough weight to in your deliberations. Until now, maybe you suppressed these feelings or were blind to them. Perhaps in the stillness, you receive a more insightful and expansive interpretation of a dream, or a new and healthier way to view a past experience.

Just as it takes time for a balance scale to reach its equilibrium, give yourself enough time to weigh all the many factors involved, to move back and forth amongst the many considerations until you find yourself coming to your center. Then, call upon Spirit or Creative Energy to reveal its higher wisdom, judgment and justice. This inspired guidance flows down the vertical pole of light into your head and pituitary gland. From within, you know that this insight is right and just, that it is the best possible judgment. Having asked, you have received. You have used right judgment and balanced the scales of justice.

Affirmations

1. I am wise and use good judgment.
2. I am compassionate with myself and release the temptation to judge harshly.
3. I make good and wise judgments in the courtroom of my mind.
4. I see clearly where I have misjudged myself or someone else, and I easily open my mind to seeing anew.
5. I am balanced in my wisdom, using my head and my heart.
6. I seek support, information and counsel in making a good and wise decision.
7. I pay close attention to my dreams and intuitions when I am making important decisions.
8. I evaluate fairly all sides of a situation and take time to make right judgments.
9. In the midst of turmoil, I am able to "be still" and listen for the voice of wisdom.
10. I wisely discern between fantasy and reality and make a new choice.
11. No matter how foolish or misguided I have been, I recover and make the decision to keep moving forward, ever forward.
12. I choose to create a heaven in my life rather than a hell.
13. God does not judge me, but God has given all good judgment to me.
14. I echo God's judgment of creation: "God saw that it was very good." (Genesis 1)

15. I desire to see justice for all people.
16. When I judge harshly or unfairly, I always ask forgiveness and seek to make restitution.
17. I refrain from being judgmental but always realize my responsibility to judge wisely.
18. I release my old pattern of making unloving or shortsighted judgments about myself or others.
19. I open my heart and the wisdom of Solomon is mine.
20. I go beyond making a snap decision to discovering the right and best way for all concerned.
21. I always have a choice.
22. My innate wisdom heals and harmonizes my body.
23. The light of wisdom and good judgment flows in and through my pineal gland, and awakens me to my highest wisdom.
24. My pituitary gland is a wise and just judge that brings harmony and balance to my whole body.
25. I make wise choices about how I express energy and power. My thyroid gland is vibrant and healthy.
26. I make loving judgments about myself and others, which energize and harmonize my thymus gland.
27. I make wise judgments about all the food I ingest, and all the thoughts and feelings I incorporate in my mind and soul. My pancreas is healthy, balanced and vital.
28. I judge wisely and with loving discernment about how to use my reproductive organs. My testes (or ovaries) manifest this good judgment in my body.
29. Wisdom and good judgment guide me in eliminating all that is imbalanced in my life. My adrenal glands are aglow with vitality and good health.
30. The power of wisdom and good judgment is always within me—I now call it forth in all my thoughts, feelings and actions.

5
The Faculty of POWER

POWER

POWER is my ability to convert an idea into words I speak, actions I take and things I build. I affirm my oneness with the Higher Power. It is not I, but the power within, that does the work. I express power through my voice and through physical movement. I need to own my power and to be poised and centered in my power. Power expresses through my larynx, muscles and limbs.

OWN YOUR POWER

David. You are a person of power! You are empowered by owning your power. What does it mean to "own your power"? We often give our power away. We dissociate ourselves from our power. We take our power and we put it "out there" in certain people, circumstances, situations and struggles. We say, "You make me mad!" That is, "You have this power—you are powerful and you are doing this to me." Or we say, "You are making me a nervous wreck!" "You are breaking my heart!" "You drove me to drink." We seem to be saying, "You are so power*ful*—you are all powerful—and I am power*less*." So we give our power away to others. Not that people don't influence us or act out or have problems. But they don't have as much power as we often attribute to them.

We also may attribute our life, happiness or security to others. We say or sing, "You make me so happy." "Without you my life would be empty and nothing." "Without your love I would just wither up and disappear." These sound nice and complimentary, but can also be a way of giving our power away. We are saying, "You have the power to make me happy, so if I'm not happy, it's probably your fault. Make me happy!"

So, we have our gift of power. But are we giving our power

away? Our airplane flight gets cancelled, and we may say, "They did this to me and I'm furious. I'm powerless!" A girl-friend dumps us and we respond, "She rejected me. The rejection is overpowering. I'm miserable. Woe is me." Maybe you are going to get up to speak somewhere and you think, "The audience out there has all the power, and it's scaring me to death."

You get the idea, right?

Now, let's reclaim this power and bring this power back into ourselves. How do we do this? Well, we go within ourselves and make affirmations. Our ways of thinking or speaking, both positively and negatively, are affirmations. They state some attribute or perspective we believe to be true about us. Therefore, we need to ask ourselves, "What am I affirming?" Remember what we learned in chapter 4: We have a choice about what we call ourselves and our situations. We make the "calls" and the decisions in the court-room of our mind.

So, we can benefit ourselves by dwelling on affirmations that own our power and use our power with wisdom and love. Our affirmative thoughts may become even more powerful and influential when we actually speak them as an audible vibration. We often need to "speak up" for what is true, posi-tive, healthy, helpful and freeing. Therefore, we affirm:

- I am a spiritual being of power.
- All power is given unto me, in heaven and on earth. This is the truth.
- I reclaim the power I have given away. I move it back into myself where it belongs.
- I have faith in God and I believe in myself.
- The airline may be delayed because of weather condi-tions. All is in divine order. I make the best of this delay.
- She or he chose to leave me and do something else with

her or his life and not be with me. I have the power to
recover from this loss and to create a new, better-than-ever
life for myself. It will take time, but I can do it.

- What you are saying and doing are disturbing to me. I
  will let you know how I feel—honestly. I will seek a resolution or solution that works for both of us.
- I feel nervous going before this audience to speak. So, I
  get still and know that a Greater Power is in me and in
  everyone who is "out there." I am safe, protected, helpful and empowered.

Remember: You are a person of power!

CONTACT THE HIGHER POWER

Power is found by getting still, by entering an empowering
silence within. This is not "suffering in silence" but contacting our Higher Power. Pure power is within. We speak the
greatest truth from this place of stillness and centeredness.
We decree:

- Let Thy highest good be manifest. Let Thy divine good
  for me and thee now appear.
- I am poised and centered in the pure Power of God
  within. Nothing can disturb the calm peace of my soul.

The more we enter this silent center of ourselves, the
more powerful we are. Silence is not just keeping our mouth
shut. Silence is turning within, breathing slowly and deeply,
getting still, centering, listening and just "being here." This
practice of silence—of physical relaxation, mental quiet and
spiritual communion—may be new to you or it may seem
somewhat strange or eerie. It is simply letting go, not being
concerned with definitions or figuring things out. It is letting

go of our mental chatter and bringing our attention back to our breathing. This simple focusing or meditation process of mind, body and spirit has been known and practiced in Zen Buddhism, yoga, Christian mysticism, Jewish prayer and many other spiritual disciplines.

You find your own natural rhythm of breathing and then breathe at that rhythm. If your thoughts flit around on trivial matters or worries, bring your attention back to your breathing.

Some people prefer various postures while practicing silence. Simply sitting with palms up, feet flat on the floor, is a good position to relax and receive Power. Some people lie down and leave palms open or put their hands over their heart. They may go to sleep, but that's okay.

We may know about these techniques for communing with our Higher Power, but we do not take time to do the contacting. Practicing this contact with God-power within will help us do more with less strain and worry, avoid burnout, handle stress better, be calmer, sleep better, digest food better, make good choices, stay healthier, heal better and faster, be more creative and enjoy life more.

Moreover, we should not make this contact just in silent meditation. In the midst of a busy day, while engaged in conversation or some activity, we can inwardly call upon the Higher Power to speak or work through us. Mentally and physically, we can step back a moment to get recentered. We can take a few deep breaths as a way to relax and to reconnect consciously with the abiding presence of Spirit within us. Then we can let go and let this Power flow through us. In this way, we can do all things with the greatest ease, mastery and joy.

INVENTORY OF POWER

As with all of our Twelve Powers, we may use our power faculty in healthy or harmful ways. We may use our power rightly, or we may abuse or misuse it. As you read the following two columns, take stock of yourself. How do you use power? What can you do to improve in this area?

Misuse or Abuse Power	Right Use of Power
1. Trying to oppress, control or manipulate others.	1. Empowering others to help themselves.
2. Trying to be a "big shot" or "top dog."	2. Holding ideals of true service, inner confidence and self-respect.
3. Feeling superior. My goodness depends on your badness.	3. Feeling unique, but not better or worse than others.
4. Power trips and games. "My Daddy is bigger than yours."	4. Humility and mutual respect. Practice peace.
5. Finding fault with others; lording it over them.	5. Helping others; not gloating over their difficulties.
6. Power struggles. Win-lose mindset. Competitive.	6. Power sharing. Win-win mindset. Cooperative.
7. Might makes right. Authoritarian. Can't admit mistakes.	7. Right makes might. Authority comes from within. Admits mistakes.

THE POWER TO SPEAK AND ACT

An old Quaker saying tells us, "Pray and move your feet!" We have the power to convert ideas into words and actions. As powerful and important as our words are, they are not enough. We must act. We must "move our feet," and that ability to move is also an expression of the spiritual faculty we call our "power." There is a time for prayer. There is a time to discuss. Then there is a time for movement, action, doing something. All these transformative activities of a human being utilize our faculty of power.

THE SWORD OF TRUTH

Gay Lynn. Have you ever considered carrying a weapon? Most of us have not; some may even be repulsed by the idea. Although we don't often think of it as such, we all carry a kind of sword or knife with us all the time. It is our tongue and voice. We often refer to someone as having a "sharp tongue," because he or she may cut someone down with his or her words. Have you ever known someone like this? I have been the recipient of a tongue-lashing, and it is awful to feel cut to shreds by someone's harsh words.

If you remove the "s" from sword and put it at the end, you have words. Perhaps if we remember the sword—the power we wield with our words—we will be more conscious of the impact that it has on our life and the lives of those around us. Once our words are spoken and their power is released, they are impossible to take back. As we mature, we understand this more clearly and work more consciously to speak words of truth. Lies, manipulations, half-truths, gossip, sarcasm, belittling comments and poisoning the well of friends or family are destructive uses of our power. So, remind yourself daily to choose your words with care and consideration, for they literally carve out your life. Choose words that are truthful, helpful, appreciative, thoughtful, kind, constructive and encouraging. "There is one whose rash words are like sword thrusts, but the tongue of the wise brings healing." (Proverbs 12:18)

Many times, some misunderstanding can be put to rest with the simple words, "I apologize. I am sorry for what has happened." Most of the time it is our words spoken in haste that get us in trouble. It is so tempting to just let our anger explode, especially if we feel the other person really deserves it!

When David and I traveled across the country on a 120-city book tour, we lived in the simple comforts of a 24-foot travel trailer. One day in San Diego we were rushing to make an afternoon book signing at a local mall. We didn't drop off the trailer at the RV park, so it was a little tricky maneuvering it through the parking lot. We always had to remember the height of the trailer. We were passing beneath markers indicating height restrictions in the lot. I warned David we would not clear the height bars. He insisted we would. I became very anxious, asked him to stop, and warned him again that the trailer would not clear the bars. He insisted it would and continued driving forward until we heard the tearing of metal and a loud crash. Like a can opener, the bar peeled back a huge hole in the top of the trailer and the air conditioner lay in shambles.

I was ready to blow my top because he had refused to listen to the warnings I had given him. I felt like giving him a tongue-lashing about how bullheaded he was. He had destroyed the trailer . . . . Then, as I looked at him, I could see the anguish and sadness all over his face. I put my arm around him and comforted him. I reassured him that the trailer was repairable, and we would get it fixed. I spoke words of comfort and care at a time when it was least expected.

We have all made serious errors, done foolish or stupid
things, damaged cars and belongings, lost things, goofed up,
been stubborn and made dumb choices. Often we spend a
great deal of time chewing someone out or deriding ourselves. In some situations this can go on for years!

The sword of truth, the words we speak, can help sculpt
our lives. We must learn to use the sword wisely and with
great care. By talking with a trusted friend, we can process
through a situation and make order out of chaos. We can
speak words that help us deal with the stress in our lives. It is
important that we be able to say "no." If we are feeling overwhelmed, stressed or burned out, we may not be using our
sword and speaking our truth. Our power is not being used
properly. We can cut ourselves off from balanced living if we
do not speak up when we need to.

The sword cuts both ways. The blade can help and it can
hurt. We are the ones using it, and the intention with which
we use it is everything. The knife in the hands of a surgeon
can cut away disease or repair organs. The knife in the hand
of a robber can hurt, maim and injure. It is a similar knife
but the intention behind its use is different.

When I was a child, my father worked as a fireman. I
remember him coming home one morning and saying that
the fire chief had died of a massive heart attack at the scene
of a big factory fire. His wife was devastated by the loss but
even more distraught over the fact that they had had an argument before he had left for work. Harsh words had been spoken that could never be reconciled. Her grief was tremendous
as she struggled with the sadness of their last words. As a
child, I never forgot this story. I always seek to resolve differences whenever and wherever I can. This is not always possible, but none of us knows when we will see someone for the
last time.

Sometimes, we need to use our power of speech to sever, release or make a shift. Perhaps you remember a time when it was necessary to cut off a relationship, change a job, move or cut the ties to the past. The power of our words can be used to carve out a new beginning. Just as in a garden, occasionally the plants must be pruned back—the dead, bug-ridden parts cut away—so in our lives we must ask ourselves these questions:

- What needs pruning or cutting back in my life?
- What is diseased, bug-ridden or dead, and needs trimming? These could be worries, fears, anxieties, blocks or hurts of the past that are still "bugging" me.
- What is no longer alive and thriving within me that I can cut out with love?

On other occasions, we are in a position where we have to use the sword masterfully to call people on their "stuff." For example, in counseling if I allow people to stay in denial, become vague or grandiose, blame others, avoid the truth or escape into fantasy, I am not doing my job. I have to skillfully assist people in seeing a clearer picture of what is going on. Sometimes, a person's behavior and his or her words conflict. I reflect this back to the person in a way that is truthful, but not judgmental. I describe what I see them doing and what I hear them saying, and ask if they see a discrepancy.

Some people say they want to be happy and live in peace, but their actions create chaos. When we see this happen, we may need to cut past the deceptions to the heart of the matter. We may not like this responsibility or position of power, and we may be rightly concerned about overstepping our boundaries. However, if we do not speak up when we are prompted from within to do so, then we become a part of the problem. Over time and with much practice, we learn to wield our power responsibly, with grace, wisdom and love.

TAKE A WALK

St. Augustine wrote, "*Solvitur ambulando*. . . . It is solved by walking." How many times have you taken a walk in order to work something out? Perhaps you have taken a brisk walk to cool off after an upsetting argument or to avoid a fight. There is great wisdom and power in moving our arms and legs to throw off excess kinetic energy in order to calm ourselves and to think more clearly. (Dr. Knapp will share more on how the power faculty relates to our muscles and limbs.) Try taking a walk the next time you have an important decision or you want to approach a situation calmly.

In the Buddhist tradition, walking with a sense of mindfulness is a spiritual practice. Thich Nhat Hanh, author of *The Long Road Turns to Joy,* has helped thousands of people in the West to understand and practice walking meditation. Originating in China, tai chi is another centering process that involves gentle, flowing movement of the arms, legs and body in order to bring forth greater balance and harmony. Western Dance Therapy likewise employs movement to calm the mind, balance the emotions and heal the body.

Another form of meditative walking was introduced to me in Grace Cathedral in San Francisco, where I first walked a labyrinth in 1993. Since that time, I have had the privilege of helping to create two labyrinths in our spiritual community. Our outdoor permanent labyrinth is seven circuits in a beautiful meditation garden setting. This ancient form of meditative walking dates back to the first labyrinths that were created over 4,000 years ago. Just imagine, our ancestors used to walk to the holy cities for their sacred celebrations. However, when wars, famine or long distances prevented such pilgrimages, people created and walked labyrinths.

Today, most people have lost the joy of walking together, although in my neighborhood the many Jewish people lovingly walk together as a family to synagogue. I often feel a longing for this walking together with friends and family as a spiritual experience of joining together on the path of life. Walking the labyrinth has filled this desire as I join regularly with friends and family, and walk the labyrinth in our church garden.

Gay Lynn walking the labyrinth at Unity of Hollywood

The labyrinth has no dead end, no wrong turns and no tricks in getting to the center. There is one path into the center and one path back out. There are three phases in walking the labyrinth. The first phase of walking to the center is for releasing and letting go. In the second phase, we are in the center where we receive new information and inspirations. The third phase is walking the path out and taking the gifts we have received back into the world to share.

In November 1998, I was leading a Women's Wisdom Weekend which I have done for many years. I entered the labyrinth with the intention of receiving whatever guidance there was to help me grow and best express the work I am doing. As I was walking into the first circuits toward the center I asked, "What do I need to release?" From within my heart and mind I could hear the words come softly, "Shed your pain." I took a deep breath and felt the pain so clearly around the relationship with my mother. I was being guided to shed it and let it go. I was willing to do this and to let the continuous healing take place inside of me. I walked into the center of the labyrinth and felt a lightening of my pain and heartache. There was great power in that walk and in my willingness physically, mentally and emotionally to release more of the hurt that was still tucked into my soul.

I have noticed that when I powerfully do this work, a corresponding shift usually takes place in my life. Sometimes, it is in the way my body feels, my health, my vitality, as if a part of the "stuck" energy has been freed up. I feel lighter, my body moves more easily and freely. Sometimes, an emotional release of sadness or tears gives me fuller access to more of my emotional life. Other times I have noticed a change that is reflected in my dreams.

That night, my dreams took me to a new level of healing my relationship. My mother came to me in a dream and she was distraught. She told me that a friend of hers was dying and she needed to get to the hospital but was afraid to drive. I said to her, "I will take you to the hospital. Mom, I remember how courageous you are. You have taught me to be courageous, to overcome my fears." My mother looked at me with some surprise and said, "You mean you don't remember the bad stuff, the pain?" I answered, "Of course not! I remember you have taught me how to be strong and to face difficulties." Then we kissed.

I realized in the dream experience that as long as I was focusing on the pain, I failed to see the good things we shared in our relationship. My focusing on the pain also was continuing an internal power struggle with my mother that had gone on for years. I was wrestling with my own use of power and wondered how I could more positively focus on our strengths. I was "dying" to my old way, just as one of the characters in my dream was dying—from seeing myself and my mother as being so different and separate. When I released the pain I could feel and experience a more positive view or perspective of our relationship. Before this release, all I was remembering much of the time was the struggle. My dream pointed to our shared courage and power to overcome in the face of difficulties.

In a powerful and sometimes extremely painful way, my mother has been one of my greatest teachers. A teacher sometimes shows us our real power not by being there for us all the time, but by letting us go, by letting us be on our own, even to leave us if necessary. We also learn a great deal from conflict and imbalances of power in our relationships.

If we resist these relationships or resent them, we lose the opportunity to grow into our power. Often, the fear of emotional pain blocks the ability to see ourselves or others differently, and we never really mature fully into our power. Running from the pain is also running away from our power . . . the power to overcome even the most difficult events in our lives.

When someone leaves us or we feel rejected, it can be devastating. We have a choice in that moment and in the days, weeks and years that follow to use our power to repeat and recycle the pain or to take a step toward freeing ourselves. That day I took a walk that began another level of healing. I took a walk that inspired me to free up more of my energies and to release my pain and rejection from the past. I gave up all hope for a better yesterday. There is no power in the universe that can change yesterday. We only have this moment to use our power in a wise and healing way.

Today, how can you let fresh ideas and new freedom come into your life? How can you identify old patterns of relating that keep you stuck in unfulfilling relationships? How can you reclaim your power and move through and beyond the pain? Why don't you take a walk and think about it?

LARYNX AND VOCAL APPARATUS

Dr. Robert. One of the major ways that we physically express power is by using our voice—we speak, sing, chant, pray aloud and say affirmations. What a marvelous ability this is! We create sound in our larynx or voice box that is located in our throat. (See Figure 5A.) The larynx is a tubular structure that is made out of hard, tough cartilage. Inside the tube are the two vocal cords that we employ to produce sound. (See Figure 5B.)

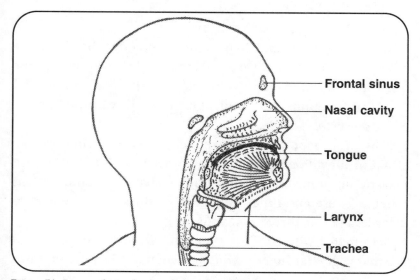

Figure 5A. Larynx (voice box) and rest of vocal apparatus

When we breathe in, muscles in our voice box hold the vocal cords open so that air can pass through them and go into the lungs. When we breathe out and we want to make sound, muscles pull the two vocal cords together. When air passes over them, they vibrate and make sound that rises up into the resonating chambers of the throat, mouth, sinuses and nasal cavity, which give the sound its distinct timbre. Then we modify the sound into specific words with our lips, teeth, tongue and soft palate.

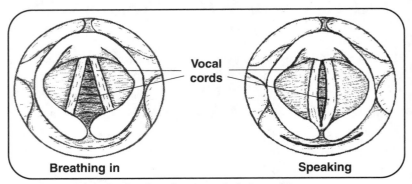

Figure 5B. Vocal cords when breathing in and when speaking

When we speak up, when we share openly what is in our mind and heart, when we speak the truth as we see it, how does our vocal apparatus work? Unless there is a structural defect, it functions beautifully. Our voice is warm, full, resonant, powerful and clear.

Now what happens when we feel powerless, when we are afraid or unwilling to speak openly or truthfully, or when we talk in an unloving, controlling or harsh manner about others? These and other difficulties with power may lead to disorders of our throat and voice box.

A woman I will call Susan felt that she had no "voice" in her marriage. Her husband did not listen to her, put her down and dominated her. She accepted this, because she felt inadequate and powerless. Moreover, she found it easier to complain and to blame him for her problems than to reclaim her power and change herself. When she was angry with him, she usually suppressed, "swallowed" or "choked back" these feelings. As a result, four to six times a year she developed a severe sore throat. Sometimes, she had to take antibiotics because she had a strep infection. Other times, she developed laryngitis and lost her voice. Through all of this, she took lots of vitamin C and other nutritional and herbal remedies, which helped some but did not eliminate her symptoms.

Finally, she decided to speak openly with her husband about her true feelings. She asked to be treated as an equal and to discuss all important family matters with him. At first, he rejected her pleas. Susan pressed on, repeatedly saying that he was the problem and that he had to change his ways, which of course only made matters worse.

Eventually, she pulled back and focused on changing herself, thereby reclaiming her own power that she had given away to her husband. In her prayers and meditations, she blessed the good within him and called upon the Higher Power to establish new balance and healing in their marriage. Gradually, over several months, he became more open, loving and communicative. He eventually agreed to go into marriage counseling, where they both had more insight about their power problems and learned new ways to communicate and to express their true feelings.

So, what happened to Susan's throat problems? Over a period of a year, the frequency of her sore throats diminished as she found her "voice" and learned to communicate openly, honestly, directly, with equal give and take. Since then, she has had only an occasional sore throat and has not had another bout of laryngitis.

What are the lessons learned by Susan that apply equally to everyone?

1. We have the power to find our "voice" and to heal our voice box.
2. We can only change ourselves; we have no real power to make others change unless they choose to do so.
3. No one has power over us unless we allow this to happen.
4. We are most powerful when we call upon the Higher Power to work through us and others. When we let go and let God Power flow through us, all things are possible. We can "move mountains."

On other occasions, when people have difficulties with power and speaking the truth, they may develop some form of speech impediment such as stuttering. Others may develop nodules on the vocal cords or even cancer of the throat. Smoking plays a major role in most instances of throat cancer.

Whatever the disease of our vocal apparatus, however minor or major it may be, the core of our plan to heal it is focusing on our inner power faculty. We speak up. We tell the truth as best we know it. We affirm and call forth Spirit's healing power within us. This power stimulates, invigorates and harmonizes our throat. At the same time, we always use the best of all effective physical treatments, such as medication or surgery, nutritional supplements or eliminating some harmful habit like smoking. In this way, we have the most powerful program to balance our mind, emotions and body.

MUSCLES AND LIMBS

Movement is power and power produces movement. In our physical body, our muscles have the unique ability to contract and shorten themselves, and then to relax and return to their original size and length. This ability of the muscles to change shape is what provides movement in all parts of our body. This includes the movement of the vocal cords in producing sound. Therefore, our muscular system expresses the faculty of power in our physical form.

When we speak of the correlation of power with muscles, we are talking about skeletal muscles, which are muscles that attach to the bones of the skeleton. Our body has over six hundred skeletal muscles. (See Figure 5C.) At each end of most skeletal muscles are tough fibrous cords called tendons that attach the muscles to the bones. For example, the biceps muscle in our upper arm has one tendon that is connected to the ulna bone just below the elbow and two tendons that attach to bones in the shoulder. When the biceps muscle contracts and the triceps muscle on the back of the arm relaxes, our lower arm moves toward our shoulder.

All skeletal muscles express power, but this is particularly true of the muscles in our limbs—our shoulders, arms, hands, and our hips, legs and feet. Moving our limbs, using them skillfully and in coordinated fashion, are major ways that we demonstrate physical power.

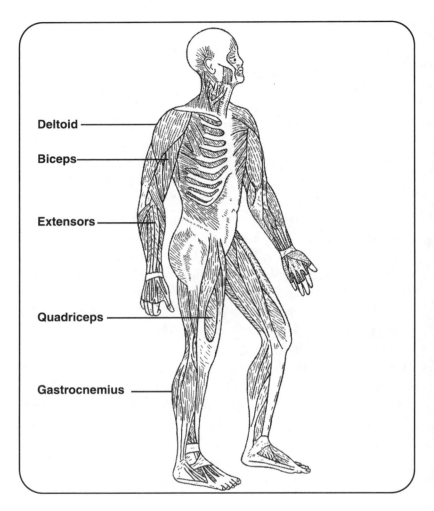

Deltoid
Biceps
Extensors
Quadriceps
Gastrocnemius

Figure 5C. Skeletal muscles

With our arms and hands we grasp, hold, lift, move and manipulate objects. We carry and transport things on our shoulders. With our hands, we can use all kinds of tools—eating utensils, pens, typewriters, computers, paintbrushes. We have the power to heal with our hands through loving touch, laying on of hands, massage, reflexology, chiropractic adjustment, auric balancing and performing surgery.

Our lower limbs provide movement for the whole body. We stand up or sit down; we walk or run, leap or dance; we stand solidly in one place while performing some deed. Visualize a ballet dancer, a concert pianist, an Olympic runner, a carpenter making a house. Here are power, mastery and dominion at work.

When we express power in a loving, balanced and masterful way, then our muscles and limbs respond accordingly. They are strong, vital and healthy. However, when we have difficulties with power—when we feel powerless or inadequate or incapable, when we try to control or dominate others, when we put people down or in their place (keep them under our thumb)—then we may develop various symptoms in our muscles or limbs.

What happens when you carry the weight of the world on your shoulders, when you attempt to shoulder too much responsibility? Your neck muscles may get tight, inflamed and sore. One or both of your shoulders may ache or develop bursitis. Maybe you think some person or situation is a "pain in the neck," more than you can handle or bear. How does this affect your body? Well, you may develop actual neck pain from your tight and tense muscles, and from inflammation of your muscles and the connective tissue around them.

We may feel that we cannot grasp or get a handle on a particular problem, that we cannot "hang on" in tough times, that we cannot handle the responsibility we have. Maybe we give our power away to others, and are unwilling to take that power back into our own hands. Maybe we try to control, dominate and manipulate others. Perhaps we try to do things all by ourselves, without calling upon the Higher Power to do them through us. At these times, we may develop problems with our arms and hands, such as arthritis in our shoulder, elbow or hand. Arthritis is inflammation of the joints, causing pain and limiting movement.

Some people have trouble taking a stand, standing on their own two feet. They can "talk the talk," but cannot "walk the walk." In these instances, they may develop symptoms and disorders in their hips, legs and feet—arthritis, muscle cramps or a lack of coordination.

To heal any muscular or limb problem, utilize techniques like medication, surgery, exercise, yoga, tai chi, chiropractic, osteopathy, acupuncture and massage. In addition to these approaches, even if the disorder has primarily a physical cause, always focus on the indwelling power that you have as a child of God. Let go and let this power flow through you. Direct it to any muscle, joint or part of your limbs that needs help. Be at one with this power and your muscles and limbs will be reinvigorated with new life and energy.

In your mind's eye, picture yourself sitting under a stream of light that pours down upon and into you, carrying with it a majestic, yet comforting power. The light stream flows into your head, throat and voice box. You may feel guided from within to tilt your head back and open your mouth, so the powerful light radiates directly into your throat. Affirm: I am filled with a Higher Power that heals my throat and voice box. I now speak with loving power and authority.

Then, let the power flow down your neck into your shoulders, arms and hands. Begin with your right side. Feel the energy flow into your shoulder, which relaxes and may feel warm. The power then flows down the upper arm to the elbow, the lower arm and into the hand. Let the powerful energy flow right through your physical hand, so that you feel it as heat or tingling or vibration within and around your palm and hand. Next, do the same thing with your left shoulder, arm and hand. Especially, direct the powerful energy into any part of your neck or upper limbs that need healing, regeneration, balancing and harmonization.

Then visualize and experience the power flowing down your spine and back into your hips, legs and feet, until it flows out the bottom of your feet. Do this with both of your lower limbs, starting first with your right leg and then moving to the left leg. Let your legs move slightly as you feel and get accustomed to the greater power that is flowing in and through them. Direct this power to any section of your lower limbs that need healing. See yourself walking, running, dancing with power and grace. Give thanks unto the Higher Power for empowering your whole body.

Finally, visualize yourself acting with power and grace, mastery and dominion, in any challenge you are currently facing in your life. Know that you can do all things by having the Higher Power do these things through you.

1. I am powerful and full of power.
2. I live, move and have my being in a limitless sea of power.
3. I share power with others in ways that are mutually beneficial and prospering.
4. I do not give my power away to people who try to abuse or use me.
5. I plug into my inner power, and miraculous demonstrations pour forth in my life.
6. I say to threatening people and circumstances: "You do not have power over me. I am a spiritual being and all power is given to me."
7. I have the power to say "hello" and the power to say "goodbye." I do both lovingly and graciously.
8. I do not take credit for my own power—all power I have comes only from the One Power.
9. The prospering power of God is at work in all my affairs, and my life is abundantly enriched in all ways.
10. I speak with power from my inner source of power.
11. I find my greatest power as I become still and enter the silence of my deepest being.
12. I can always succeed, for I now realize that the power within me can do all things.
13. I use my power to encourage and to empower others to realize and express their greatest potential.

14. I am becoming the powerful, fearless person that I am created to be.

15. From the center of power within me flows a mighty current of healing, life, love and peace.

16. I do not use my power to be a "top dog" or "big shot." My power is expressed in committed service.

17. I work to create a shared power where everybody wins and grows together.

18. Rather than playing power games and engaging in power struggles, I seek greater humility and sharing of life with others.

19. I use the power of positive prayer each day.

20. I think before I speak and unleash the power of my thoughts.

21. I move all parts of my body with power and grace.

22. I lovingly use my hands to help and heal, never to hurt or harm.

23. Power pulsates in my throat and heals my voice box.

24. I speak openly, honestly and lovingly from my heart.

25. I shoulder just the right amount of responsibility and power, and carry it with dignity and ease.

26. I speak the truth and call myself and others to accountability.

27. I resolve differences and bring reconciliation with my words.

28. I walk as a means of creating peace and power in my life.

29. Today I take a stand for truth and right action.

30. I am never alone—my Higher Power is always with me.

6

The Power of IMAGINATION

IMAGINATION

IMAGINATION is my ability to form thoughts, mental pictures and positive images. This is often called "visualization." I also have the ability to be aware of the flow of images and inspirations that just come to me. When I say, "The Lord is my shepherd," I am praying with an image as well as words. Imagination externalizes in my body as the thalamus of the brain.

OUR PICTURING POWER

David. Imagination is our picturing power. Often it is called visualization. Images are the language of the body. We "talk" to our body with images. Our body doesn't "hear" words as much as it hears or feels images.

If I take out a lemon and suck on it, and you watch me doing this, you probably will start to pucker and salivate. I do not give you any direction to do so, but the image comes to you and you have a physical reaction. Our imagination powerfully affects us physically.

In the same way, if I was injured and wanted to recover and walk again, I would picture myself standing and walking. This would send a signal to my muscles to work in accomplishing this.

Albert Einstein, the great quantum physicist, said, "Imagination is more important than knowledge." He also said we live in a sea of energy. Einstein and others have shown that we live in a universe where everything is existing at various rates of vibration. We often say, "Where our thought goes, energy flows." Energy takes on the shape or pattern of the "self-image" or "mind-set" into which it flows.

Bottles of various shapes and colors can represent the way we imagine ourselves to be. If we pour clear water into each of them, the water looks red, green or blue—like the color of the bottle. The water also takes on the shape of each bottle. In similar fashion, we are always giving shape and color to our lives by our power of imagination. Remember, we shape and can reshape our lives. We are always shaping a life—a home, a career, a business, a  marriage, a project, a school experience, a retirement.

Plato cautioned over two thousand years ago to be careful of the images we put into our mind. He said that we are not to put images of terror, violence or fright into our minds, and especially not into our children's minds. Rather, we are to put in pleasant images of beauty, joy, peace and harmony.

THE POWER TO BRING FORTH

The American transcendentalist, Ralph Waldo Emerson, said, "What we can conceive and believe, we can achieve."

Of course, we have to use our imagination in a balanced, coordinated way with all of our spiritual powers. Imagination is powerful. We can image and form in our life what we picture consistently or hold in our strong feelings. Some books and speakers tell us, "You can have whatever you want! Just make a clear mental picture of it and hold it." But there is no discussion of any ethical or moral dimension in the use of this powerful ability we have. Someone could hold the image of being the biggest, richest drug dealer in the city. We want to use this powerful, creative ability to produce or achieve only good, as guided by our other powers such as wisdom, love, order and understanding.

People sometimes say, "Oh, it's just your imagination."

Don't trivialize your power of imagination. When joined with your power of faith, imagination is especially great in bringing forth the things you hold in your mind.

The great artist Michelangelo took an old discarded piece of marble and carved out his famous statue of David. When asked how he created such a marvelous statue he said, "I just took away everything that was not David!"

James Allen, who wrote a popular little book called *As a Man Thinketh*, wrote a poem years ago:

> *Mind is the Master-power that moulds and makes,*
> *And Man is Mind, and evermore he takes*
> *The tool of Thought, and shaping what he wills,*
> *Brings forth a thousand joys, a thousand ills.*
> *He thinks in secret, and it comes to pass:*
> *Environment is but his looking glass.*

An old saying goes: "Thoughts held in mind produce after their kind." What are you holding in your mind? What do you feed into your imagination?

Shakespeare wrote of our power of imagination in *As You Like It*:

> *[We] find tongues in trees,*
> *books in the running brooks,*
> *Sermons in stones, and*
> *Good in everything.*

Open your eyes and your imagination to see a world of wonder and miracles all around you!

SPECIFIC AND OPEN-ENDED IMAGINATION

Imagination is the "scissors" of the mind. We are "cutting out" our life from the universal bolt of divine material, which we mold and shape as we will.

Often, people use a helpful technique called a "treasure map" to picture what they are seeking to have made manifest in their life experience. They cut out pictures and words that form a kind of prayer map that helps to stimulate and focus their power of imagination on what they want. Some people make an "image book" that also helps them to focus on the positive qualities they want to incor- porate and express.

Treasure map

We call this "visualization," "mental programming" and "name it and claim it." Most methods of goal setting and achieving use this technique: See it, claim it, picture it happening, feel it strongly as real in the here and now.

This kind of visualization is especially useful in health and healing work, as pioneered by physicians Carl Simonton, Norman Shealy, Bernie Siegel and others. We focus our thoughts and mental picturing power on "seeing" and feeling ourselves being strong, healthy, whole and well. Many coaches and athletes use visualization to improve their abilities. They practice "mental rehearsal"—seeing themselves at peak performance. This mental focusing often works in quick and spectacular ways.

A caution about this specific kind of visualization: I may

"treasure map" and picture myself getting what I have been "programmed" or "taught" to want by advertising, peer-group pressure or other conformity. This may or may not be what is really best for me. Again, we have to use our powers of wisdom, love and understanding, to know what is best for each of us and for the highest good of all.

To review, "specific imagery" includes:

- Visualization
- Scissors of the mind
- Treasure mapping
- Setting a goal and seeing it being achieved

There is another way we can use our power of imagination. It is best summed up in the familiar phrase, "Let go and let God." This is what I call "open-ended imagination." We open ourselves to a flow of images rather than consciously thinking them up and holding images. It goes beyond what we know about and want, to the realm that we don't know about. This is the truly creative realm where artists, inventors, scientists, writers, musicians, poets, visionaries and ordinary people open themselves to images or thoughts that just "come."

These images come to us as inspirations, in outer signs, in dreams, in a flash of feeling or intuition, as something we "run across" or a "song we hear." These can be powerful and transformative. They come as images, just as the inspiration that came to the poet-psalmist, who wrote in the Twenty-third Psalm:

> *The Lord is my shepherd;*
> *I shall not want.*
> *He maketh me to lie down in green pastures,*
> *He leadeth me beside the still waters,*
> *He restoreth my soul.*

How comforting, strengthening and encouraging these powerful images have been to those in distress, grief and confusion over many centuries—simple images of protection, care and serenity.

In the open-ended, unconditioned way of imaging, we pray with images—we don't just play with images. We make responsible use of our creative ability to shape and mold our life and world. We hold a positive life-affirming vision for ourselves and humanity. We receive and learn from the images that come to our open mind.

To develop our imagination faculty, we can affirm:

- I see myself as God sees me: whole, free and happy to be alive!
- I am glad to be who I am!
- I am developing a better self-image each day—my self-image is based on my knowledge that I am created in the image and likeness of my Creator.
- I have the power of imagination to form my own thoughts, to color my own feelings and to take charge of my own life.

MESSAGE IN THE SAND

Gay Lynn. We often use the phrase, "Can you imagine that!" Imagination shapes out of the raw material of our daily activities a life . . . my life . . . your life. Our imagination plays an essential role in designing our lives, in literally creating our lives. How does this work? How can we be more aware of how this power of imagination functions?

When David and I were traveling on an extensive two-year book tour, we both received signs and inner promptings that it was time to stop the tour and settle down. This was different from our plan because we still had a number of speaking engagements left on our calendar. These signs and signals took the form of dreams, feelings of completion, and images of our new home being built on the east coast of South Florida, often called the "Gold Coast." These intuitive images also came in the form of daydreams and of processing what it would be like to be in that new life. Fantasy images danced around in my brain.

As I was receiving these intuitive impressions, my practical side wanted to sort out the information, and to ask for clear guidance and direction using more of my powers like wisdom, order and understanding. David and I shared our thoughts and feelings and, although our tour was not complete, we both felt it was time to stop.

Have you ever been in this situation, feeling as though a change is ready to happen in your life? A new relationship is coming? A new beginning in a career or a fresh start is needed and you are receiving the inner promptings? It does not necessarily mean that something has gone wrong or turned sour. You just feel as though there is something new that is going to emerge that will need your cooperation or assistance.

At these times, I especially tune in to my intuition, psychic talents and extrasensory perception. I ask for messages and signs, and I say, "Make them as big as a billboard so I don't miss them!" As David and I were asking these questions and imagining what the next phase of our life might be, we were walking on a beach. I strolled along the sandy shoreline, asking the question, "Is it time to follow a new path and make a fresh start?"

I looked in the sand just ahead of us, and there was a big message literally written in the sand. The message said, "Gold is here. Follow up." I couldn't believe my eyes. I had never seen a message actually written in the sand, and it was so appropriate to our question. I pulled David over with great excitement and said, "Look. Gold is here. Follow up." Thankfully, with all the other messages and signs we both saw, we made a life-changing decision to begin a new life.

We moved to the Gold Coast of Florida. We finished the manuscript of our book, *Golden Eggs*. We started a radio program, and a wonderful ministry opened up in Hollywood, Florida. This truly began one of the most fulfilling and joyful times in our lives. We renewed our friendship with Dr. Robert Knapp, and together we produced a TV/video series and this companion book, *Twelve Powers in You*. All of this was possible because we tuned in, listened to our intuition, and received the messages from within and without. The wonderful message in the sand said, "Follow up." In other words, this is the time; your gold or your good is here.

What kind of messages are you receiving? What kind of life are you imagining for yourself? What signs and intuitive impressions are coming to you? Listen. Your good is here. Follow up!

PAINTING OUR LIVES

Have you ever heard yourself or someone else say, "I can't do that, it's impossible"? "Why does this always happen to me?"

While working with people in counseling, I have heard these statements many times, and I often use the illustration of a palette of paints. We are the artists of our lives. We are the artists in residence, and we have all these wonderful colors to choose from, a wonderful range of greens and reds and purples. Many times, we are only painting with a few colors, like blue. We even say, "I'm feeling blue, blah. I'm depressed. Nothing changes."

Sometimes, we fall into a rigid or fixed way of seeing ourselves, our lives and our relationships. Has this ever happened to you? Have you felt like you are in a rut? Your imagination has become inactive? You lack foresight and vision? You are stuck in one track of thinking? This is like using only one color to paint a picture! Pretty dull and boring.

We need to stretch, experiment and imagine new possibilities, to try new colors. Embrace the risk of doing something different. Add some new blends of color and contrast to our lives.

Many people I have counseled have actually used paints to express their healing process. One woman traumatized by childhood abuse literally painted her way, with abstract art and photographs, through years of anguish and hurt. She could actually see her metamorphosis in her own artistic expression. As the months went by, what she could not talk about or express verbally was captured by the various colors of paint and the lens of her camera. She literally took the power of imagination and became the artist of her healing journey.

We can do this for ourselves with crayons and paper. Allow the feelings to be drawn, without judgment or concern for artistic quality. Many times, much can be revealed and released in this imaginative and creative process.

What new healing can you envision? What new life would you like to create? What new colorful changes can you imagine for yourself? "I am in the pink, feeling good!" And then the world I live in and the people I see also look different, and I bring new vision of hope and life into the world.

This is how you begin to heal your body. This is how you start to heal your emotional wounds. This is how you recover from feeling depressed and abandoned. Paint a new portrait of your life. Just imagine! Just imagine!

IN THE IMAGE AND LIKENESS OF GOD

For the past two thousand years, people in the West have primarily been given a male image of God, even though references to the feminine aspect of God have been represented in the Hebrew scriptures as the Shekinah, and in the Christian scriptures as Sophia and Mary the mother of Jesus. In many cultures around the world, female deities such as Kuan Yin (China), Gaia (Greece), Bridgit (Celtic Britain) and Athena (ancient Greece) are honored.

These feminine aspects of the Divine have helped men and women know and recognize themselves as being made in the image and likeness of God. "God created man in the image of himself, in the image of God he created him, male and female he created them." (Genesis 1:27) So whether you are in a male or female body, you have within you both aspects of the Divine: male and female. In recent years, there has been a resurgence of interest in the Motherhood of God, such as in the form of the Goddess that predates and has heavily influenced Christian doctrine and religious celebrations.

You are a spark of divinity made in the likeness of our Father-Mother God. To embrace the feminine aspect of the Divine Creator is to creatively embrace more of your own God essence and how you co-create with this magnificent Power.

One of the meaningful ways I continue to explore my relationship with God is by having an image of God as mother as well as father. Have you ever imagined God as mother? I never even considered the feminine face of God when I was young. In my Baptist upbringing, I focused only on a male image of God. Mary, mother of Jesus, was mentioned and played a role in our Christmas pageants, but that was the extent of it. Many years later, I had an experience with the mothering aspect of God in the form of the patron saint of the Mexican people, the Virgin of Guadeloupe. She is sometimes referred to as a "Black Madonna" as she is portrayed with beautiful brown skin tones. She became a new way for me to image God expressed as a woman. My journey has continued to develop for many years and part of this journey is chronicled in our book, *Golden Eggs.*

My image of God and my tenderness toward the Divine have been transformed by being able to image God as a female figure with all the qualities of a loving mother. In Isaiah 66:13, the Lord says, "As a mother comforts a child, so I will comfort you." I felt deeply moved by the experience of having inner communion with the compassionate Mother who would hold me, rock me and draw me close to her softness. Charles Fillmore, cofounder of Unity School, said, "We must think about and worship the Holy Mother and talk to the Holy Mother consciousness within us. We must become, in other words, meek and lowly, just like a little child crawling to the Mother and getting into her lap and resting on the breast of the Mother."

Can you imagine God this way? It was hard for me at first, but the more I allowed the image of the Holy Mother to come to me, the easier it became. She also helped me to heal some of those places where I felt I needed that special "mother's touch."

One man with whom I worked had such a painful and rejecting childhood—his mother had been particularly critical, cold and judgmental—that he anticipated this from every relationship. His dreams were filled with images of people who were attacking and chasing him. He was always on the defensive and moved often from job to job because he imagined that his coworkers were "out to get him." This man lived in a great deal of distress and his physical body was large and overweight—a protective shield he wore around himself.

One of the keys to transforming himself was learning to receive feelings of love and tenderness. He began to imagine a feminine figure as the Divine, whom he could trust and with whom he could have positive interactions and warm emotional experiences. Soon, she began showing up in his dreams, where she opened him to feelings of joy and expansiveness. In one dream, she took him to a mountaintop, showing him a different way to image his life.

Slowly, the relationship with his feminine side gave way to tears and much healing of pent-up rage and anger. He embraced a new image of himself and was able to share and express his feelings more freely. He added new colors and dimensions to his life through creatively experimenting with his imagination, even imagining that which he thought was impossible for his life, through a positive experience with the mothering side of God.

As you are moving forward in your life, imagine that the Holy Mother—the Creative Love—is with you. Imagine that you are totally loved and supported. Picture her with you. Experience this in your imagination as vividly as possible. Imagine the outcome you would like to see happen as you are giving birth to the divine ideas you hold in your mind's eye. Invite her to help you, and her compassionate love will support you and activate the power of imagination as you conceive and give forth new life.

Maybe there are things that you think could never happen to you. If you begin today to imagine the impossible, soon it moves into the realm of the possible. We are the artists of our lives. We could even be like the Queen in Lewis Carroll's classic *Alice in Wonderland*. Here is how she responds to Alice's claim that, "One can't believe impossible things."

"I dare say you haven't had much practice," said the Queen. "When I was your age, I always did it for half-an-hour a day. Why, sometimes I've believed as many as six impossible things before breakfast."

Try this today: Imagine at least six impossible things before you eat breakfast. Enter into a new Wonderland in your own life and create a new world of wonder!

THALAMUS OF THE BRAIN

Dr. Robert. Have you ever looked into a crystal ball to see the future, to see a vision, or to see into your past? Well, you don't need an actual crystal ball to do this, because you already have one right in the center of your head. It is called the thalamus, an ovoid or egg-shaped structure that is located just below your cerebrum. (See Figure 6A.) Actually, there are two thalami, each of which lies beneath one of the two cerebral hemispheres. The two thalami are joined together on their middle surface.

Scientists and researchers currently know that the thalamus serves as a relay and integrating center. All of the data gathered by our five physical senses, except for smell, travels along sensory nerves to specific centers in the thalamus. From there, the sensory information gets relayed to specific sensory centers in the cerebrum, where it is perceived, analyzed and understood—where we "make sense" of it.

What most scientists are not yet aware of is that the thalamus also serves as a relay or way station—a "crystal ball"—for our psychic senses. These psychic talents have been called our extrasensory perception, or ESP, to indicate that they are beyond or in addition to the five physical senses. However, there is nothing "extra" or "extraordinary" about

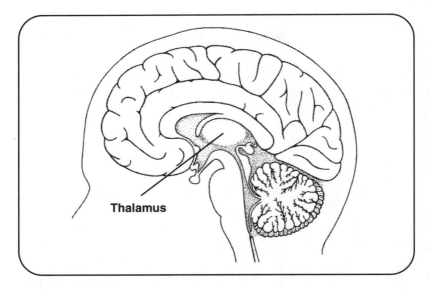

Figure 6A. Thalamus of the brain

them, since we all have them to one degree or another, just as we all have five physical senses. Therefore, a more appropriate name for ESP is elementary spiritual powers. Commonly, some of these powers are called clairvoyance or clear seeing, clairaudience or clear hearing, and clairsentience or clear knowing (intuition).

How do these powers work? And how do they involve the thalamus? Think back to a time when you saw a vision or an image in your meditation, or when a new idea suddenly came to you, when you intuitively knew something. That image or intuitive impression registered first in the area just in front of your forehead, which legend calls the third eye. In the East, it is called the third-eye chakra and is represented symbolically as a large, all-seeing, cosmic eye. In the United States, this esoteric understanding has even been depicted on the back of a one-dollar bill, which pictures a single or third eye at the top of a pyramid. Sometimes, the third eye is called the third-eye screen, because it is like we have our own "television screen" or viewing area in the region of our forehead.

Pyramid and third eye on dollar bill

We have all heard numerous stories of a mother who knows inwardly when her child is in danger, although the child is miles away. She senses it intuitively or psychically. Maybe an image suddenly flashes in her mind's eye. Maybe she has a prophetic dream. In each of these instances, the image or intuitive flash registers first in the third eye and then anchors into the physical body at the thalamus in the center of the head. The thalamus serves as an integrating center, registering the psychic impression or image in the physical body. The thalamus is a way station, in that it relays the psychically received impression to the cerebrum of the brain, where it can be interpreted and analyzed.

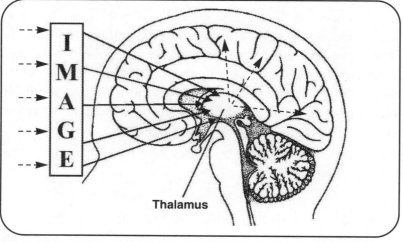

Figure 6B. Psychic images/impressions relayed from third eye to thalamus, then to cerebrum

How does all this relate to the use of a crystal ball? The crystal-clear ball simply serves as an outer focusing device. It is placed in front of the user who peers intently and single-mindedly into it. This helps the person to keep his or her eye single, to be focused on the inner impressions and not on all the things the physical senses perceive or on the ramblings of the conscious mind. We do this same thing in our meditations and visualizations—we clear our mind, focus our thoughts, and peer inwardly onto the screen of

For our imagination to work at its best, it must be crystal clear. In other words, we cannot cloud our mind and imagination with our selfish desires, worries or fears, expectations of what we will receive, or the need to feel that we are special because we are psychic or have some supposedly unique powers. Then we are clouding our imagination—what the Apostle Paul called "seeing through a glass, darkly." Rather than receive clear, accurate impressions and guidance, we may make things up out of our subconscious desires or we may "color" or distort what we receive.

What we want to do is to receive clear images, ideas, symbols, colors and impressions that are constantly radiating to us from our own spiritual Self, the Christ within us—to let go and to let our God Self impress its ideas and images upon us. The third-eye screen is the window or doorway through which these images pass as they come to our conscious awareness. Such images and higher ideas then guide us in our business, relationships, healing activities and artistic endeavors—in every aspect of our lives.

WHAT WE SEE WILL BE

We not only receive new images, but we also create new images by way of our imagination and thalamus. Think of the thalamus as being like a television picture tube. In our mind and cerebrum, we create new ideas and images, and then we project these images by way of our thalamus/picture tube onto our third-eye screen. From this screen or sending station, we project these images out to others. Those who are receptive and psychically intuned "pick up" these images, just like a radio or TV receives the invisible radio waves or TV signals that are broadcast through the air.

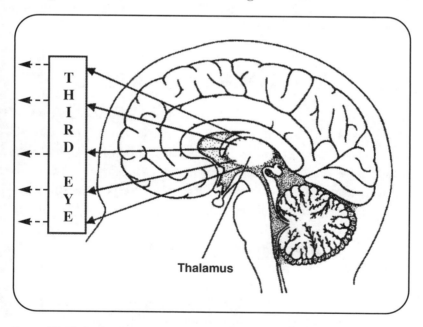

Figure 6C. Thalamus, broadcasting new images to third-eye screen

When we create and hold a new image, we also send it via our thalamus to the rest of our physical body. The image is converted into nerve signals that the thalamus relays along motor, sympathetic and parasympathetic nerves to every part of the body. Nerve messages from the thalamus also travel to the hypothalamus located just below it, which controls the release of pituitary hormones that regulate the whole endocrine system. In these ways, what we envision becomes a physical reality.

Why is this so important, this ability to create new images? Because this is how we grow, how we change, how we heal ourselves and others. First we create a new image and then in due time we manifest it in our lives and our physical bodies. Here is the key principle: What we see, will be. In fact, this ability to visualize a new image is one of our most powerful healing techniques.

KEEP YOUR EYE SINGLE

Years ago, I had pain in my right shoulder after I fell on it. With rest and time, the pain went away. Then, periodically my shoulder would start aching again. I'd be playing golf and suddenly I could hardly swing my club. X-rays showed no structural problem. Stretching exercises helped, as did physical therapy, chiropractic adjustments and massage. But the pain always returned.

Finally, I started working more with my imagination faculty. In the stillness of my meditation, I was shown a vivid, green, ethereal light, which to me represented healing and harmony. So, I envisioned that green healing light flowing into my shoulder. Each time I did this, my shoulder felt better.

During one of these visualizations, it dawned on me that my shoulder pain usually flared up when I was feeling that I couldn't "shoulder" my responsibilities, when I felt like my load was too heavy and more than I could bear. With this new insight came a visualization: I imagined myself being seven to ten feet tall. I saw myself rising up into this tall body, which was composed of a finer energy or frequency vibration—it was a body of light. As I rose into the light, I gained a new and higher perspective of myself and my challenges. I left behind the feelings of "poor, little ol' me; I can't do this." Instead I felt like I had the power to do all that I was given to do. My shoulders were broad, strong and powerful. I could "see" myself shouldering all the responsibilities that were given to me, but letting go of those problems and difficulties that I did not have to carry. I developed greater faith that the Higher Power would do the work through me. In response to this new image, over many months, my shoulder pain gradually diminished and eventually disappeared.

In working on my shoulder, I was following the guidance that Jesus has given to us about healing: "If your eye is single, then your whole body will be filled with light." What is this eye that he referred to? It is our third eye, our all-seeing cosmic eye. How do we keep it single? By focusing only on the good, the harmony, the love, and the wholeness and holiness within each and every one of us. Then, our whole being and body are filled with light.

When I was first learning how to keep my eye single, my dreams guided me to work with my parents. You see, so much of our self-image, of how we see ourselves and others, comes from our early experiences with our family.

As I shared previously in the chapter on Faith, my baby sister died when I was seven years old. My mother became acutely depressed and was admitted to a psychiatric hospital. My older brother and I were taken to live with our aunt and uncle. Needless to say, I felt abandoned, lost, alone and unable to make sense of what had happened to my mother, whom I loved dearly.

When I was twenty-nine, I dreamt that I was back in my childhood home. The doctor had come to take my mom to the psychiatric hospital. Being both in the dream and observing it from above, I heard a wise and all-knowing voice say that I had been so hurt by this experience that I had decided never to love anyone again. It was just too painful to lose my mother, so I shut down emotionally and put a protective shell around myself. From that time on, I "saw" myself as being separate from her and others.

As these old, deep, painful feelings resurfaced, I was given a visualization technique, which I used particularly with my mother, but also with my dad and brother. In meditation, I focused first on the top of my head, on my crown chakra and brain, where I felt the influx of light and the communion with my spiritual Self. Then I saw and felt the power flowing into my third eye, my imagination center in the forehead region. Then the flow of power traveled down my neck and out my arms into my hands, which are used to lovingly manipulate and transfer the higher energy. Next, my heart center became stimulated and filled with love. Then the power flowed down my spine, down my legs and out my feet. Now I was grounded and anchored in the Higher Power. My eye was single and my whole body was filled with light.

Next, I envisioned my mother sitting right in front of me, just a few feet away and I focused on the good within her. I visualized her being filled with light, and this light poured out of my third eye into her. I opened my heart and loved her unconditionally; I forgave her and asked for her forgiveness. I lifted up my hands and transferred power through them to her, until I saw her being completely filled with this Higher Power.

These sessions commonly lasted ten to fifteen minutes and were repeated hundreds of times over the years. In some of them, I felt an incredible sense of love and oneness with

her, as I came to "see" and to become one with her as a
fellow child of God. Here were the new images that were
bringing about my healing, as well as hers. For healing begins
with a new image, a healthier image, a more loving image.

Robert sending light to his mother

Other times, in the meditation or afterwards, my heart
ached as I inwardly bonded with her, as I felt the searing pain
of my childhood loss and family trauma. Before the new
images of love and oneness could become a reality, I had to
release the past images, the feelings of abandonment, the
desire to keep myself separate from others. Believe me, this
was not easy to do. It involved counseling. It took many talks
with Mom. It required that I repeatedly express my love for
her—that I put my love into action. Gradually, as I did, the
pain of my childhood was replaced with the eternal bond of
love that I felt for her. We became dear and close friends, a
loving mother and son, two children of God who loved one

another. What had begun as a new image became a living reality for both of us. And the same thing happened with the rest of my family.

How about you? Who is the key person in your family that you are to "see" in a new and higher way? What you see, will be!

AS WITHIN, SO WITHOUT

When we use our power of imagination in a balanced way, then our thalamus likewise is healthy. When we have difficulties with imagination—when we see through a glass darkly—then we may develop thalamic disorders. For example, there may be headaches in the forehead and temple areas. Current medical technology, however, has yet to delineate additional thalamic diseases. Even brain scans (including CT, MRI and PET scans) have not revealed common thalamic problems. The only thalamic disease generally listed in medical texts is death of thalamic tissue caused by a stroke that blocks blood flow to this organ.

In time, it may be discovered that hallucinations are caused in part by thalamic imbalances, since the thalamus serves as a relay or way station for the psychic senses. Some theories already have been proposed about this, involving the imbalance of the neurotransmitter serotonin in the thalamus. Also, it is well known that hallucinogenic substances such as psilocybin (found in some mushrooms) and lysergic acid diethylamide (LSD) are similar in molecular structure to serotonin. (We definitely do not recommend the use of these or other hallucinogens.) Moreover, in people with schizophrenia, who may have hallucinations, the thalamus commonly is smaller in size than in normal brains, but other parts of the brain likewise may be smaller.

We look forward to the day when medical science unravels

the mysteries of our thalamus, our ESP and our imagination faculty. In the meantime, we use our imagination and thalamus to receive clear guidance and to visualize health, balance and harmony. When we do this, our mind, soul and body are filled with light.

Visualize yourself within a pyramid of light. The apex of this pyramid is a couple feet above your physical head. The four sides of the pyramid are a foot or two away from your physical body. Imagine each side of the pyramid: one side in front of you, one side behind you, and one side to either side of you. You now are safely enclosed and protected within a pyramid of light, which represents your own spiritual Self.

Now, visualize yourself rising up into the apex of the pyramid. As you rise up in consciousness, leave behind your worries and concerns, your usual way of thinking about things. Instead, imagine that you are thinking in your higher consciousness. Your thoughts become clearer, more inspired, more insightful. When you ask a question of Spirit, you receive a flow of clear ideas. New images come into your mind. You find yourself thinking about things from a new and higher perspective.

In this consciousness, receive and co-create a new image for yourself or someone else, an image that pictures something healthy, wonderful, uplifting, good, positive, constructive, happy and beautiful. Create new scenarios for your life, your work, your creative endeavors. Create these new images and then see them coming to life. If there is something that you do like about yourself, your past or your relationships, then re-create it now in your imagination. See it as you wish it to be.

If you have any physical imbalance, visualize that part of

your body being healthy, balanced, full of energy. Keep your eye single on this new image. Know from within that as you see it, as you image it, so it will be.

In due time, slowly come out of your meditation and give thanks unto Spirit for all that you have received and imaged.

1. I am created in the image and likeness of my Father-Mother Creator.
2. Via my imagination and third eye, I now receive the cosmic ideas emanating from the Father aspect of God.
3. As a mother loves and comforts her child, I see myself being embraced, nurtured and loved by the Divine Mother.
4. I am the artist of my life.
5. I shape and color my life with my imagination.
6. My mind pictures health and my body reflects it.
7. I am one with the Creative Matrix of divine ideas and inspirations.
8. I avoid images of terror, violence and fright for myself and my children. I hold images of beauty, joy, peace and harmony.
9. I am inspired by my dreams and intuitive promptings.
10. What I conceive and believe, I will achieve.
11. I think in secret and it comes to pass; my environment is but my looking glass.
12. I let go and let God guide and move me.
13. The thoughts I hold in my mind produce after their own kind.
14. I see myself as whole, free, healthy and happy to be alive.
15. I listen to my inner tutor, my intuition.

16. I am developing a better self-image each day, which is based on knowing that I am made in the image and likeness of God.
17. I am in the flow of images and thoughts that expand my life.
18. I am willing to stretch and to imagine new possibilities.
19. I am thrilled to be who I am.
20. I look for messages, signs, dreams, meaningful coincidences and things that just "come" to me.
21. I tune into good ideas that come to me and I follow up.
22. I imagine myself doing the seemingly impossible with grace and poise.
23. I see myself already doing what it is that I long to · attain.
24. I mentally rehearse skills I want to develop and see myself successfully doing them.
25. I use a full palette of colors to paint a new portrait of my life.
26. I visualize healing of my heart, nerves, digestive system and all other parts of my body temple.
27. I envision healing for everyone in my family.
28. I see harmony, balance and happiness in all my relationships.
29. I visualize peace, love, cooperation and coordination for all peoples of the world.
30. I keep my eye single and I fill my life and the world with healing light.

7

The Power of
UNDERSTANDING

UNDERSTANDING

UNDERSTANDING is my ability to make sense of all my other Powers and of life. It allows me to know that Divine Mind stands under all things. It is being aware that what stands under me is the eternal growth process. "With all my getting, give me an understanding heart." (I Kings 3:10) The power of understanding correlates with my five physical senses and the analytical aspects of my conscious mind.

OUR BASIC NATURE IS GOOD

David. Our power of understanding helps us to make sense out of all the other Powers with which we are endowed and out of which we are forming our life. We have said that all of our Powers are designed to work together—to coordinate and function together in a balanced way. When our Powers function in an integrated and harmonious manner, we are capable of reaching our full potential as a spiritual being. However, when our various Powers are not in balance, we get a distorted life expression.

We believe that people are divine beings, made in the image of God, so we are basically good. The medieval Catholic mystic, Meister Eckhart, wrote: "The seed of God is in us all. Given a hardworking farmer, it will thrive and grow up to God whose seed it is, and accordingly its fruits will be God-Nature. Pear seeds grow into pear trees, nut seeds into nut trees, and God seeds into God."

Knowledge of "potential maturity" exists within a seed. The seed contains the template or instructions that "know" what the tree is meant to be and how it can get to be that fulfillment. The texture of the bark, the shape of the leaves and the general structure are all genetically encoded in the seed.

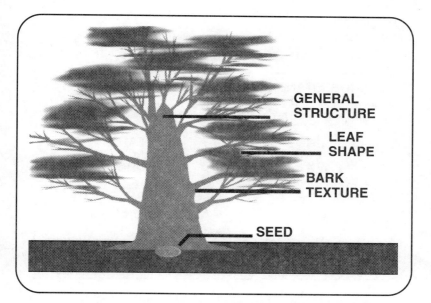

So, likewise, knowledge of potential maturity exists within a human being. Just as a seed for a plant or tree somehow "knows" what it will someday become, so also do human beings have within them a pattern—a basic knowledge of what and how we are intended to express via our Twelve Powers.

Jesus said, "I am the vine, you are the branches." He could be referring not just to himself as a visionary person who saw many people branching out from his teachings, but also to the I Am or the Christ within that is the core or vine within each individual. For out of this core grow our Twelve Powers, which branch out as us, according to our level of understanding.

Thus, we are organic in nature, seeking to unfold or develop according to the inherent pattern that is contained in what Meister Eckhart called "the seed of God." As we grow and mature, we are like a tree that has twelve major branches, one for each of the powers, including faith, love, strength, wisdom and understanding. When all of these branches or powers are well-developed, strong and in balance with all the other branches or powers, then we are healthy and well-balanced. We are expressing our wholeness.

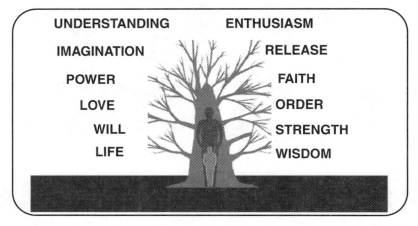

UNDERSTANDING	ENTHUSIASM
IMAGINATION	RELEASE
POWER	FAITH
LOVE	ORDER
WILL	STRENGTH
LIFE	WISDOM

If people are basically good, if they have the seed of God within them that grows and expresses by way of the Twelve Powers, then how can we understand why people do terrible things? How can we reasonably believe in and hold to a view of ourselves and others as basically good when we experience such things as cruelty, murder, slavery, genocide, corruption and greed? We look around and often wonder: "How can this happen? How can people do the violent acts they do? I just don't understand. Is there a devil? Are we evil?" If we don't believe that there is a power of evil that is separate and apart from God and is trying to control us and use us for its malevolent purposes, then how do we understand what we often call "human nature"?

Rather than perceive us as inherently good, many people see our basic nature as "volcanic" or "evil" with negative or sinful drives that must be controlled by threats, fear, bribes, force, chastisements, punishments and rewards (such as grades, money, contests, promotions, awards). This "sinful person" view says theologically that we do not deserve anything good, but because God loves us, God wants to save us anyway. This view of human nature says that we are rebelling against God because of our sinful or ego-driven nature.

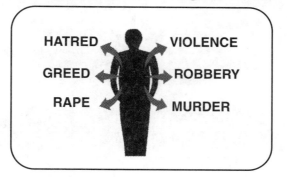

Such an emphasis or belief is a misunderstanding of the basic nature of people. We are not victims of the devil or ego. Rather than "volcanic" or "evil," we are inherently growth-seeking children of God. We are basically "organic." We are systematically moving toward wholeness. The divine seed—the I Am Self—that is our God-nature is seeking to be fulfilled in, through and as us.

So let's look at the tough dilemma: If we are children of God, growth-seeking beings and basically good, how can we understand the "evil" that people do? How can Anne Frank, a Jewish teenager caught in the midst of the Holocaust in World War II, living in a hidden attic in Holland, write in her diary, "I still believe that people are really good at heart"? Are these the hopes of an idealistic, romantic teenager, or the realization of truth even amidst the Nazi horrors and concentration camps?

What has been called a "sinful nature" or "being taken over by ego" is actually the result of cutting off growth in much the same way that a tree is badly pruned. A healthy, balanced, mature tree might look like:

If too many branches are cut from one side, however, then there may be so much growth on the other side that the tree ends up out of balance. The life forces flow into the other branches, and the tree is strained and has problems. Growth is "frustrated" and directed mainly into certain branches.

So we can understand that "evil" is not a separate "power" in and of itself—not an entity personalized as Satan or the devil—but results from the ways we use the divine gifts or divine potential for growth and unfoldment with which we are endowed. Evil can be understood as a frustration or misdirection of our divine potential, rather than a devil or outside force. Therefore, when we pray, "deliver us from evil," it means, "I want to be free from the erroneous or wrong use of my own spiritual powers."

The life force in the tree that is struggling, flopped over and strained still has the same growth-seeking potential. The life force is basically good. The seed is the same. The inherent pattern in the seed is the same. The life energy is the same. In his book *Jesus: The Son of Man*, Kahlil Gibran wrote, "A seed hidden in the heart of an apple is an orchard invisible, yet should that seed fall upon a rock it will come to naught."

If certain branches of our expression of God are not allowed to grow or are cut off for any reason, we have an imbalanced, strained, difficult situation. We don't say, "This is an 'evil' tree, cursed by a satanic force." Rather, we see the organic pattern being misdirected. For example, without the counterbalance and right use of love and wisdom and life, which have been cut from the tree of life, the powers of strength, imagination and will may become imbalanced, distorted, excessively developed and misapplied. In this case, we may get a person who is cruel, dictatorial, domineering or abusive.

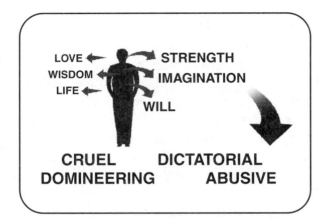

In another instance, if a person is loving, imaginative and enthusiastic, but lacks wisdom, strength and power, this person may not be able to stand up for himself or herself. He or she may get used, abused, dumped on, scammed or drained. This individual may be a "pushover" or be taken advantage of by "users."

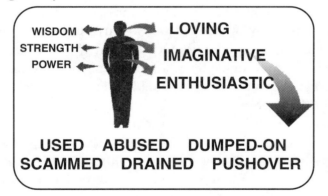

So, ideally our divinity or fulfillment is the balanced co-ordination and expression of all of our spiritual powers, from the God Seed within us.

Now we *understand*. We have something natural and scientific to stand on. We see what *stands under* our existence and growth process. We behold the basic goodness that is seeking to get expressed through our Twelve Powers in balanced, coordinated and cooperative ways. (The drawings in this section are adapted from *Human Be-ing* by William Pietsch.)

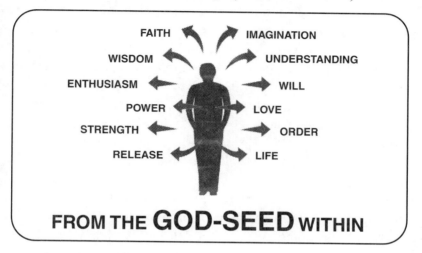

FAITH
IMAGINATION
WISDOM
UNDERSTANDING
ENTHUSIASM
WILL
POWER
LOVE
STRENGTH
ORDER
RELEASE
LIFE

FROM THE **GOD-SEED** WITHIN

QUEST FOR UNDERSTANDING

Understanding is never final. We may "see the light" and exclaim at times, "Ah, now I understand!" However, we always are evolving and growing in wisdom and stature.

Doubt is not sin. Certainty is not a virtue. The word "quest" obviously is stimulated and driven by the word "question," with both coming from the Latin *quaerere* meaning "to search." Jesus certainly was pointing us in this direction when he counseled people "to become as a little child."

The most famous questioner in the Bible stories (outside of Job) was the disciple Thomas. He represents the search for understanding in us. Thomas didn't mind asking questions, and he listened to Jesus' answers and learned. He wanted to know and understand. He knew the benefit of a doubt.

Understanding is not handed down. Creeds, doctrines,

definitions, dogma, opinions, teachings and writings are handed down. Alfred Lord Tennyson wrote, "There lives more faith in honest doubt than in half the creeds." All the great seekers have discovered their own map—Gautama Buddha, Jesus, Lao-tzu, Socrates, Moses, Isaiah, Paul, St. Francis, St. Theresa. Each one had his or her own road map that can help point the way for us, but we still have to travel the road of our own illumination and understanding.

Thomas was a questioner. He had to ask, search, knock, probe, experiment and seek proof. He was the most "scientific" of the disciples. He wanted firsthand experience, and he wanted to verify and validate what is true by seeing and touching it.

The story of Jesus appearing to the disciples after the resurrection is a classic example of Thomas' desire for outer evidence. When some of the other disciples claimed to have seen Jesus, Thomas said he would not believe until he put his fingers into the nail holes in Jesus' body. A few days later, he had the opportunity to conduct his own "scientific" experiment and he did so. He became convinced by so doing that some kind of phenomenon had taken place, which was difficult to explain but which was experienced as a reality to him and his physical senses.

As was pointed out previously in chapter 3, Mahatma Gandhi called his autobiography, *The Story of My Experiments with Truth*. The famous Greek philosopher, Socrates, said that the key to life was to "know thyself." Jesus may have seen Thomas as the bright one who, like him, was not satisfied with hand-me-down convictions and others' beliefs. Thomas was a quester—a questioner—and when he received a confirmation he understood and was changed.

You who are experimenting with Truth;

You who are searching and studying;

You who are on a quest;

You who are not satisfied with worn-out explanations or easy answers;

You who feel there is a better way to live;

You who don't want to repeat old negative patterns that you or others have gotten enmeshed in;

You who want to have firsthand experience;

You who know that understanding is never final:

May all Power be unto you as you continually search for and gain greater knowledge, illumination and understanding.

As Kahlil Gibran wrote in *The Prophet,* "Say not, 'I have found the truth,' but rather, 'I have found a truth.'"

BE STILL AND KNOW

Gay Lynn. It is so beautiful to look into a calm lake and to see the reflection of a tree as it grows next to the bank. When the water is rough or churning, you can no longer see the image. If the wind is blowing and you throw something into the lake, you are not able to see the image of the tree.

There is an old Chinese saying, "Muddy water let stand becomes clear." Many times when people come to me in counseling they are all churned up. Their emotions are at a high pitch; they feel as though they are on sensory overload, taking in so much from what is happening around them. Many times they are struggling to make a decision in the midst of this turmoil, and it is impossible. How can they see the reflection of the tree when the water is all stirred up? The beauty of the tree cannot be seen in churning water, and the understanding and guidance of our heart, mind and spirit cannot come clear while the mind is all mixed up.

Understanding can be increased as we practice becoming still. Sometimes, the best answer is to take no action, to let things calm down around you, to allow your senses to take a rest, and to let your mind become quiet. A quiet mind can see more clearly what needs to be done. Remember, "Muddy water let stand becomes clear." If you are feeling confused and you need greater understanding, practice stilling your mind. You can do this by simply holding a single word in your mind, such as "peace." Repeat the word over and over, breathing deeply and exhaling with each repetition. You may want to light a candle and just watch the dancing flame. Let your mind simply rest and keep your focus on the flame. Practice going into a prayer state where you give your worries over to a Higher Power. The rabbi, Jesus, illustrated how to do this when he looked at the troubled waters. His disciples were all anxious and afraid, and so Jesus said to the waters (and perhaps to the disciples), "Peace. Be still." *Peace. Be still.* We can say this as a calming affirmation to ourselves, until our mind becomes calm, uncluttered and clear.

Understanding does not always mean that your life turns out the way you planned it. Changes can take place beyond your control. One loving father in Florida named Chris was greatly distressed when he found out the mother of his three-year-old daughter, Amy, was moving to Philadelphia. Chris could not understand why this was happening to him. He was very upset and all churned up inside. He did everything possible to try to delay and prevent the move from happening, but eventually he had to say good-bye.

Chris called Amy every single day to say, "I love you and I am here for you." For two years, he traveled regularly to see his little girl. He also spent considerable time working on and understanding himself, being determined to stay in a healthy recovery program, attending church, and having support from friends and family.

One of the special services he attended at his Unity church designated a time to write a "God Letter." Chris had been working daily to surrender, to understand more deeply his relationship with Spirit's will, and to find clarity in his life. On this occasion, people had the option of writing a letter to God or of being the recipient or secretary or stenographer who received a letter from the Higher Power. Chris prayed and wrote a simple letter that he felt was coming from the Divine:

Dear Chris,

I will put Amy back into your life, living close to you again so you can be together.

Love,
God

Chris then wrote his own name and address on an envelope, put the letter inside and sealed it. Finally, he put the "God Letter" in a basket, knowing that in six months the

church would mail it back to him at his home.

Three months later, Chris had long since forgotten about the letter when Amy's Mom called to say that they would be moving back to Florida. Within the next few months, Amy was

back near him and was spending time regularly with her Dad. One day, they walked hand-in-hand to the mailbox and found inside a strange letter from the church with his own handwriting on the envelope. Chris opened the letter with his precious little girl by his side and read:

Dear Chris,

I will put Amy back into your life, living close to you again so you can be together.

Love,
God

In shock and amazement, Chris hugged his beautiful daughter and cried, realizing the power of prayer and feeling the presence of an understanding Father working in his life.

Understanding often takes time, not to mention love and patience. You can see how Chris could have cursed his situation and, with upset and anger, churned himself up and everyone else. Instead, he turned the situation over to the Higher Power and worked steadily to create within himself an understanding heart.

UNDERSTANDING AND CELEBRATING OUR DIFFERENCES

In exasperation, have you ever said, "Why can't you just understand me?" My husband, David, and I certainly have said this to one another. We have had our share of difficulties understanding each other in our years of marriage and parenting five children. Fortunately, we discovered a book many years ago that really helped: *Please Understand Me* by David Keirsey and Marilyn Bates. There is an inventory discussed in the book that helped us to know our unique ways of being in this world. It is a simple inventory that can be taken by anyone, one that is not at all complicated or difficult. And we have each taken an inventory of ourselves.

My way of thinking and feeling, my aims, purposes, values,

drives and impulses are different from David's. David's are unique and different from mine . . . and that is good. If David doesn't want what I want, it is important that I not try to make him be wrong. He sees things differently than I do and I need to embrace those differences.

For example, I am more outgoing than David; I become energized by being around people. I am very social, love to interact, and have many friends and relationships. David is quieter. He likes being around people, but after a while, he is ready to leave and go home. He is more energized by spending quiet time alone or with a few close friends, rather than being in large gatherings for long periods of time. Now, you can see how this could result in a big disagreement if we are at a large gathering, and I am just getting started when he is ready to leave. So, we compromise. It is very important that I understand and not take it personally that David needs his private places in his thoughts and in his surroundings. Of course, both of us need to have quiet time and social time, but our preferences for the amounts are different.

David is much more the visionary. He is great at seeing the big picture. He likes to keep things open-ended, gather more information, "go with the flow," wait and see what might happen next before finalizing things. This is very valuable and makes it possible for some wonderful things to emerge. I am a detail person. I run my life by my day planner. I like decisions made, lists written. I like to "wrap it up," "get the show on the road," "make closure." Well, again, you can see how different we are. But together! Together, we bring a unique blend of talents and skills to all that we do, as long as we make that extra effort to understand and appreciate the unique differences.

Saying that this requires "extra effort" does not mean that David doesn't love me or that I don't love David. We are different in some ways, but we are also quite similar in other areas, such as having strong intuition, an inclination to act on hunches, being very imaginative and having big dreams. Working together through our differences actually helps us develop these similarities and achieve our dreams.

So, if I believe something other than what you believe, if I don't want what you want, please try not to tell me that what I want is wrong. Please understand that it is just "different." This is a key to staying in a long-term, growing relationship with family, coworkers, anyone: honoring our uniqueness, sharing our diversity.

If both of us are trying to make one another into a copy of the other, we are not really using our power of understanding. Really listen to hear what I am saying. See things through my eyes for a moment. Understanding says, I am not irritated or disappointed with you because you are different from me. I don't want to change you to be like me; I embrace you as you are. I respect and even nurture our differences. This is true understanding!

Body

FIVE PHYSICAL SENSES

Dr. Robert. How do we understand ourselves and the world around us? In large measure, we do this by gathering a vast amount of information by way of our five physical senses—taste, touch, sight, hearing and smell—and then by carefully analyzing and computing this data. Therefore, our power of understanding externalizes and expresses via our five physical senses and the reasoning, analytical aspects of our conscious mind.

In many ways, understanding is the counterpart to the power of imagination, which involves our psychic senses (ESP) and the thalamus. Using clairvoyance, clairaudience and clairsentience (intuition), we gather information about the invisible realms, the realities beyond the vibrations or frequencies of the physical dimension. Then we complement our visions, dreams and intuitive impressions by analyzing and interpreting what we see, hear, touch, smell and taste with our physical senses. The two powers—imagination and understanding—must work closely together in full harmony if we are to have a complete view and comprehension of our whole existence.

Some spiritual teachers and pathways warn against getting entangled in psychic matters and experiences. They say things like, "Beware of psychics, channels and past-life readers."

It is true that we can overemphasize or misuse our elementary spiritual powers (ESP). But the point is to use them properly, for they are an integral, inherent part of us. What would we do without our intuition, our ability to dream, our power to "see" beyond the physical realm? Charles Fillmore wrote that most of his early spiritual guidance came to him in his dreams, many of which were prophetic. Dreams are a major way we use our imagination faculty.

Other spiritual leaders and teachings present a similar belittling attitude or warning about our five physical senses. We hear them saying, "I don't want to live in sense consciousness." "The world of earthly sensation is a trap." "The five physical senses are part of our animal or lower nature." Here again, however, the goal is to use our five senses in a balanced, healthy, illumined way. You would not be reading this book if you could not see. You could not begin to function in the physical realm or come to understand your right place in it if you did not have a means of gathering all kinds of physical data and then analyzing and interpreting this information. Look at all the extraordinary technological advancements in healing that scientists have made by using their understanding faculty.

When talking about the five physical senses, we are using a general classification, since some senses have subdivisions that might be considered as separate senses. For example, there are numerous sense receptors that record different types of touch including vibration, temperature, position, size and shape of objects, pain, and light and heavy touch. Moreover, inside the ear, which generally is thought of only in regards to hearing, is the inner ear that contains the labyrinth; this gives us our sense of balance. Thus, when we use the term five senses we are not limiting the number of physical senses but rather are using the traditional description.

Each sensory organ records a different type of information and sends it by our sensory nerves to specific centers in the cerebrum. For example, in the eyes, the cornea and lens bend the light coming into the eye, so that an image forms on the retina at the back of the eye. Rods and cones in the retina—which respond to black and white and color, respectively—convert the light into bioelectrical impulses that are transferred along the optic nerve to the thalamus and then via other nerves to the back of the cerebrum. Only when the impulses reach the visual centers in the cerebrum do we actually "see" something. And only when the visual input is transferred to other surrounding cerebral centers do we begin to comprehend and understand what we have seen. (See Figure 7A.)

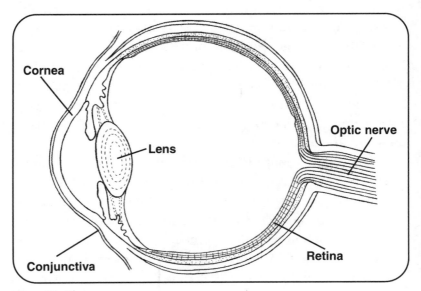

Figure 7A. The eye

Take a moment now to imagine what it would be like to be without your sight—no sunsets, no faces of loved ones, no

visual warnings of impending danger. You could compensate, as blind people do, by developing your other senses. However, you would be missing a majority of the information that the senses record, because the eyes gather 80 percent of the total sensory data.

And how about your sense of hearing? It can be so uplifting to hear the words spoken by a friend, a talk given by a spiritual teacher, a favorite melody, the sound of the wind and the rain and birds chirping. Each sound wave travels through the outer ear to the tympanic membrane, which vibrates and moves three small bones in the middle ear, called the hammer, anvil and stirrup. The vibration of the stapes at the oval window creates waves in the fluid of the cochlear of the inner ear. These waves move tiny hair cells, which then send a signal via the cochlear (auditory) nerve first to the thalamus and then to the hearing center in the cerebrum. (See Figure 7B.)

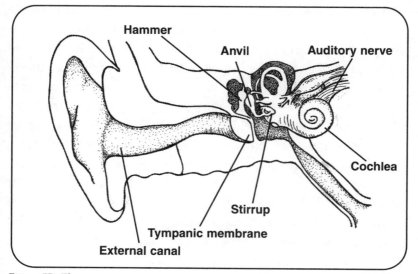

Figure 7B. The ear

In like fashion, our taste buds and touch receptors convert taste and touch sensations into nerve impulses that travel via sensory nerves to specific centers in the thalamus, which then relay them to specific taste and touch centers in the cerebrum. Smell is the only sense whose information travels directly via nerves to the cerebrum, bypassing the thalamus. Seventy-five percent of the ability to taste relies on the ability to smell. For example, when you have a cold that clogs your nose, you lose much of your ability to taste food.

Isn't it interesting that all of the senses except smell relay their information first to the thalamus and then to the brain? Remember, we said that imagination (thalamus) and understanding (five senses) work closely together. We can see this close interaction in the physical body, where both our psychic senses (ESP) and four of our physical senses transfer their information by way of the thalamus to the cerebrum.

Do we understand something just because we have seen it or heard it or sensed it? Obviously not. Five people may see the same accident and report five varying versions of what happened. Twenty people may hear the same lecture and respond in twenty different ways as to what "spoke" to them.

Moreover, understanding does not rely only on our five senses, as glorious as they may be in providing information about our physical world. Deeper, higher, more expansive understanding often comes in times of quiet contemplation, reflection, self-analysis and meditation, when we deliberately are not paying attention to our physical senses or our usual way of thinking about things. In these moments, we understand the underlying universal principles, lessons and realities of what we are experiencing. Then we are truly wise, illumined and understanding.

Gautama Buddha took great joy in looking at the countryside and sunsets, but he was not deceived into believing that the things of this world were permanent and unchanging. He and all the great masters have realized that behind all outer phenomena and physical activity is a corresponding spiritual principle and reality. This is the cosmic understanding that scientists are beginning to realize now that we are entering a new millennium. We are letting go of the limited, illusory way of thinking that we are just a physical being who can think and feel because we have a brain, that our body and spirit are separate, unconnected parts of us.

Rather, more and more, all of humanity is starting to comprehend that we are a spiritual being who is endowed with Twelve Powers, each of which externalizes via a particular part of the body. In other words, our body has a cosmic, holistic design. Here is the new model, the new paradigm, the new understanding that will be the basis for future healing research and treatment.

SYMPTOMS OF IMBALANCE

When we have difficulties with our understanding faculty, we may develop physical symptoms with one or more of our five physical senses, including pain, irritation, inflammation and infection in our eyes or ears. Maybe we have a "blind spot" in the way we see ourselves or others, and thereby develop some type of visual problem: nearsightedness or far-sightedness, astigmatism, cataracts, glaucoma or blindness. When we have ear disorders such as infection or loss of hearing, we can ask ourselves, "What am I not listening to and 'hearing'?" Difficulties with understanding also may lead to problems with conscious reasoning, as in learning disorders (such as dyslexia) and mental imbalances (including severe ones like psychosis).

Whenever you have any difficulty with your five physical

senses or your reasoning and analytical ability, focus on your power of understanding to treat this disorder. At the same time, however, consider every possible physical cause and treatment of your disease. For any major or chronic symptom, always consult with a licensed health-care practitioner.

When a person is nearsighted or farsighted, has astigmatism or needs bifocals to see when he gets older, does this always mean that he has a problem with understanding? Not necessarily. There may be a genetic predisposition to eye problems. There may be numerous other physical causes, which medical science currently does not understand. The need for corrective lenses to see things up close often is a normal part of the aging process.

Moreover, we all know someone who has 20/20 vision and excellent hearing but is "blind" to his or her own shortcomings, or does not "listen" because he or she already "knows it all." As Jesus put it, this person does not have "the eyes to see or the ears to hear." Conversely, people who are visually or auditorily impaired, such as Helen Keller, may have incredible comprehension of themselves and all aspects of life. Therefore, we need to be careful when we attempt to discern and to analyze what may be the corresponding imbalance in the understanding faculty, which may be causing or contributing to a problem with the five physical senses.

SIGHT RESTORED

One of the classic healing stories in the Bible involves Saul of Tarsus, who was called Paul after his conversion (Acts 9:1-19). Saul was a learned man who studied with the prominent rabbis of his day. Yet, his understanding was tainted with self-righteousness, for he persecuted unto death the Christians, whom he considered heretics. Then, when he was traveling on the road to Damascus, Saul had a vision of bright light coming down from the sky and heard a voice saying, "Saul, Saul. Why do you persecute me?" When Saul asked who was speaking, he was told it was Jesus. Shaken and shattered by his experience, Saul became blind.

Saul had seen this vision by way of his imagination faculty and his psychic senses. His third eye had opened to the higher, invisible planes of reality. Clairaudiently, he had heard Jesus speaking to him. This interdimensional communion revealed Saul's "blindness" to, and lack of understanding of, Jesus' teachings and demonstration. In response to this shattering revelation, Saul actually lost his physical sight for the next three days.

Saul continued his journey to Damascus where Ananias had a vision of Jesus (which Bible scholars say may have been a dream, since in the Bible dreams commonly were called visions of the night). In the vision or dream, Jesus gave Ananias detailed instructions of where to find Saul, so that he could heal him. (Here is yet another vivid example of clear receiving by way of the imagination faculty and the thalamus.) However, Ananias first had to carefully analyze and understand his vision before he acted upon it, because he had heard of Saul's previous persecution of Jesus' followers. Then, convinced that he had received accurately, he went to Saul, placed his hands on him and prayed for his healing. In response, the Biblical account says that something like scales were shed from Saul's eyes and his vision was restored. Saul, who now took the name Paul, went on to become one of Jesus' foremost apostles.

We can take heart from this extraordinary example of transformation. When we are "blind," stubborn, insensitive or dogmatic, when we hurt people emotionally or physically, we can call upon the Higher Power to give us new insight in our dreams and visions or via our intuition. When we "see the light" and hear the "still small voice" speaking to us, we can transform our way of thinking. We can repent, which means simply to rethink or to turn around. We need not wallow in guilt or remorse. Rather, we can use our new understanding to move forward, to heal ourselves and to help others, especially those who are facing similar challenges that we have overcome.

How has this happened in your life?

As in the visualization on imagination, see yourself within a pyramid of light. The tip or apex of the pyramid is a foot or two above your physical head. The capstone or upper part of the pyramid surrounds your entire brain. The remainder of the pyramid encases the rest of your physical body, with one side of the pyramid in front of you, one side in back of you, and one side to either side of you. You now are enclosed in a pyramid of light. You are surrounded by, and imbued in, the light of your spiritual Self.

Next, visualize bright light flowing down from the top or apex of the pyramid into your head and brain. You can coordinate this influx of light with your breathing. As you breathe in, imagine that the light is flowing into your eyes, your ears, your nose and your tongue. When you breathe out, relax and let the light be absorbed and assimilated by your sense organs. If you are having difficulty with any of your senses, focus there until you feel that your eye or ear has been fully filled with light. See the light going to every part of your body, because you have touch receptors throughout your body.

As the light flows into and through your five senses and your brain, call upon the Spirit within you to reveal some new understanding. Ask a question of this Higher Intelligence and wait to receive the answer. Be patient. Be still. Let your mind be attuned to the influx of new ideas, new ways of seeing things. Listen carefully as the Spirit "speaks" to you, guides you and lifts you into a heightened state of awareness and consciousness. Be still and know that you are one with God, that the "seed" of God is growing within you and as you. Be illumined in the light of your God Self.

In due time, slowly come out of your meditation and think of ways to apply your new understanding in your life.

1. I understand who and what I really am.
2. I am developing a more understanding heart.
3. My understanding grows as I see, hear, touch, taste, smell and analyze accurately.
4. I understand that at my core I am a good person.
5. I see myself as a lovely tree whose branches are all developing in a balanced way.
6. "I still believe that people are really good at heart." (Anne Frank)
7. I ask questions, I seek answers, I am illumined.
8. My life is an experiment with Truth.
9. I do not say "I have found the Truth," but rather "I have found a truth."
10. I practice stilling my mind so I can see clearly and reflect calmly on what I need to understand.
11. Peace. Be still.
12. I understand that the Higher Power is always at work to help, heal, prosper, illumine and enlighten me.
13. I understand that differences between others and myself are normal and interesting.
14. I value others because they have their own individuality and ways.
15. I combine my creative imagination with my keen understanding, so I am both visionary and grounded.
16. My physical senses are precious gifts that I use with wisdom and discernment.

17. I give more attention and time to understand and appreciate the unique qualities in those I love.
18. I love my physical senses and I realize how much I gain by using them carefully.
19. I have "the eyes to see and the ears to hear" what I need to learn and understand.
20. I understand that people are not inherently "evil" but that they may use their Powers in imbalanced ways.
21. I understand that the seed of God is in me and that I am growing up to God whose seed I am.
22. I understand myself as a part of the cosmic design of the universe.
23. I understand that it is natural for me to express all that is contained in the divine pattern of my God-likeness.
24. I understand my Twelve Powers and how to use them together.
25. I view others and myself with understanding eyes.
26. I am in touch with the Divine.
27. I love to understand myself, others and everything in my life.
28. I am illumined in the light of my being.
29. I know that I am systematically moving toward wholeness.
30. I understand why I am here and what I am to do.

8
The Power of WILL

WILL is my ability to be willing toward God. Will is the executive faculty of my mind. I am God's executive. I am the CEO of my life enterprise. I am the one who can get the job done with God. Will externalizes in my body as my respiratory system: sinuses, trachea, bronchi, bronchioles and lungs.

CEO OF MY LIFE

David. Will is a spiritual power—one of our twelve primary powers. It is our executive ability. Have you ever thought of yourself as an "executive"? Or even more, as the Chief Executive Officer of your life? The CEO? You may not work in an executive office and have a desk and that kind of job, but you are an executive. I see us all as being in a partnership with the Higher Power. We are all part of, and a partner in, a great enterprise—a universal incorporation of All-Good. It's a dynamic and multinational, multicultural, multiracial, multi-everything enterprise.

I am appointed and charged with being the CEO of my life. I have executive power over how God's limitless good is managed and allocated in my life.

My executive power is my "will power." We have all heard about the type of "will power" needed to stay on a diet or to stop smoking. But I'm talking about a greater understanding of our "will power" than just those efforts we may make to stay on a diet or stop smoking—as important as these are.

Will is the spiritual power that enables us to do things. I make executive decisions and then I execute—that is, I carry out those decisions:

"I *will* successfully run the business of my life."
"I *will* be prosperous."

"I *will* make it through school."
"I *will* get to places on time."
"I *will* be orderly in organizing my life."
"I *will* choose relationships that are positive."
"I *will* stay in a healthy recovery program."
"I *will* look for the good in myself and others."
"I *will* keep my sense of humor."
"I *will* let peace begin with me!"

These affirmations are acting as an executive—a CEO.
These are ways I cooperate more fully with the divine will,
called God's will. And remember, God's will is always "good
will"—a desire that only the very highest good comes to me,
to you and to all people. That is the will of God.

At the same time, you and I have "free will." I can will—
choose and do—that which rejects my good. For example, I
may try to operate strictly on my own, to hurt myself or
others. Or, I can co-operate with my Higher Power-Partner
and flourish, prosper and find fulfillment in amazing ways.

Our power of will needs to be strong and directed by the
highest and best that is in us. Being of strong will, however,
does not mean that we are to impose our will on others. Then
we are domineering, stubborn, bossy, rigid. We all know folks
like this—they badger, harass or persecute. We have all experienced "power struggles" that are a "clash of wills." These
are negative uses of our power of will.

The flip side of being overbearing is being weak-willed, not
feeling able to assert ourselves, being wishy-washy and indecisive, allowing others to make our decisions for us, getting
along by always going along.

Again, we need to have a strong will, which we then
can turn over to the Higher Power. In his book *Christian
Healing*, Charles Fillmore wrote, "The idea of giving up the
will to God's will should not include the thought of

weakening it, or causing it to become in any way less; it properly means that the will is being instructed how to act for the
best."

So, in our approach to being a whole person and living
fully, we are developing and balancing and coordinating our
Powers, not weakening or cutting them out. We don't say, "I
have to get rid of my will power or my judgment or enthusiasm." We say, "Thy will be done," as a way of affirming the
Universal Good expressing through us as a whole, well-
balanced person, because that is God's will for us. When we
pray, "Thy will be done," we are asking to be a channel for
Infinite Good to pour through us out to humanity and the
world at large.

Our will, used in this creative and inspirational way, is a
great mobilizer and energizer. Through our power of will, we
can take charge of our lives, make sound and clear decisions,
and follow them up with decisive action that is positive and
productive.

GOD'S GOOD WILL

God's will for me is good. Do we remember this often
enough? Do we really believe this? Think about what is going
on in your life right now. Whatever is happening, believe and
know for yourself, "God's will for me is good. God desires for
me health, love, companionship, prosperity, financial stability, peace of mind and peace in the world. I am willing to
accept all of these."

All of us have grown up with little phrases that we may
have erroneously come to believe as true. An accident happens, a death occurs or someone gets sick and people say, "I
guess it was God's will." Do we really believe that God has
some perverse "need" to have us suffer and be punished?

One time I visited a patient who was recovering from an operation in the intensive care unit. I walked into the room and he had all kinds of IVs in him. Monitors were checking his body constantly; he was all hooked up to sophisticated technology; and medical experts were watching him day and night.

I said, "How are you getting along?" He replied, "Oh, I don't know, I guess it's just God's will that I have this problem—and I ought to just accept His will." I purposely tried to shock him out of such a ridiculous attitude. I said, "Wait a minute. If it's God's will that you be ill and stay ill, then why are you in here with all these IVs and monitors to help you— it's costing thousands of dollars a day! All this care and technology is trying to get you over the illness. If it's really God's will for you to be sick, then why all this? You should be doing the opposite of all this and just try to be *sicker!*"

He didn't really believe "God's will" is sickness. He just was repeating an old, negative superstition without really thinking about how it flew in the face of his efforts to get well.

Dr. Bernie Siegel, author of *Love, Medicine, and Miracles,* said, "Science is catching up with good feelings. When you are happy, every cell in your body knows about it. Feelings are chemical. If God told you to be happy for the rest of your life, what would you do?"

We also need to remember, as Dr. Siegel often says to patients and colleagues, "Death is not a failure." Life extends fully in a continuity beyond our current "lifetime." We don't fully understand the entire life process, but what we see of it in this segment we are living in now is only a small part of our ongoing life. So we can add these affirmations:

- My will to live is strong. I see much in life worth living for.
- I believe we can know that God's will for us is always

good—and we are immortal beings—life extends beyond this lifetime and particular incarnation.

- We are always in the light, protection, love and life of God. In that consciousness we can truly say, "Thy will be done."

RELATIONSHIPS OF THE SOUL

Gay Lynn. Before David and I met, I had chosen to be with people in my life that "I" thought would be good for me. I met with a fair share of hurt, pain, frustration and upset. If this story I am about to tell you had not happened to me personally, I probably would doubt its authenticity! But this really happened one day as I was sitting in church after the midweek service. There was a deep sadness in my heart. I was divorced, not in a relationship, and feeling a great deal of doubt about any future relationships in my life.

As I sat in church, I was praying in a way I had never prayed before. I remember so clearly saying, "God, I surrender." Tears flowed. "God, I have done a poor job choosing people to be in a relationship with, so I surrender that to you, dear God." Tears ran hot down my cheeks. I thought of how important a good relationship was to me. I am a partnership kind of person. I work best in a team. I love the companionship and nurturing a good relationship can bring.

I ended my prayer by saying, "God, you choose. You tell me who my partner is and guide and direct my way." A voice behind me spoke and made me jump a bit. Before I could turn around I heard, "David Williamson." When I looked behind me, to my amazement no one was there. I felt this incredible deep peace come over me. I really didn't know who David Williamson was, but I had this calm assurance I would find out in the right way and at the right time. Did I know him? Had I seen him somewhere? Had someone told me about him? How would I find and meet him? What is supposed to happen, when and where? All I had was a name, mysteriously received in a moment of openness and humility. And then, in a series of wonderful synchronicities, we came together.

The only difference between this prayer and many others I had prayed was the degree to which I had surrendered my will and my efforts to make things go my way over to God. I said with my whole heart and soul, "Thy will be done, Lord." And in that one magnificent moment of total surrender, my prayers received an immediate response. I yielded to God's calling, and I heard what I have come to clearly understand and recognize as the voice of Spirit, for me.

My experience of having an immediate response in this way is not common. I work daily to stay in that flow of conscious awareness. The time was right, and the Higher Power truly answered and put me in touch with my beloved David. A relationship I probably would have never even thought of for myself came to fruition. The words you are reading right now would never have been spoken. Our TV/video program on the *Twelve Powers in You* would never have been produced, if I had not surrendered to God and had not been open and willing to follow God's will for my life and my relationship.

Maybe you are looking for a relationship, wanting to make a change or seeking a new direction in some area of your life. Ask today, "What is your will for me, Lord? Thy will be done."

I AM WILLING

How willing are you to keep going when you are given some challenging news? You and I face varying degrees of challenges and hard times. It is tough to overcome some of these setbacks.

What do I do if I am fired or "let go" in a company merger or downsizing? What if I am in debt and having financial problems? What happens if someone I love, maybe a family member, girlfriend or boyfriend, rejects me and refuses to talk to me, or walks out on me or wants a divorce? What do I do? How does "will" play a role in helping me?

I had a girlfriend I was very close to, whom I valued as being a part of my life. We had had a rocky relationship with some ups and downs for years. I sent her a gift for her birthday, a book I enjoyed called *Love and Survival* by Dr. Dean Ornish. Dr. Ornish had been in town and I had the book personally autographed to her and sent it along with a beautiful card. Well, the following week the package was returned in the mail and the card was unopened. This hurt me. I felt sad that we could not be in a caring relationship. I felt rejected and hurt.

Sometimes when this happens to me, I shut down inside. Have you felt this way? Unwilling to reach out, fearful of having to go through the pain of rejection again? Not wanting to risk opening yourself emotionally again because you don't want to feel hurt?

So, I put the book on my shelf and every time I would look at it, I would be reminded of this hurt and rejection again. And I thought, this is ridiculous! I have to stop feeling this way. Then an idea came to me. I could give the book to someone who *was* very special to me. I wrote a note inside the book sharing my love and enclosed a card to explain what had happened.

She joyously received the book and said many caring and

loving things that my heart longed to hear. She was so appreciative and receptive. I was thankful I had made another
choice to reach out and share my love. A *willingness* that
was more powerful than any pain of rejection helped me to
overcome past hurts.

Where in your life can willingness help you? Are you willing to try again? Call upon that power of will and let it
breathe new love and abundance into your life.

Take a deep breath right now and say to yourself, *"I am
willing!"*

Body

RESPIRATORY SYSTEM

Dr. Robert. Our executive ability, our power of will, externalizes in our physical body as our respiratory system, which includes our nose, nasal cavity, sinuses, throat, trachea (windpipe), two bronchi, bronchioles and two lungs. (See Figure 8.) We breathe in air and life-giving oxygen, and we breathe out air and carbon dioxide.

In the Biblical story of creation in the Book of Genesis 2:7, it says, "The Lord God formed man of dust from the ground, and breathed into his nostrils the breath of life; and man became a living being." Thus, our Father-Mother Creator willed us to live. He-She breathed this divine will or breath right into our respiratory system. And our Creator's will is that we be healthy and filled with energy, and that we live life abundantly. Each time we breathe in oxygen-laden air, we are fulfilling this divine will. We are breathing energy, the fire of life, or prana (as it is called in Hinduism) right into our lungs. Ancient Egyptians called this breath of life *ka*, whereas Hawaiian kahunas refer to it as *ha*.

During inspiration, we draw air and oxygen through our nose's two nostrils into the nasal cavity, which is located over the roof of the mouth. Via small passageways, the air then may enter into four pairs of sinuses—frontal, maxillary,

ethmoidal and sphenoidal—which are air-filled cavities in
the bones behind and above the nose. The sinuses and the
nasal cavity warm, moisten and filter the air as it travels
through them.

Next, the air flows through the throat (pharynx), the voice
box and the trachea, which divides into two tubes that are
called bronchi. Each bronchi carries air into one of the two
lungs. Inside the lungs, the bronchi divide into increasingly
smaller air passages called bronchioles. At the end of the
smallest bronchioles are clusters of tiny air sacs or alveoli.
The lungs contain an estimated 300 million alveoli. Cut open
and laid out flat, the surface area of the alveoli would cover
an area of approximately seventy square meters.

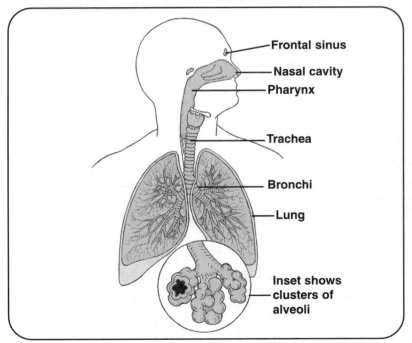

Figure 8. Respiratory system

In the alveoli, the oxygen diffuses through the alveolar walls into the surrounding blood, which carries it to every part of the body. Oxygen is the spark of life, the fire of life. When it combines with glucose in the cells, it provides the energy, the life force, which powers all cellular activities. The waste product of this oxidation of glucose is carbon dioxide, which diffuses from the cells into the blood. The blood transports the carbon dioxide to the lungs where it diffuses into the alveoli. When we breathe out or exhale, the carbon-dioxide-rich air travels via the respiratory tract to the nose, where it is expelled from the body.

BREATHE IN THE WILL OF GOD

We have free will, so we always have a choice as to how we incorporate and utilize the divine life force. One of our first acts when we come out of our mother's womb is to breathe. If not, we are stillborn and we die. For without oxygen, we cannot live. Then for the rest of our life, we make a multitude of choices. Just as we breathe in and out an average of about fifteen times every minute, so too do we make many decisions every minute, every hour, every day. Each choice we make affects the functioning and health of our respiratory system and our whole body.

What happens to your breathing when you feel anxious, upset, afraid? At these times, your breathing becomes shallow and rapid. How about when you feel relaxed, at peace, that God's good will is expressing in your life? Now your breathing becomes slower and deeper. You breathe deeply from the diaphragm and draw abundant air and oxygen into your system. In fact, when you feel nervous, agitated or fearful, you can change your state of mind just by taking a couple of slow deep breaths, and letting go of your anxiety and worries when you breathe out. This is one of the simplest ways of entering into a calm, meditative state: to consciously slow down and to deepen your breathing, which in turn helps to quiet your mind and emotions.

In the East, yoga teaches a series of breathing exercises called pranayama, which are designed to increase and to regulate the flow of prana or life force throughout the body. In a common form of Buddhist meditation, one simply concentrates on the breath as a focusing device, without trying to change the breathing. This is practice for learning how to be in the present moment, to live in the here and now.

We need to be fully aware that our current choices may have long-term consequences. Consider smoking, for example. It begins as a free-will choice. Then, people continue to smoke even when they know that it causes all kinds of respiratory diseases, including lung cancer. Tobacco companies make the choice to produce and promote their product. Is this the will of God, who breathes life into us? Obviously not! When people around the planet stop smoking, this one collective decision will do more to heal humanity than perhaps any other physical action. So, let's visualize this taking place, and let it be soon!

Allowing others to impose their will upon us, to make our decisions for us, also can affect our breathing and respiratory system. In counseling, I have heard several people say that they felt like they were "suffocating" in their marriage. Others said it felt like they could not "breathe" in their relationships, because they were not allowed or given the room to think for themselves, to make their own decisions, and to make changes in their lives. In several instances, such a suffocating relationship led to respiratory problems, including frequent colds, allergies, bronchitis and asthma. However, when the affected individuals properly asserted their will and made healthy choices for themselves and others, their respiratory difficulties disappeared.

As adults, our power of will has a particularly strong influence on children. In asthma, the bronchioles in the lungs narrow or shut down completely, making it hard or impossible to breathe. In one classic study, researchers found that a group of asthmatic children saw their parents as being domineering, as harshly imposing their will upon them. And if the children did not meet up to their parents' will for them, then the parents were rejecting and cold. We might say there was too much will and the wrong kind of will, and not enough wisdom and love. The researchers noted this and decided to send the parents on a paid vacation. Guess what happened to the children? Half of them improved dramatically without any other treatment!

In another compelling study, twenty asthmatic children had a medically documented allergy to the dust in their homes, which set off asthmatic attacks. However, when the children were taken out of their homes, placed in a hospital room, and then the same dust from their homes was secretly added to their hospital room, only one of the twenty children developed asthmatic symptoms. Here, again, the psychological influence of the parents obviously played a key role in their children's health.

Of course, in asthma as with all respiratory diseases, numerous physical factors may be the primary or a contributing cause of the illness. Moreover, if symptoms persist or are serious, professional health care and treatment are essential. Underlying the illness, however, may well be a difficulty with the power of will, because the faculty of will expresses by way of the respiratory system. Difficulty in making good, healthy, life-affirming choices may precipitate any number of respiratory disorders: frequent colds; allergic rhinitis (hay fever); repeated bouts of sinusitis (inflammation of the sinuses); bronchitis (inflammation of the bronchi); asthma; pneumonia (inflammation of the lungs); tuberculosis; and pleurisy (inflammation of the pleura or lining around the lungs).

To one degree or another, our free-will choices directly influence the health of our respiratory system. So, let's make good choices, healthy choices, loving choices, wise choices. We always want to remember and reaffirm that God's will for us is good. It is good will, not ill will. And when we breathe in, let's breathe this good will right into our lungs. Then our entire respiratory system will be healed.

TURN TO SPIRIT WITHIN

When Georgette first learned about spiritual principles and her Twelve Powers, she eagerly applied these teachings to her business. Seeing herself as a CEO with the power to do great things and to live life abundantly, she rapidly expanded her employment agency. Riding the wave of her initial success, she added two more business ventures to her already full schedule. Lacking the necessary discipline and not taking the time to listen carefully to the will of the still small voice within her, she overextended herself to the point that all of her business ventures came to a crashing halt. At this time, depressed and feeling defeated, she developed bronchitis that worsened and became pneumonia, whereupon she was hospitalized.

During her ensuing treatment and recovery over several weeks, Georgette reflected on her past choices, her tendency to be impulsive, and her willfulness in pushing ahead when caution would have been a better choice. Deeply disappointed at first about her apparent failure, she gradually came to see the whole episode as a wonderful learning opportunity. She turned inward, surrendered her will to Spirit, and asked for new direction in her life. Cleansed and renewed, weeks later she met her spiritual partner with whom she eventually founded a spiritual-educational organization. All of her will power now was redirected into her new business—the "business" of helping others to grow spiritually.

How about you? Have you gone through a similar healing crisis, a redirecting of your life, a turning within to discover God's will for you? Did you come to see that your seeming failure was actually a stepping stone, which helped you to realign your personal will with the will of Spirit within you?

With some individuals, this healing crisis becomes a life and death struggle. This was the case with Ken Williamson. He was born addicted to heroin because his mother was a heroin addict. From the age of thirteen, he smoked cigarettes. Despite his unstable family background, he did well in high school, going on to college and becoming a social worker. However, he experimented with and became addicted to numerous illicit drugs. Raging within him was the battle between that part of him that was healthy, positive, productive, loving and service-oriented, and the part of him that maintained self-destructive desires and actions, his feelings of

Ken Williamson

worthlessness, and the deep pain of his childhood that he tried to dull with drugs. What would he choose? Would his will to live and to care for himself and others be stronger than his will to destroy himself?

In his late thirties, no longer able to manage his drug habit, he "hit bottom" and entered a drug treatment program. Here he learned about the twelve steps of

Alcoholics Anonymous, and about how to turn his own will and power over to a Higher Power. Slowly, in individual and group counseling, and in AA meetings, he came to see how and why he had been committing a slow form of suicide through his use of drugs, alcohol and tobacco. He stopped using drugs and gave up smoking a year later.

Meanwhile, he got married again, and one year later his son was born. He began going to a metaphysically-based church where he learned about and began to apply his Twelve Powers. Previously, he had been suspicious of anything religious or spiritual, and he had perceived himself as being separate from any alleged Higher Power. Now, through AA, the church and his study of the world's religions, he came to see himself as a child of God, who desired only good for him. He continued to transform his life by breathing the divine will into his consciousness. However, his greatest challenge was yet to come.

Three years later, he was diagnosed with lung cancer, an adenocarcinoma that was located primarily in the upper lobe of his right lung and had spread to the adjacent lymph nodes. Immediately, he sought out a cancer specialist who would provide the best possible medical care, but who also would support his other healing efforts through prayer, visualization, hands-on healing, nutritional supplementation, herbal remedies—whatever would enhance his immune system. The oncologist said that Ken had about a twenty-percent chance of living five years.

From the start, Ken held strong to his conviction that God's will for him was harmony and healing. He thought of himself as being filled with light and vital healing energy. He visualized his T cells destroying and removing the cancer cells in his body. Not that he didn't have his doubts and dark moments of despair. He questioned why this had happened now after he had finally gotten his life in good order. He wondered if the cancer simply was the result of decades of smoking and other self-abuse through drugs and alcohol. He received no answer other than he was to marshal all of his energy for the healing process.

A surgeon removed the cancerous portion of his lung. Then Ken underwent two series of chemotherapy, after which no cancer was detectable. Six months later, however, the cancer had returned and spread to additional parts of his body. Conventional chemotherapy was no longer an option, so Ken entered an experimental, radical program in which large doses of chemotherapy were used to destroy the cancer cells, but which also destroyed his body's bone marrow and immune system. Therefore, after the chemotherapy, he received a blood transfusion of blood cells from his own bone marrow, which had been extracted and frozen prior to his chemotherapy. From these cells, his immune system grew anew.

In the midst of this harrowing experience, Ken prayed fervently to God. Before he had tried to outline how and when his healing would take place—he dearly wished to remain on Earth and to be with his physical family. Now he came to a deeper realization that he might die physically and that his healing might continue after his transition. His death would not be a "failure." Rather, he envisioned an ongoingness and believed he could continue his work beyond this present lifetime. His prayer became, "Not my will, oh Lord, but Thy will be done as to the way and time in which You bring about my healing."

Meanwhile, he kept up his spirits—his will to live—by reading inspirational literature, surrounding himself with positive and loving people, finding joy and humor in the "small" things in his life, sharing openly and lovingly with

family and friends and especially with his wife, who was his
greatest supporter. He enlisted the prayer support of
numerous prayer groups of different religious denomina-
tions. He exercised daily, when possible.

Having asked that God's will be done, Ken now felt the
inspiration to become a minister. To others, this may have
seemed like a foolish thought, a form of denial. But to Ken,
this simply was the right thing to do. He was not doing this
to gain favor with God, to bargain for his healing. Rather, he
simply knew from within that this was his calling, that this
was Spirit's will for him in his healing journey, and that he
was going to live. In yet another life-affirming decision, he
and his wife went ahead with plans to adopt a child.

Ken's guidance turned out to be accurate. Following his
radical chemotherapy and recovery, Ken's cancer has not
recurred for eleven years (at the time of the publication of
this book). Moreover, he has become a dynamic, loving minister and parent. Repeatedly, he has shared his extraordinary
story of healing with others who have so-called incurable illnesses, inspiring them to turn within and to express their
Twelve Powers, in conjunction with utilizing the best of all
available treatments. He speaks with authority, for in the
depths of his soul, he has breathed in and demonstrated the
will of God in his thoughts, feelings and actions.

Repeatedly in his life, and especially in dealing with his
cancer, Ken faced the choice of giving up, giving in to doubts
and fears, giving himself over to his own self-destructive
urges and desires; or of choosing to see himself as being
healthy, holy, worthy and wise, lovable, capable of being
healed and made whole. He developed a remarkably strong
will when he came face to face with the specter of death.
Time and again, he chose life and acted on that choice by
employing every effective healing technique. Perhaps the
most powerful thing he did at each step of the way was to

align his personal will with the will of the Creator. Following that higher will, breathing in that Life Force, he passed through the crucifixion of his cancer and resurrected into a whole new life.

Isn't it interesting that right in his name, *Will*iamson, was the keynote of "will" for his lifelong journey and transformation?

Not my will, but Thy will be done!

Relax and let your mind come to a state of peace and rest. Then imagine yourself being outdoors, perhaps in your favorite place in nature: in a garden, at the beach, in the mountains. In your mind's eye, or with your actual physical eyes if you are outside, look up to the expansive blue sky above you. The air is all around you, everywhere present. The air is free, just as God's will is free.

Take a few deep breaths. Breathe the sky-blue air right into the depths of your lungs. When you breathe out, let go of any tension, upset, fear or concern. As you breathe rhythmically, slowly and deeply, you are energized, vitalized and filled with the life-giving power of oxygen or prana, the divine breath of life.

The vast sky above you represents heaven, the higher consciousness, the will of God. As you breathe in physically, imagine that you are breathing in the will of Spirit. In other words, think of the divine will being implanted into your lungs and being radiated to the rest of your body. Remember and affirm that the will of our Creator is good will: harmony, balance, abundance, peace and love for all of its creations. Breathe this will into your mind and body.

If you are having some difficulty with any part of your respiratory system, visualize the sky-blue light entering into and transforming and healing your nose, sinuses, windpipe, bronchi, bronchioles and lungs.

Filled with the divine presence, call upon the Spirit within you to reveal its will to you. Affirm: Not my will but Thy will be done. Wait patiently, silently, expectantly as the Creator breathes its will into you. Know that having asked, you will receive, whether in this meditation, in a dream or in some totally unexpected way.

Then, as you are guided from within, come out of your meditation knowing that God's will is being done in your life.

1. I am willing.
2. I will to be well, strong and whole.
3. God's will for me is good and only good.
4. I place myself and all my affairs lovingly in the hands of God.
5. My will to live is strong. I see much in life worth living for.
6. I am free from discouragement and weariness. I desire to open the door to new energy and accomplishment now.
7. I am willing to see good come to everybody.
8. I am willing to hear other people's point of view.
9. I am determined to make this a great day in my life.
10. I am the Chief Executive Officer of my life.
11. I make good executive decisions in directing my life.
12. I will live my life in accord with God's Good.
13. I choose to be optimistic, pleasant and open-minded in the midst of trying circumstances.
14. I do not attribute troubles or problems to "God's will." I see every challenge as an opportunity to learn and grow.
15. I realize I am blessed with free will. I am free to make mistakes, improve and make my life whatever I will.
16. I take the responsibility to make my own free-will decisions.

17. I encourage others to make their own choices. I do not try to force my will upon them.

18. Thy will be done on Earth as it is in heaven.

19. I am willing to move past rejection and hurt to love again.

20. It is God's good pleasure to give me the kingdom of All-Good.

21. I do not waste my time begging God for what has already been willed to me. I accept my divine inheritance.

22. I am a willing giver and a willing receiver.

23. I yield to a higher calling.

24. I make the choice today to reach out and to share my love.

25. I visualize a smoke-free world.

26. With each breath, I breathe the Creator's will into my life.

27. My nose, sinuses and bronchioles are vibrantly healthy.

28. I surrender my will to a Higher Power that directs my life.

29. The will of God, the breath of life, fills and heals my lungs.

30. I choose only that which is for my highest good and the highest good of all.

31. I am inspired now to do the will of Spirit within me.

9
The Power of ORDER

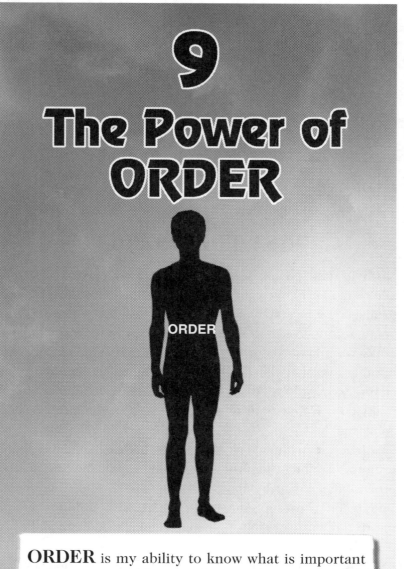

ORDER

ORDER is my ability to know what is important and to put my life in order. I begin to put "first things first." I seek first the kingdom of heaven (spiritual consciousness and values) and then I add all things unto this. I put God first. Order helps me to establish and maintain worthy personal and social priorities. Order externalizes as my digestive system, skin and bones.

Spirit

FIRST THINGS FIRST

David. Our power of order is mainly concerned with our ability to clarify our values, to set priorities for our lives, and to discern what is really important. How do we order and organize our lives? How do we decide what is most important? We make executive decisions in managing and directing our lives (as the CEO of our lives, as we looked at in chapter 8). We put "first things first" as we center on spiritual values rather than on material things, trivialities or ego concerns.

A teacher in New York decided to honor her high school seniors by telling them the difference they made. She used a process developed by Helice Bridges of Del Mar, California. The teacher presented each student with a blue ribbon imprinted with gold letters, which read, "Who I Am Makes A Difference."

From there the ribbons went forth to many others as the students circulated them. One of the young men presented a ribbon to a junior executive, who had helped him with career planning. The junior executive decided to give a blue ribbon to his boss, who was kind of a grouchy fellow. He presented his surprised boss with the ribbon and put it on him, praising him for his astute qualities.

This made him feel important, that he mattered and that people cared about him. He was given an extra blue ribbon with the request that he pass it along to someone else, who would also be affirmed by receiving it from him. So, he decided to give this ribbon to his teenage son, who he had not been paying much attention to and who had become increasingly distant.

When he went home, he knocked on his son's bedroom door. His son yelled through the door, "Yeah," and wondered what his dad wanted. The father came in and said, "Son, I've been busy and occupied with my work and other things. I know I yell at you about your grades or messy room. I haven't given you the love I feel 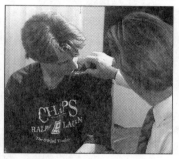 for you, and I want you to know you mean a lot to me. I want you to have this ribbon because you really do make a difference in my life. You're a great kid and I love you."

The startled boy began to sob and couldn't stop. His whole body shook. He looked at his father and said through his tears, "I was planning on committing suicide tomorrow, Dad, because I didn't think you loved me. Now I don't need to."

(If you want to order some of these blue ribbons, see Resources on page 329.)

We need to check our values to make sure we are placing people first in our spending of time and money. We say we love each other but we yell at our loved ones over a light that's left on, a broken dish, or a scratch or dent in the car. Companies put people out of work to make their bottom line look better to stockholders. These are "order" concerns and issues. We need to "put our own house in order." That is, to establish a divine order of what and who is really important.

I had a man say to me about another man that we both knew, "He takes better care of his lawn than he does his marriage." He spent long hours weeding, trimming, planting, watering, fertilizing and watching his lawn. He lavished a great deal of time and money. He was proud of his lovely green lawn, but his marriage could have used some of that energy, devotion and care to help it grow and flourish.

Every day, we say "yes" and "no" to many things. On what basis or ordering do we make these decisions? How do we decide what is important? What do we put first, second, third? How do we decide how we are going to spend our time and money? Do we engage in "impulse buying" or tell ourselves that we love plants and then not water them? Do we make a conscious prioritizing and then follow those values? Are spiritual values and people central in the ordering of our days? How do we decide who and what comes first for us and then make that a daily basis for ordering our life commitments?

Let's compare these decisions to a gallon jar. I put a few large rocks carefully into the jar. Then I ask, "Is this jar full?"

People may reply, "Yes, it's full."

Then, I take some gravel and dump it into the jar, shaking the jar so that the gravel goes down into the spaces between the big rocks. Then I ask once more, "Is the jar full?"

Now you are catching on, so you say, "Probably not."

"Good," I comment, and I get a can of sand and pour it into the spaces left between the rocks and the gravel. Once more I ask the question, "Is this jar full?"

"No!" you exclaim.

"Good," I congratulate you, as I take a pitcher of water and pour it in until the jar is filled to the brim.

What is the point of this object lesson? One overachiever thinks he gets it. He says, "No matter how full your schedule is, if you try really hard, you can always fit more things into it." But, is that the point?

This illustration teaches us that if we do not put the big rocks in first, we'll never get them in at all!

What are the "big rocks" in your life? Quality time with your loved ones? Learning and growing? Time for meditation and physical exercise? Helping others grow and succeed? Serving a cause beyond yourself?

Remember, these are the "big rocks," and if you don't put them in first you will never get them in at all. So today, tonight, reflect on this parable of the jar and how it gets filled by you. Ask yourself, "Who and what are really most important to me?" Put those first in the way you live your days and nights.

First things first. Spiritual values matter. People matter. Helping each other matters. Having arts and music in our schools matters, as well as sports and field houses and playing games. Individuals and families matter. Workers and colleagues matter. Supporting a spiritual work and spiritual leaders matters. The environment and caring for the Earth matters. Taking care of our health and well-being matters.

Clarify your values and put first things first!

THE GOSPEL OF CONTINUOUS IMPROVEMENT

People in organizations or institutions who are original thinkers, whistle-blowers or who question the status quo have often been considered troublemakers. But today, innovators commonly are rewarded and honored. To be a trailblazer is now valued; to be an agent for change is considered an asset. Many corporations have established incentive programs for creative entrepreneurs and seek to keep them with the company. We all don't have to fit a traditional role.

Families, organizations, companies, governments and religious communities find themselves needing to go beyond pouring "new wine into old wine skins." The old paradigms are breaking up and are no longer adequate. Men, women and young people of vision will lead us forward in the new millennium.

Jesus' concept of order was considered disorderly by the Pharisees and Sadduccees of his day. They were the religious and legal establishments of that time and place. What was important to them was trivial to Jesus. And what was important to Jesus was considered irreverent and blasphemous to the authorities. Jesus was a free thinker, reformer, innovator, originator, prophet and nonconformist. He was branded a blasphemer and a renegade from traditionalism. And yet he made it crystal clear that he had come to fulfill the law, not to defy it or the orderly teachings of earlier prophets. However, he said, let's get clear about what the higher law is: It is love. This is the fulfillment of the law.

SPIRIT HAS A PLAN

There is a little song I used to sing in Sunday school to the tune of "Farmer in the Dell"—it was called "Spirit Has a Plan":

Spirit has a plan,
Spirit has a plan,
Spirit has a perfect plan,
Spirit has a plan.

Some people believe that God plans our whole life and we follow a preset order of events or blueprint. That's called pre-destination. Whole religions believe that "it is written" and "kismet" rules. The more all-powerful God is conceived to be, the more the tendency toward this autocratic view of predestination.

I believe in a kind of predestination. I feel God's "plan" for us is unlimited growth and good. We are to manifest or demonstrate this divine destiny, but we can ignore it, post-pone it, take our time about it, or get on with it in great ways every day. The plan is for us to express our divine potential for a full life in all ways. That's our destiny or evolutionary goal. These are the marching orders that we receive from our Father-Mother Creator.

We are free, and yet there is an evolutionary urge in us that calls us to keep moving forward individually and as a species to a spiritual fulfillment of shared abundance, health and peace.

William Shakespeare wrote, "There's a divinity that shapes our ends, rough-hew them how we will." (*Hamlet, Act 5, Scene 2*)

It's somewhat like being dealt a hand of cards that we may play any way we choose. We can hold them, fold them, dis-card or share them, maybe pick up other cards, play them out any way we decide. We hope for and expect a divine des-tiny of abundant life and growth, and we play it out day by day according to our understanding and our will to express this destiny.

When I spoke one time with a friend, Jon Wesley, about

our life being like a game of cards, he wisely commented: "Will moves us off the fence of indecisiveness. Jesus told us that if we are not with him it is better to be against him, rather than neither. That says to me it's better to make a wrong decision and learn from it, than to make no decision and flounder about, going nowhere. If my life is like a game of cards, it's up to me how I play them. I can make sound, wise decisions and gain cards or I can make poor decisions and lose cards but learn how to play my next hand better. If I fold, I have gained neither cards nor lessons."

Here are the orders for today:

- Start what you need to start.
- Work on what you need to work on.
- Finish what you need to finish.
- Make sure that what you do is worthwhile and valid, that it serves a good purpose.

WHAT WILL I BE REMEMBERED FOR?

Have you ever heard the story behind the Nobel prizes, those prestigious awards for excellence in the arts and sciences? Alfred Nobel, a Swedish chemical genius, became incredibly wealthy by inventing dynamite and blasting gelatin. He originally had hoped the high explosives he created would serve peaceful purposes, but the military of many countries quickly adapted them for devastation of their enemies. Nobel licensed his formulas to governments, who made their weapons of mass destruction.

One day, Nobel's brother, Ludwig, died and a French journalist mistook Ludwig's death for Alfred's. The obituary called Alfred Nobel "the merchant of death." When Alfred read the obituary about his life in the newspaper, he received a psychic wound so deep that he never recovered from it. He was pictured as the man who made a fortune by enabling armies to achieve new levels of mass destruction. Having been faced with this negative appraisal of what his life amounted to and what he would be remembered for, he took his fortune and willed it to establish the prizes, which still bear his name.

He is thereby remembered for his legacy of honoring great achievements in various fields, which benefit humanity, and hardly anyone outside of chemistry class thinks of Nobel as connected to explosives. The unique opportunity he had to see his obituary and reassess his life caused him to give the last part of his life an entirely different direction, which has left an enduring impact on humanity.

LIVING IN COMMUNITY

Gay Lynn. There is an amazing order to all of life. Even the Hebrew Bible points to order in the most humble of creatures, the ant. "Look to the ant, O sluggard; consider her ways and be wise." (Proverbs 6:6) I grew up in Michigan. As a little girl I was fascinated with the ant mounds that were in the cracks of the sidewalk. Now living in South Florida, I have a much closer relationship with the ants because they keep appearing everywhere *inside* our house—in our bedroom and kitchen, on the walls, marching in a grand parade through the windows and along every crack possible.

Ants have an amazing order! Did you know that ants have changed very little in over 60 million years? The same kinds of ants that roam the world today inhabited the world of *Tyrannosaurus rex*. Ant fossils have been found more than any other insect. Ants have thrived successfully for a very long time. No wonder the Bible says, "Look to the ant!"

Ants are social creatures just like wolves, gorillas and, of course, humans. "Social" means that they work together and help everyone in the colony. Every ant has a job: farmers, engineers, construction workers, soldiers and babysitters. There are no unemployment lines in an ant colony. So you see in the tiniest creatures there is interrelatedness, interdependency, with all ants working together in an orderly way that brings harmony to the whole group.

If in looking at the most miniscule, almost insignificant creature we see simple orderly systems operating, how much more so must we as humans, co-creators with the Divine, function in an orderly way?

To me, order is active; it is "yang" energy in Chinese terminology. And sometimes we all can be lazy. The Hebrew scriptures called it like it is: "O sluggard!" How do we get lazy? I believe it begins in our thinking and feeling. Sometimes we begin to feel separate and apart, isolated and lonely, thinking that we don't belong or have a part to play. Pretty soon we begin to act as if this is true, not being a part of community activities, growing apart from friends and other people. Remember, order is part of a group consciousness— we experience it more fully as we are engaged in life and are taking part in community activities.

By being with the community we are saying, "I am here, I am willing to show up!" Fifty percent of success in life with anything is just showing up. And then when we show up we are a part of the whole, part of the wholeness of life. We are growing in ways of valuing ourselves and knowing our value as being part of the community of life! There is a powerful vortex of energy when we are energetically a part of one another's lives. This can be communicated through touch, words, songs, movements, and being in service to one another and the planet.

Albert Einstein once said, "The belief we exist separate from each other is an optical illusion." We only look like we are separate, but in reality we are all one. We all exist in relationship to one another. Perhaps that is partly why Jesus said, "Where two or more are gathered, there I am in the midst of them." There is a cosmic order where I exist through you, and we all exist through each other, infinitely related and together.

When I get lazy I forget my connection. I forget to value myself and others. I forget to come together to experience the bonds and benefits of being in community. Like the ant, I know I cannot do it all by myself. Rather, we thrive in community, we do much better in being an integral part of the whole.

Value the part that you play in your colony/community. You are important. You can get things done, find solutions, meet the challenges of the world. You are here to own your power and use it in an orderly way.

ORDER AND PROTECTION

Sometimes, I am home alone at night and I hear every little bump and creak around the house. I can let my imagination run wild and scare myself. "Personal protection" is one of the top concerns the majority of people have reported.

Pat Reese, a dear friend of ours in Detroit, was a single mom raising three girls in the middle of the city noted for its crime. One night she heard someone in the yard obviously trying to steal the lawn mower from the back of the house. She immediately turned on all the lights outside and around the house, and scared the person away.

Although she had averted the robbery, her anxiety about being home alone with the girls heightened dramatically. Friends in the neighborhood gave various suggestions of support: Get a gun, a big dog, a house alarm system and so forth.

Pat is a very creative and deeply spiritual person. It came to her to create a stained-glass window sticker with a simple message: THIS HOUSE IS PROTECTED BY GOD. She placed it by the front door and around the back door. Each day as she walked into her house, she would affirm in her mind the statement on the window sticker. This initiated a shift in the way Pat began to feel, as she put the thought of God's protection first and foremost in her mind. The ordering of Pat's

Window decal

thoughts in this way brought her calmness and confidence, which radiated throughout the home to her children. Her neighbors came by, loved the window sticker and asked Pat to share the message of protection with them. She ended up manufacturing these attractive decals and calling them the "Home Blessing." (See Resources, page 329).

Pat never had another attempted robbery, and she uplifted her whole neighborhood by having stickers on all the homes. Each created a divine sense of protection by ordering their thoughts to think of the loving presence of Spirit watching over them. They each created a new order by putting their focus on faith rather than fear. The decals have now gone out to thousands of homes far and wide.

How can I reorder my thoughts so that I feel safer? What do I give priority to first: my fears or my faith in a Higher (Protecting) Power?

Each of us has the choice and the power to change one thought at a time. I can create a new life, a new sense of protection and divine order. Once I have put "first things first," then I can add other methods as may be wise to my whole protection program, such as using locks and other security devices, being part of a neighborhood watch team and working cooperatively with the local police.

It has been shown in studies of transcendental meditation (TM) that when numerous people who live in an area meditate on a regular basis, there is less crime in that area. Thus,

a group of people steadily meditating on peace and protection can have a dynamic effect on what actually takes place
in their neighborhood. We can also extend this prayer and
meditation out to surround our entire planet in peace and
order.

One of my favorite protection prayers, which we have said
for years in our home with our children and in our spiritual
family, is called The Prayer of Protection. It was written by
James Dillet Freeman.

> *The light of God surrounds us.*
> *The love of God enfolds us.*
> *The power of God protects us.*
> *And the presence of God watches over us.*
> *Wherever we are, God is!*

Share this prayer with those you love and care about.
Each of us can participate in creating a more peaceful world.
It begins with one orderly, peaceful thought at a time!

Body

DIGESTIVE SYSTEM

Dr. Robert. What is your favorite meal? Take a moment now to visualize yourself eating a feast of your favorite foods. It probably makes your mouth water just thinking about it!

From the time you start chewing the food, you are engaged in an orderly, systematic, step-by-step digestive process that brings water, vitamins, minerals and nutrients to every cell in your body. The body uses all of these vital substances to build, maintain and repair its cells and organs in an orderly fashion, to form and re-form all the structures of the body. Therefore, the power of order-organization-system externalizes by way of the digestive system.

First things first: In your diet this means first choosing healthy and vital foods, lots of fruits and vegetables and whole grains, low-fat foods, foods that are free of toxic chemicals, not eating devitalized "junk food." It also means picking the foods and following the diet that is right for you. Beware of rigid dietary systems that say everyone should eat only certain foods in particular combinations or at specific times of the day. These may seem like orderly guidelines, and they do help some people. However, they do not take into account that everyone is different and has unique nutritional needs. Find out what works best for you!

Chewing the food in your mouth breaks it down into smaller particles. Your saliva contains enzymes that initiate the digestion of starches. Then you swallow and the food passes down your esophagus into your stomach, where hydrochloric acid and pepsin are released to start the digestion of proteins. When the food moves out of the stomach into the duodenum, which is the first part of the small intestine, digestive enzymes from the pancreas and bile from the gallbladder pour into the duodenum. The enzymes continue

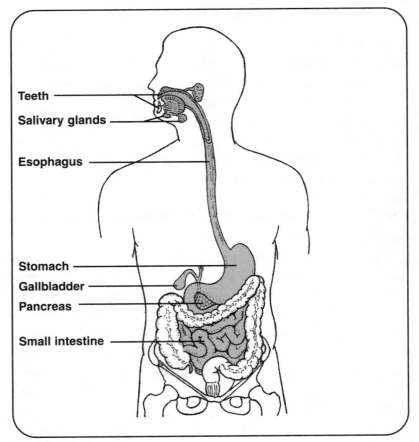

Figure 9. Digestive system

the breakdown of proteins, carbohydrates and fats, whereas the bile is needed for the assimilation of fats. The walls of the entire small intestine—the duodenum, jejunum and ileum, which together are about twenty feet long—have additional enzymes that complete the breakdown of the various nutrients. Then they are absorbed through the walls of the small intestine into the blood, which carries them throughout the body. (See Figure 9.)

What happens when you think, feel or do something that disturbs this orderly, systematic digestive process? In a hurry, upset about something, eating to "fill" your emotional needs, you may bolt down your food or stuff yourself. In response, you may develop indigestion or "heartburn," which is caused by the reflux of acidic stomach contents into the esophagus. Maybe you have taken in too much information or had several trying emotional experiences without "processing" or "digesting" them. Afterwards, you may feel nauseous or vomit.

How about when you cannot "stomach" something in your life or when something "eats away" at you inside? Then you may develop gastritis (inflammation of the stomach) or an ulcer of the stomach or duodenum. Infection with a bacterium called *Helicobacter pylori* is now known to be a principal physical cause of many ulcers. However, problems with order may be the underlying cause that sets the stage for the growth of this bacterium.

Have you ever felt like you were all "tied up in knots" inside? When you have been fearful or have "swallowed" or suppressed your anger, have you felt tightness or a burning sensation in the "pit of your stomach"? The result may be gastroenteritis (inflammation of your digestive tract) or problems with your pancreas. Difficulties with the power of order also may cause or contribute to gallbladder disease, eating disorders such as anorexia nervosa and bulimia, and obesity.

Since we are part of a greater whole and interconnected with all life, we also may sense the disturbance, dysfunction or disorder of those around us. Have you ever walked into a room of strangers and felt that something was amiss or just not right? Where did you feel this disturbance in your body? Probably in the abdominal, solar-plexus region, which is the center for order. Some individuals note solar-plexus disturbance before or at the time of natural disasters like earthquakes, volcanic eruptions, tornadoes or floods. In response, they may even experience nausea, vomiting, loss of appetite or other digestive disturbances.

If you have digestive difficulties, regardless of the cause, focus first on your power of order-organization-system. Affirm: All is well; all is in divine order; all is in right balance and harmony in my life, in the lives of others and in my body. Then consider any psychological or physical causes for your digestive disease and correct these. As part of your treatment, you may want to visit a nutritional physician or counselor who can help you with your diet and with taking the right nutritional supplements. When you have firmly established new order in your life, your digestive system will manifest this harmonious order in your body.

SKELETAL SYSTEM

Order and organization also externalize in our body as our skeletal system, which includes the bones, ligaments that hold bones together at joints, and cartilage. Our two hundred and six bones form the solid, organized framework for our whole body. Just think, if our body had no skeleton, it would become a shapeless mass, incapable of moving, and unable to protect its delicate internal structures like the brain, spinal cord, lungs and heart. Moreover, it would have no red blood cells because these are formed in the marrow of some bones. Bones appear solid and unchanging, but actually they are constantly and slowly being remodeled. In like manner, our core beliefs form the solid framework or order of our consciousness. However, we need to continually refine our core ways of thinking, feeling and acting. On the one hand, order and organization require structure, rules, systems, tried-and-true methods for getting things accomplished. On the other hand, to be orderly requires us to be fluid, to give and take, to change, adapt, refine and grow.

People can become set in their ways, rigid, dogmatic, crystallized, clinging to the status quo. This may lead to problems with bones, ligaments or joints, including bone infections and bone tumors. Other individuals are disorganized, lack structure, have too many things going at the same time, or do not take the time to sort out their thoughts and feelings. Sometimes, this will cause people to be "accident-prone." Their many bumps, bruises, mishaps, falls or even broken bones are manifestations of their internal disorder.

A dear friend and successful corporate consultant who leads training seminars on cultural diversity all over the world had an unusual accident. Returning from a trip, walking on the sidewalk to the front door of her own house, she rolled her ankle and fell, tearing some ligaments and breaking a bone in her foot.

Over the next few days, her lower leg in a cast, walking around on crutches, she pondered the reason for her mishap. The realization came that she had been rushing around from project to project with such intensity that she never took the time to relax, to assimilate all that was happening in her life, or to spend sufficient time with family and friends. Looking back at her fall, she remembered that she had been so charged up, so preoccupied with thoughts of her last trip and her next trip that it was like she was not really in her body.

Now, as she recuperated, she had no choice but to slow down. For months she had to walk more carefully and deliberately. Even after the cast came off, she received regular therapy for her torn ligaments. During this time, she restructured her life, giving herself more time for meditation, quiet reflection, unhurried talks with her loved ones, walks on the beach and just goofing off. As she did this, she became more centered and balanced, more in tune with what was essential and most important in her life. She stopped rushing, pushing and forcing. And yet, she still accomplished as much or more as she had previously, because she had developed a whole new level of order and organization in her life.

When was the last time that you had an "accident" or hurt yourself or made some mistake? What was out of order in your thoughts or feeling or memories or physical activities that caused this to happen? What did you do to reestablish harmony and order in your life?

SKIN

Here's another way to see if your attitudes and emotions are balanced, harmonious and in good order: Examine your skin. Perhaps no other organ so clearly reflects and reveals your state of mind and your true feelings. For example, what happens when you are frightened? Your skin may blanch and become white. How about when you are embarrassed? Your face gets flushed. How about when you are furious inside but try not to show it? Your skin may get red or inflamed.

The skin is the body's largest organ. It serves as an outer shield or boundary, which protects and holds the internal organs in their right place. It holds blood and other fluids in the body, except during sweating which helps to regulate the body's temperature and removes a small amount of toxins. The skin also provides the body with its outer appearance, shape and form. In all these ways, the skin expresses the power of order.

It is well known that a large percentage of skin diseases are caused or exacerbated by psychological imbalances. When people are angry, anxious, afraid or ashamed, this may cause or contribute to dermatitis (eczema), acne, psoriasis, hives, warts, boils, sebaceous cysts or cellulitis.

The skin also is particularly sensitive to toxic chemicals and other irritants. So, with a skin disorder, always consider these and other physical causes. For treatment, use any effective ointment, medication or nutritional supplement. At the same time, always focus on your power of order to revitalize your skin.

Begin to picture in your mind that you are about to eat "manna from heaven." You may want to see this as a very special loaf of bread, which is imbued with higher energy and all the spiritual nutrients you need to solidly build the light of Spirit into your mind, emotions and body.

Hold out your hand and visualize the manna or bread in it. Then place the light-filled bread in your mouth. Chew it and sense its flavor. Swallow the bread and visualize it moving down your esophagus into your stomach. Feel it being digested and assimilated into your system, just as your pancreas, gallbladder and small intestine work together to absorb physical food. As you assimilate the manna, affirm: I am receiving and absorbing all that I need to bring about divine order in my life.

Next, visualize the light-filled nutrients traveling from your solar plexus and small intestine to all of your bones. Feel the higher energy being absorbed and anchored into your whole skeleton. Direct the light particularly to any bone or joint that needs healing. Affirm: I feel divine order in my bones; divine order flows throughout my consciousness and throughout my body.

Then, visualize the nutrients of light and energy flowing from your solar-plexus center to all of your skin. See your whole body radiating with light that shines in and through your skin. Focus for a few moments on any part of your skin that needs reinforcement, revitalization, regeneration and reinvigoration. Think about divine order being reestablished in that section of your skin.

Now consider any part of your life where you may need more order and organization. Affirm: I see and bring forth divine order in my relationships; I invoke divine order in my work; all is in right order in my home; harmony and balance and order now reign in my community and all throughout the world. Then, in due time, come out of your meditation, knowing that all is well.

1. My life is filled with divine order.
2. I do not believe in or trust to luck, chance or fate. I know what is important and I put that first.
3. Trust is important to me. I will not deceive myself or others.
4. Being faith-filled is an order in my life choices.
5. Being loving is an order in my life choices.
6. Being strong and steady is an order in my life choices.
7. Being wise is an order in my life choices.
8. Being powerful is an order in my life choices.
9. Being imaginative is an order in my life choices.
10. Being understanding is an order in my life choices.
11. Being of good will is an order in my life choices.
12. Releasing is an order in my life choices.
13. Affirming life and renewal is an order in my life choices.
14. Some say, "Don't sweat the small stuff," but I know a great life is composed of small acts of integrity and spiritual values.
15. I see through the "bigger is better" hype to know that simple, small and significant can be beautiful.
16. Money is not the bottom line. An Earth fit to live on is the ultimate bottom line.
17. I am orderly, but not fussy.
18. I value and learn from the past, but I do not need to keep everything just as it used to be.

19. The divine plan for me is to live fully, meaningfully and productively.
20. I bless my digestive system with divine order and harmony.
21. My physical structure is sound and strong.
22. My life has structure and purpose.
23. My skin reflects a calm and peaceful mind and heart.
24. I accept the perfect plan of good in my life.
25. I observe the amazing order in all of life.
26. I recognize my infinite connection to all people and all life.
27. I am divinely protected and surrounded by peace.
28. I radiate orderly, peaceful thoughts throughout my home and neighborhood.
29. I digest my food and my life one bite at a time.
30. I am wise and use my prayers and common sense to keep me safe.
31. I recognize the signals my stomach gives me to create new order and balance in my life.
32. I create order in my life and it is reflected in my healthy skin.

10
The Power of ENTHUSIASM

ENTHUSIASM

ENTHUSIASM is the power that fires me with energy. It is my starting power and staying power. It is my urge to stretch, my drive to excel, my desire to improve and contribute. *En-theos* means "on fire with God" and "filled with God." Enthusiasm expresses physically through my hypothalamus and medulla oblongata at the base of my brain.

JOYFUL EXUBERANCE

David. Enthusiasm or zeal is that power in us that moves us forward, that fires us with energy. It is the fuel that is necessary in our growth and development. It is the urge to stretch, the drive to excel, the desire to improve and contribute. Remember, this is a power you already have. You have the power of enthusiasm now. You have all you will ever need or can use.

Maybe you feel bored, dull, burned out, exhausted, defeated, sad. We all have those feelings at times. If you seem to lack the power of enthusiasm in your life, return to the silence, that state of quiet and inner contact with your unlimited Source that supplies you—God within.

Some people try to pump up or drum up enthusiasm. They are told to shout in the mirror in the morning, "Wow, I am enthusiastic!" That may be one way to find enthusiasm. However, there is a deeper well of enthusiasm. Even the origin of the word itself indicates that this is a divine attribute that is closely connected to a cosmic energy that burns within us. Enthusiasm comes from the Greek *en* meaning "in" and *theos* meaning "God." It is being "on fire" or "possessed by God."

There is a framed piece of what looks like rough school construction paper in the library at Unity School. Charles Fillmore wrote on it back in 1948 with what seems to be a crayon:

*I fairly sizzle with zeal and enthusiasm and
spring forth with a mighty faith to do the
things that ought to be done by me.*

He was ninety-four years old when he wrote that on a
scrap of paper. It was a few months before he died, but he
was still enthusiastic. He was still in love with life and living.
He still wanted to accomplish and serve. He said that enthusiasm is "the impulse to go forward, the urge behind all
things." (*The Twelve Powers*, p. 130)

We need enthusiasm to accomplish anything. Rightly
understood and wisely channeled, our enthusiasm brings
zest for living, joy, exuberance, and the ability to convert
good desires into successful outcomes that make a positive
contribution to the world.

ORDERLY ENTHUSIASM

Our spiritual faculty of order is the partner of enthusiasm.
Together they form a complementary team. Our order faculty enables us to put "first things first" and set positive priorities in our lives. Remember, order is our ability to know
what is most important, to set priorities, to budget, to set

healthy boundaries, to organize, to make schedules and plans.

Some people get "fired up" with enthusiasm and ride off in all directions at once. Enthusiasm has to be channeled in an orderly way if we are to do our best work. It's like people who have great talent but can't "get their act together" and can't organize their lives enough to capitalize on their abilities. Their talent is not fully realized or expressed. All of us have known people with marvelous abilities, who are passionate about singing or computers or writing or landscaping, but they have never been able to organize their talents and efforts in a successful way.

Overzealous people tend to be overly active, overly involved in myriad projects, unable to set healthy boundaries to others' demands and needs, have too many irons in the fire, and drive themselves "full speed ahead." Overzealous people, who are not balanced by using their faculty of order, can crash, burn out, break down and lose people they care about. An old saying goes, "No one ever complained on their death bed that they wished they had spent more time at the office."

Our enthusiasm can get swept up and carried away in egotism, materialism and ambition, at the expense of our health, family and spiritual values. Being enthusiastic and enjoying what we have is probably even more important than the enthusiasm to get new things and attain bigger success. For the acquisitive person, more is never enough.

THANK GOD IT'S MONDAY!

Employers love to have enthusiastic workers. They value people who look forward to coming to work. They often reward initiative.

I once had a person working for me who complained whenever the phone rang, "Oh, another call. I have enough to do already. Who is it now?" When there was money to count, she complained, "There's more here than last week." When people came in to buy something, she grumbled, "Oh, another customer." I eventually had to replace her, because her negative attitude set up a resistance to the ability to serve and to the potential of the organization to grow.

Enthusiasm creates a positive consciousness of receptive and welcoming greater good. "Wow, another customer!" "Great, more money to count and take to the bank!" "We're doing so well, the phone just keeps on ringing!"

Some people burn out and some rust out. Both troubles are often found in long-term situations: A marriage of many years, a job we have been doing a long time, a routine such as always going to the same place at the same time of year on vacation. Enthusiasm, wisely channeled, can often prevent both conditions.

A classic movie with Robin Williams, *The Dead Poets Society,* has a scene where the teacher shows his students the glass showcases with pictures of students long past. Then he says, "Can you hear them calling to you? Live an extraordinary life!" He tells his students: *"Carpe diem!"* Seize the day! Live with zest and enthusiasm.

ENTHUSIASM OVERCOMES BOREDOM

I heard that someone conducted a survey which asked the question, "Which is worse, ignorance or apathy?" One person responded, "I don't know and I don't care!"

George Bernard Shaw wisely observed, "The opposite of

love is not hate, but indifference." Enthusiasm is our power to go forward, to accomplish great things, to be engaged in life, to be involved, to love, to care, to make a positive difference.

The lack of zeal or enthusiasm is experienced as apathy, boredom, expecting others to do our work for us, thinking things will change for the better without our help, looking to outer events to entertain us. Some people feel "bored" and are always looking for other people or outer stimulation to entertain them or make them perk up. Some people seem incapable of enthusiasm because they feel trapped in a dull routine, or see their lives as just busy with mundane responsibilities that "have to be done." They feel "stuck" and depressed. They may need counseling and medical help with their depression.

There are changes we can make in our attitudes and actions that bring forth a greater enthusiasm. The boredom is not necessarily in the job, marriage, school, town or church. We often say, "This is a boring job." The question then becomes, "Can I get unbored? Can I get more interested or interesting? Can I be more enthusiastic about this job? Are there ways I can engage myself to make this more stimulating, exciting and meaningful?"

Walter Toscanini, son of the famous symphony conductor Arturo, was asked what his illustrious father was most enthusiastic about, what was the most important thing in his life, what really turned him on the most. He replied, "The most important thing in Toscanini's life is the thing he happens to be doing at the time, whether it is directing a symphony or peeling an orange."

We can be enthusiastic about anything: playing with our children, having fun with our dog or cat, finding ways to improve our work, being in a successful recovery, doing well in school, exploring our town, changing our routine, finding ways to be more romantic in a long marriage, or being fascinated while peeling an orange. Henry David Thoreau, the American transcendentalist and naturalist, said, "I have traveled much in Concord." Well, Concord was a small village; there were hardly any places to go. But Thoreau could be enthusiastic about observing the slightest things, such as a colony of ants, a patch of flowers or a spider weaving a web.

Our enthusiasm for living engages us not in just the "big" things, but in the "little" everyday things, as well.

IDEALISM AND ENTHUSIASM

I once visited the grave of Dr. Martin Luther King Jr., which is beside Ebenezer Baptist Church in an area of Atlanta called Sweet Auburn. I felt like it was a pilgrimage to the shrine of a modern seer and prophet. It is in a national historical district. A small museum contains one of King's handwritten sermons beside his well-worn Bible in a glass case. The sermon is on the power of enthusiasm. I copied down the introduction.

> *No greater tragedy can befall a people than to be circumscribed to the dark chambers of pessimism. Pessimism is a chronic disease that dries up the red corpuscles of hope and slams down the powerful heartbeat of action.*

This from the man who said we could remember him as "a drum major for justice"! This minister-activist gave one of the most remembered and visionary addresses as he challenged America to *be* America because, "I have a dream." He was a person of enthusiasm, who was not deterred or overcome by all the insults, arrests, church bombings, police attack dogs and clubs. He refused to give into pessimism and give up. His assassination marked a terrible loss of leadership in the work for nonviolence, justice and peace. When we honor his day and his dream each year in January, let us remember his tireless optimism and enthusiasm.

"I have a dream." Dr. King was one man who maintained his enthusiasm for "liberty and justice for all."

Keep the dream alive.

Hold the vision of a world that works for all people, and act passionately on that vision.

Energetically stay committed and enthused and we will get to the mountaintop of peace and caring for all people and our whole planet.

Soul

ON FIRE WITH GOD

Gay Lynn. I am alive, I am alert and I am enthusiastic about life! How often do you feel this way? Occasionally? Seldom? Often?

Enthusiasm is truly the energy that propels you, urges you, entices you to take the next step forward in your life. Enthusiasm says "Yes" to life, "Yes" to your good, "Yes" to being in the flow of energy. Moment by moment you decide with your own thoughts whether you are saying "Yes" or shutting down the life flow.

What happens when I shut down the flow? My body tenses up. I hold back my feelings. I think of the worst and become pessimistic. I am afraid to try new things and become self-conscious. I hold myself back and maybe those around me. You and I have a choice to live in the flow or to shut ourselves down. One of my favorite affirmations is, "I am enthusiastic in all that I do because the energizing power of Spirit fills and thrills me now!"

Enthusiasm activates our other powers like faith, imagination and love. It is the power that says "Yes" to what has not been seen but we know can come forth or manifest. When we experience being stuck, congested, restricted, closed off or shut down, and don't feel energetic, we may need to do some letting go and releasing work to start the flow again. How do we do this?

We have the capacity to reprogram ourselves, to have mastery over our automatic subconscious reflexes. I have seen many examples of how yogis and other spiritual adepts such as fakirs have command over their bodies to perform in seeming impossible ways. Much has been documented on how they can stop breathing, arrest their heartbeat, live for a time without air, lie on nails and other jagged sharp objects, walk on fiery coals unharmed, or impale their skin and not bleed or be wounded.

Most of us would not want to attempt these things. However, the example is certainly there to show us that with desire and practice you and I can raise our body, mind and spirit to higher vibrational levels. There is a potential for mastery and reprogramming of our habitual subconscious reflexes.

Out of curiosity I decided to take a trip with my friend Toni Boehm who is a Unity minister. She had also been a nurse and had had a wonderful corporate career. We joined Edwine Gaines, also a Unity minister and a wonderful workshop facilitator, for an experience of "fire walking" and meditation in the depths of a cave, in total darkness. I am only going to touch on the "fire-walking" experience because it relates so directly to our enthusiasm. Fire is like our enthusiasm. It is our passion, our flame, and it is powerful. Enthusiasm literally means "on fire with God."

When we tap into our passion, it must be balanced with our other Powers like wisdom and good judgment, order, love, understanding and strength, or else we will get "burned" or we will "burn out." Balance and discernment are critical. We need to tune into our inner guidance and realize how we are to be enthused but not overzealous. At the "fire-walk" experience, the question I asked myself was, "Do I have the guidance to walk across the fire or not?" I was the only one who could answer this question. After all, it was my feet! I had to tune in for me and be all right with my inner guidance, really honor it and hear it clearly. "Yes," I walk across the fiery coals or "No," I don't walk, and either way is okay.

Sometimes the answer from our inner self may be, "No, don't do that." If you or I get this message it is okay to stand in that truth with strength and power, even though others around us might be doing what we would "like" to be doing. Some examples of "No" are:

- No, don't go out with that person.
- No, don't charge any more on the credit cards.
- No, don't eat that unhealthy junk food.
- No, don't marry that person.
- No, don't take that job.
- No, don't become obsessed with work.

In other words, don't be swept up in the passion, fire and enthusiasm of the moment and get burned! Don't get consumed with toxic relationships or unhealthy obsessions and burn up or burn out. Don't go foolishly where angels fear to tread. You have the power to say, "No."

Even when there are people around you who may be doing the things you "wish" you could do, it is important for spiritual and mental health and the well-being of your body to listen and honor the answer "No" when it comes to you. Sometimes, I have stubbornly done something anyway and really have gotten burned. This time, under a beautiful, star-filled night sky, I searched my heart and soul and wrote pages in my journal asking whether I should walk across these red-hot cinders. I had actually helped to start the fire hours before and had been watching it burn now for many hours. A whole range of red glowing embers stretched before me like a jeweled path of fire.

My question was about my own belief. Did I believe that I could walk across hot burning embers and not get burned? My answer was "Yes." The answer was clear and it was from the place inside me that I receive my best guidance. That vibration of "Yes" filled my body as I took long, deep, strong strides across the expanse of burning coals, eyes focused ahead, hearing in every cell of my being, "Yes," "Yes," "Yes" . . . until I had walked all the way across and did not get burned. I had taken conscious control of an ordinarily automatic response, "fire will burn you," and I had defied a well-accepted law of cause and effect that I had once believed was immutable.

JOY OF LIFE

There is a spark of aliveness that is kindled when we are enthusiastic about our relationships. Many years ago, David, my wonderful husband, was leaving on an extended trip. Before he departed, he put a number of little Post-it notes in secret places around the house, so that when I opened a closet or cupboard or drawer, I found a little love note. One of them said, "Remember 1,000 times a day that I love you!" That "sticky note" stayed up in my closet for eight years until we sold that house, and then I still saved that precious note!

Is there some small way you can express your enthusiasm for someone in your life today? David and I have continued for  many years to tuck little notes in cards, luggage, pillows, lunch bags, books and day planners. When you are enthusiastic about your family and friends, your relationships stay invigorated, energetically connected and wonderfully alive!

As children, we can all remember that special feeling when Mom or Dad or someone in our lives like a grandparent showed enthusiasm about something we did or accomplished. Perhaps it was a teacher who enthusiastically responded to our work or told us we were talented and asked us to display something we had created. Enthusiasm plays a vital role in the development of our confidence and our ability to enjoy our lives. As children, when we sang a song, read a poem, performed a dance or made a great science project, these moments of being applauded and receiving recognition from the special people in our lives gave us the courage and ability to take another step. Even when we were babies going from crawling to walking, someone stood us up, looked us in the eye, and said, "You can do this. Take a little step. I'm right here . . ." And when we finally took that step, there was such enthusiasm! We knew we had done something special and we could do it again. In every step of our lives, we need to enthusiastically cheer ourselves and others on. We all need this encouragement.

Enthusiastically support someone you love today. Tell her what a good person she is and how much you value her, and find one totally positive thing you can share with her. Watch the glow of a smile spread across her face and feel the energy of life increase for both of you. Tell her that you are proud of her, and you enjoy watching all the success that she has earned. What a great gift we give when we give the gift of our enthusiasm!

HYPOTHALAMUS AND MEDULLA OBLONGATA

Dr. Robert. When your life is in good order, when you are in a good flow, how do you feel? You feel terrific, enthused, filled with energy, full of zest and zeal.

This shows the close interaction and interdependency of the powers of order and enthusiasm. Actually, all of our Twelve Powers work together. Each one influences the others and is affected by the others, just as all of our physical organs work together in a harmonious and integrated fashion.

The power of zeal-enthusiasm externalizes in our physical body via several organs at the base of the brain, including the hypothalamus and the brain stem, which consists of the midbrain, pons and medulla oblongata. (See Figure 10.) *Hypo* means below, so the hypothalamus is positioned below the thalamus. Specific centers in the hypothalamus and brain stem regulate all of the body's automatic functions and cyclic activities that are under subconscious control. These include temperature, water balance, heart and respiratory rate, appetite and the sleep-wake cycle. These organs at the base of the brain also regulate our energy level, our mood and our libido.

What happens when we get excited, enthused, filled with zeal? These attitudes and emotions activate the hypothalamus, which then sends out nerve impulses via the sympathetic and parasympathetic nerves to all parts of the body. For example, the hypothalamus regulates heart and respiratory rates by transmitting nerve impulses to cardiac and respiratory control centers in the medulla oblongata, which then relay them via the nerves to the heart and lungs. So, when we are "on fire," joyous, stimulated or impassioned about life, our heart beats with greater force and at a quickened rate. We breathe more deeply, evenly and rapidly.

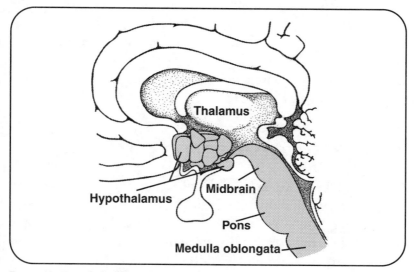

Figure 10. Hypothalamus and brain stem

What happens when we ingest too much information, feel overwhelmed emotionally, have "stuffed" our anger or have eaten some spoiled food? Certainly, it is difficult to be enthusiastic and full of energy at these times. Instead, we may feel nauseous and vomit. This reflexive response is mediated by swallowing and vomiting centers in our medulla oblongata.

The hypothalamus also manifests our zeal and enthusiasm by regulating the secretion of pituitary hormones, which in turn regulate the other endocrine glands. For example, when we affirm and believe that we are filled with abundant energy, then the hypothalamus responds by releasing a hormone that directs the pituitary to release its hormone that regulates the thyroid gland. With the resulting increase in thyroid hormone, we experience greater energy and vitality.

You probably have heard the term "runner's high," which describes the feelings of joy, well-being and peace that people may feel after exercising. This is produced in part by the release of endorphins from the hypothalamus. Endorphins are the body's own morphine-like substance. They eliminate pain and elevate our mood. The hypothalamus apparently also releases them when we laugh and when we feel love, joy and oneness with the Divine.

SUFFICIENT UNTO EACH DAY

What do you think is the most common complaint of people who visit a doctor? It is tiredness, a lack of energy, not having much "get up and go." Why and how do people come to feel this way? Like so many other conditions, this lowered-energy state has numerous possible causes.

The body's energy level and rate of metabolism are "set" or programmed in a particular center or group of cells in the hypothalamus. However, that programmed "setting" is influenced by how we use all our other powers. For example, if someone lacks faith in himself or herself and in the abiding presence of Spirit, then this fractured faith contributes to a lack of zeal and enthusiasm, which in turn lowers the body's energy level. Conversely, when we are in love and we love our work, then our love power positively influences our hypothalamus and enhances our energy level. We can see how the use or misuse of all our other powers likewise programs our subconscious and reflects into our hypothalamus, thereby increasing or decreasing our energy level.

One woman in counseling who had chronic fatigue syndrome was always feeling divided within herself. She invested monumental amounts of energy in her current love relationship, but it was not working out, just as previous relationships also had soured. She tirelessly gave to her job and was always on the verge of burnout. Her relationship with her parents was challenging; she felt depleted when she visited them, but she would not stop out of a sense of obligation. Her excessive and misdirected zeal clearly was the central cause of her chronic fatigue.

If you have lowered energy, even as low as in chronic fatigue syndrome, what should you do? Certainly, consider all possible physical causes and treatments, and see a physician if your depleted state persists. However, at the same time, evaluate all of your Twelve Powers to see if some imbalance in one or more of them is contributing to your lack of "pep." Pay special attention to the power of order. Ask yourself: What is out of order, out of synch, not in its right place in your life? When you discover and correct this, and put things in proper order, then your energy level will improve automatically.

With lowered energy, concentrate particularly on your power of enthusiasm and zeal. Have you "burnt the candle at both ends"? Have you allowed yourself to become overstimulated, overextended, hyperactive, going in six different directions at once, burnt out? Have you been working at a "feverish" pace, not getting sufficient rest and relaxation? Have you always been a giver and not a receiver? Or, on the other side on the scale, are you too "laid back," a "cold fish," bored, blasé, unwilling to commit or dedicate yourself to any project or activity or relationship? What is needed is a

254 THE POWER OF ENTHUSIASM

balanced zeal, a flame that is not too high or too low, but that is at the right heat for the task at hand.

In your prayers, visualizations and meditations, see yourself being filled with abundant energy that flows evenly, smoothly and harmoniously through you. Affirm: Sufficient unto each day, I receive all the energy I need to do all the things that Spirit would have me do.

RESTORE YOUR ZEST FOR LIFE

Another common reason why people seek medical help is depression. Studies indicate that from one-quarter to one-half of visits to primary care medical doctors are by people who have minor or major depression. Everyone has ups and downs in life, times of sadness and grief. However, these do not constitute clinical depression, which may be marked by a loss of appetite or overeating, loss of libido, sleep difficulties, lowered energy, persistent pessimism, hopelessness and helplessness, and suicidal thoughts. Many depressed people consume excess alcohol or take illegal drugs.

Here again with depression, the core focus needs to be the power of enthusiasm, which externalizes partly by way of pleasure and pain centers that are situated in the midbrain. Electrical stimulation of the midbrain pleasure center produces feelings of joy, euphoria and well-being. These same feelings can be produced by injecting the neurotransmitters serotonin and dopamine. Midbrain nerve cells normally release these brain chemicals when we have pleasant, uplifting thoughts and emotions. Antidepressant medications like Prozac, Zoloft and Paxil work by elevating serotonin levels. In people who are prone to depression, there may be a genetic predisposition for lowered levels of serotonin, dopamine and other neurotransmitters.

Electrical stimulation of the punishment center in the midbrain causes feelings of unpleasantness, fear and loss of control. So, we have the neural programming to feel pleasure or pain, joy or sadness, enthusiasm or boredom, hopefulness or hopelessness, optimism or pessimism. It is a matter of what we choose, of how we program our subconscious, of how we use our power of zeal.

Teresa was feeling blocked, pressured and exhausted. She began to successfully work through this by simply recording her thoughts in her personal journal, such as in the following entry:

"I have come to a 'mental brick wall.' I desperately need to make a choice of which direction to go—but feeling like I am stuck to that wall with Velcro thoughts—thoughts of nothing better to do than go back to the familiar routine—all doors closed—my mind frozen in fear of which I can't define. Chaotic thoughts have crowded out the sanity—too many decisions depend on fate—to move or stay? I feel time is running out—the timer is ticking, the bell is going to ring and I will have to run back to my old life feeling once again like I have failed to meet the challenge. Disappointments of well-meaning people tend to make me regress. I need to take a mental hammer and tear down that mental wall."

In part, Teresa had constructed this "wall" with her power of order. She had built it brick by brick, until it was solidly in place, in much the same way that the body builds and maintains its solid structures like bones. So, in her counseling, she needed to review how she had done this, and then remove the bricks (thoughts and feelings) one by one. Each time she did, her enthusiasm and energy level increased. The energy had been there all along, but it was invested primarily in maintaining the wall—as she had written, it was stuck to the wall like Velcro. It took many months, lots of soul searching and rethinking, but finally the whole wall came tumbling down.

By the time people become clinically depressed, we cannot expect them to just "snap out of it" by abruptly changing their thoughts or saying a few affirmations. Rather, it almost always takes a multi-pronged treatment approach to alleviate the depression. The right antidepressant medication may be very helpful. German studies indicate that taking the herb St. John's Wort (hypericum) may be equally effective. Counseling helps, as does social support and exercise. Dietary changes and nutritional supplements may be essential. All of these complement the central focus on the right use of our power of enthusiasm.

Jason had a tendency to feel "blue" and to expect the worst in his life. He meditated, said his affirmations, ate healthy foods, exercised regularly and took St. John's Wort, but his underlying, low-grade despair continued. Finally, in counseling, he realized the root cause of his despondency. As a child, his father had been depressed and his mother had had a series of serious illnesses. In response, Jason had decided that his own lot in life, like his parents, was to suffer.

This realization hit him like a bolt of lightning: He was "supposed" to suffer. He had programmed this belief so deeply into his subconscious that no affirmation could touch it. Now, over a year's time, as he released and reprogrammed this conviction with expectations of peace, joy and happiness, his baseline mood gradually brightened until he was filled with joy and a zest for living.

A BALANCED ZEAL

Think back to a time when you were all charged up and burning with enthusiasm. Where did you sense this "fire" in your body? One place may have been in the back of your head at the base of your skull. Maybe you felt heat or tingling or some discomfort there. Moreover, you probably had trouble slowing down your thoughts, relaxing and resting. All of these signs and symptoms indicated an overactive or over-stimulated hypothalamus and brain stem. They pointed to the need to turn down the heat, the fire, the flame of enthusiasm.

At its extreme, excessive zeal and enthusiasm may lead to mania, which is the flip side or polar opposite to depression. Mania is characterized by undue elation and excitability, rapid speech, even delusions of grandeur and hallucinations. Some people are manic-depressive (bipolar), meaning they swing back and forth between depression and mania. With mania, medication usually is necessary to balance the brain chemistry. Genetic factors may be involved, since mania and manic-depression commonly run in families. However, med-itating on and building in the balanced use of zeal-enthusiasm is the key to healing this disorder.

If we are depressed or overaccelerated, we may also expe-rience difficulty sleeping. This may involve trouble going to sleep or getting back to sleep when we wake up in the middle of the night. When we are "down" and despondent, we may sleep more than usual. An estimated one-third of the popu-lation in the United States has sleep problems.

Our sleep-wake cycle is governed by the hypothalamic sleep center. Therefore, with sleep difficulties we need to focus on our power of enthusiasm and on its partner, the power of order. Reestablish balance and order in your life. Deal with any underlying depression or overstimulation. Then you will sleep like a baby!

In the middle of your head, in the area at the base of your brain, visualize a small pink rosebud. Think of this rosy-pink bud as representing the joy, enthusiasm and zeal that are always within you and that are about to flower now to a greater degree. Rosy means "hopeful" and "promising." This is how you feel when you reach the stage where your life is in good order and you are able to express a balanced form of enthusiasm.

Imagine the rosebud starting to open. As it does, you feel a lifting of your spirits, an opening of your mind and soul to greater joy, a flow of new energy and inspiring ideas about how to enthusiastically live your life. Envision the rosy-pink light radiating into all parts of your head, beginning to fill it with the warmth, passion and vibrant energy of your indwelling power of enthusiasm.

Do not be in a hurry. Do not try to force the bud to open too quickly. Let it open at its own pace. Zeal and enthusiasm cannot be forced any more than you can force open a flower without harming it in some way. Rather, let joy and happiness well up within you. Feel a greater passion to love God, to live life to the fullest, to love all other human beings. Know and affirm that you have all the energy and passion that you need to do all that Spirit would have you do in this moment of now.

Think also of the rosy-pink bud as representing the talents and abilities that are already present within you in latent form, programmed into your subconscious mind. As the bud opens and flowers, these innate talents begin to open to your conscious awareness. As you zealously and enthusiastically develop these unique talents, you will be following your bliss.

Envision the rosy-pink flower opening such that it fills your whole head and inner vision, radiating its warmth and enthusiasm throughout your whole consciousness and body. Then, in due time, come out of your meditation, giving thanks unto Spirit.

1. I am alert; I am alive; I am enthusiastic.
2. I zealously and joyously follow my bliss.
3. I am balanced and wisely use order and good judgment with my enthusiasm.
4. I enthusiastically say "yes" to life and "yes" to my good.
5. I have the power over automatic responses that block my enthusiasm for life.
6. *"Carpe diem!"* Seize the day!
7. I take time to enthusiastically share my love for family and friends.
8. I get "high" on life.
9. I don't get in a rut. I welcome new ideas and I am willing to be enthusiastic about them.
10. I am looking forward to seeing the good that will come out of this situation.
11. I avoid pessimism. I am deeply optimistic about the possibilities for all the good that will come into my life.
12. I express my enthusiasm in loving ways to the people in my family, workplace, church, friendships and all around me.
13. I am on fire with a passion and enthusiasm for living my life.
14. I am a winner and have a zest for living.
15. I give cards, notes and other reminders of my affection to many people in my life.

16. I release lots of endorphins in my body as I laugh, love and live with zest.

17. I avoid burnout by using my power of enthusiasm in a balanced and constructive way.

18. I see myself as a talented and resourceful person who is able to bounce back from disappointments.

19. I don't have to pump up my enthusiasm through outer things because I find the joy of living within myself and in many wonderful interactions with others.

20. I have follow-through as well as start-up power.

21. I am a child of God and I "let my child out" in safe, fun, creative ways.

22. Things don't have to be a "big deal" for me to be enthusiastic and excited.

23. I am a "fan" of life, not just a fan of famous people, sports or entertainers.

24. Life is for living and I live fully.

25. I don't ask, "What's in it for me?" I ask, "What's in it from me?"

26. I live enthusiastically from the inside out.

27. Sufficient unto each day, I receive all the energy and joy that I need.

28. The fire of God burns brightly within me.

29. I sleep deeply and soundly, and I awake restored and energized.

30. I fairly sizzle with zeal and enthusiasm and spring forth with a mighty faith to do the things that ought to be done by me.

11
The Power of RELEASE

RELEASE

RELEASE is my ability to give a "no, thank you" response to the untrue, undesirable or worn-out. It is my ability to forgive, free myself, break bad habits, not be controlled and let go. Release uses the "vacuum principle" by letting go of mental and physical "stuff," so that God has space and place to be realized. What is released may not be "bad," but it needs to be eliminated and replaced with something better. Release expresses physically via my colon and urinary system.

RELEASE AND REPLACE

David. Release is our power or ability to change our mind, to change our beliefs, to let go and let God. What are some obvious limiting beliefs we may need to release? About God: God is an angry judge. About people: We are worthless, helpless sinners, destined for hell if we don't repent. About the human condition: It's a dog-eat-dog world, revenge is sweet, and wars produce peace. This is "error thinking" and must be released and replaced with truth. I can know the truth that God is Love, that I am loved and of infinite worth, that I am at my best when I live in cooperation and peace.

IF THE SHOE FITS

I go into a shoe store and try on shoes that I may want to buy and wear. Some of the shoes look sharp, but they hurt my feet. I'm tempted to get them anyway and suffer. (Sound familiar?) However, I have a choice. I can also choose to get shoes that fit well, are comfortable, and will wear well (usually). Maybe a salesperson or others tell me I should get a certain pair of shoes, but I'm the one who will wear them. The shoes that I "let go" are not for me. They may be okay for someone else, but they are not mine.

Can you see how we are continually faced with such choices? To accept or let go. To buy into something or to say, "No, it's not for me."

I may also have some shoes that I have worn a long time. They have been great shoes, but they are worn or faded or unusable. I don't call them "bad" or "wicked" or "sinful" or "sick." I simply realize that I need to let them go. So, I give them away or put them in the trash.

LETTING GO BY LETTING GOD

You see, releasing something isn't just for what we consider "bad stuff." We often have to let go of ways of thinking, beliefs, patterns, places, jobs, things that have been a good and helpful part of our lives, but now it is time to give up the lesser for something greater.

We can use what has been called "creating a vacuum" by periodically cleaning out our closets, garage, car trunk and storage locker. We give things away or have a yard sale to recycle or put things in circulation, so that we can create a vacuum to receive new good in our lives.

Originally, the term used for this "letting go" process was "renunciation" or "elimination." Mr. Fillmore may have used "elimination" in his Twelve Powers philosophy because he was relating the powers to bodily functions, and we ordinarily refer to the organs of elimination. Our power to let go includes physical elimination and also extends beyond that. Obviously, we know the problems in our body which may occur when we're having trouble with elimination. (I'll let Dr. Knapp deal with that!) But release or letting go is also a natural process of sometimes "letting go and letting God." For example, we let go of our anxious hold on some person or situation and "put it in God's hands." This is releasing it to God-the-Good.

We all have had the experience of having to release a friend, loved one or colleague when they died. We know that this releasing is a process that is not just done quickly, once and for all at the memorial service, but is worked out through stages over a considerable period of time. We don't just "eliminate" the person or relationship but we do go through a "letting go" experience. A friend of ours, Dr. Melba Colgrove, coauthored an excellent book called, *How to Survive the Loss of a Love*. The authors suggest a powerful affirmation to help us in recovery from loss: "I am alive. I will survive."

KNOWING WHEN TO SAY "NO"

I went to a workshop with John Bradshaw. He asked us to practice saying "no" to people who kept asking us to do things. I often have difficulty saying "no" to people, so I had to work at the assignment.

Some teachings say that we need to "deny" certain thoughts, suggestions, opinions, beliefs and feelings a place in our life. That is, we need to say "no" to them. We may just inwardly reject an opinion such as, "You're going to come down with what everyone else in the office has. Just wait." Or, "You know you cannot trust people with brown (white, black, red, yellow) skin." Or, "Shame on you." We may say to ourselves, "I reject that. I don't accept it and I won't buy into it."

We often have to renounce negative things that we think or say about ourselves—our negative self-talk. Knowing the power of our words, I work on not saying something that I used to exclaim all the time: "Give me a break!" I don't *want* to break something, so I've stopped affirming it to my listening subconscious.

The problem with the word "denial," which has often been

used for this decision to say "no" and not to accept something, comes into play when we carry it into "psychological denial." This is when we try to tell ourselves or others that we don't have a problem that we obviously *do* have. Pretending to myself or others that I am not thinking, feeling or acting negatively doesn't cleanse that negativity out of me. It just suppresses it down into my subconscious realm of mind, where it may cause physical illness or further emotional problems.

Release requires the honesty, humility and courage to face what I may be doing to myself or others. I let it go by admitting it, talking it out, defusing it and forgiving myself. I make courageous, honest self-analysis a continuing part of my spiritual practice. It is positive to face up to, and to let go of, the negative.

A major part of learning is recognizing and releasing what we have believed to be true but which is really not true. We have all been exposed to a lot of superstitions, old wives' tales, "flat Earth" views and error consciousness. Sometimes, I hear people say, "Just hold a positive thought . . . just keep knowing things will work out."

That's fine, except it leaves something out. I may have to do some releasing before all these positive thoughts and affirmations can have a place and take hold. Dumping and pumping them into my mind is like putting fresh, clean water into a dirty sink, full of old greasy water. I have to release the old water to make a place for the new good I want. I can't just keep pouring in positive thinking and affirmations, and expect them to work. I first have to clean out my mental and emotional house. I pull

the plug on my old, worn-out, negative, limited patterns of thinking, speaking, feeling, acting and choosing.

The dirt may be stubborn and require some steady work on my part to loosen it and let it go. Some old prejudices, superstitions, self-discounting and self-destructive patterns don't disappear or get released overnight. They may be stubborn and multilayered, and may take time and effort to cleanse. But no one would try to wash dishes in a sink full of old, messy water that had been standing there for days. We know that water has to be drained and replaced to effectively do the dishes. We, too, have to keep letting go of what needs to be released or transcended.

This two-stage process of change also needs to have a flow of fresh water to replace what has been released. It is not enough just to stop or cleanse something. Then we must put something really positive and good in its place. You will notice that some of the statements at the end of our chapters contain a thought of release and an affirmation of what we want to now think, have or do.

Life is a flow. Life is dynamic. We are constantly changing. Every day is a new day. No one can be static or fixed. The past is not "bad," anymore than the old water in the sink is "bad." We release and replace. We reinvent ourselves every day in some way. We find God anew, in different ways, every day. We stay in the creative flow of life.

CASTING OUT A LIFE OF DRUGS

A young, attractive woman named Michelle asked me if she could help start a Narcotics Anonymous group at our church. She said she had been going to a group across town and would like to have a fellowship in our side of the city.

Michelle said, "David, I never told you how I let go of

cocaine. I came to a New Year's Eve 'Burning Bowl Service' at your church a couple years ago. We were supposed to write on a paper what we wanted to let go in our life. I was still using cocaine at the time, and my life was a disaster. When you asked what we wanted to let go of that night, to release, I heard inside me the words, 'I think I want to let go of cocaine.'

"I didn't even have a pen in my purse so I wrote it with my lipstick liner. I was shaking all the way up to the Burning Bowl, but that one sincere desire was enough, and that night became a turning point for the rest of my life.

"I saw myself letting go of my coke habit. I saw myself free. I knew I would find help. I knew God was with me in this and would bring me through getting over coke. I put the paper in the fire and saw it burn. I took a deep breath of freedom and walked away from it forever. I joined Narcotics Anonymous. I went back to college. I started a whole new life."

I saw Michelle years later, and she was a new person—clean and sober—living a whole new life.

In your overcomings, one sincere desire can be the turning point in creating a successful life. Always remember, you are empowered from within to live fully and freely now. You are free!

AND STILL I RISE

Gay Lynn. Who or what do I need to stop fretting and worrying about? When I ask myself this question, most often it is my family or kids I am worried about, no matter how old they are!

A young mother came to me a number of years ago, concerned about her teenage son, Michael. She discovered that Michael had been skipping school, hanging out with the wrong crowd and earning failing grades. A recommendation was made to place Michael in the "at-risk" program at his high school. As part of a special service at our church, the mother had received a "phoenix medallion" I had created and minted. I put "And Still I Rise" on it, the title of a poem by one of my favorite poets, Maya Angelou.

The phoenix comes from Egyptian mythology. The miraculous bird was said to live for 500 years and then, after its death on an altar of fire, rose in youthful freshness to live again. The phoenix is often used as a symbol of immortality and of rising out of the ashes to new life, to a fresh beginning.

The mother gave her son the phoenix medallion and told him that she believed in him. She said that she knew he could rise out of any difficulties and that she loved him very much. Michael accepted the medallion and his mother's love and confidence. He started the "at-risk" program and joined other youths on the verge of dropping out. Each year students in the program chose an emblem and motto for their class. All the students were asked to participate in creating a design that would be inspirational and help them to succeed. Since Michael had just received the phoenix medallion, he invested a great deal of time in drawing a beautiful, large rendition of the phoenix with the quote, "And Still I Rise."

The class voted on the best emblem, and Michael's phoenix made the semifinals. In his final presentation, Michael read Maya Angelou's poem to his classmates. The final vote was taken and the announcement was made. Michael stood in awe as they voted his drawing and motto the winner. He had never won anything in his life. The affirmation from his classmates inspired him as he realized that he had positively influenced and helped the people around him. He was not just Michael, the troublemaker; he was a talented artist whose drawing had inspired his class. For the first time, he could see how his life and his art could

have a great impact on others. He discovered in his adversity, at a time when he was ready to quit, his talent and his power.

Michael's mom gave medallions to all of the students. The beautiful phoenix was hung on the wall of the classroom and all the students signed their names around it. Out of the ashes of failure and doubt came a new vision of hope and another way of life.

You and I may be like Michael, facing our own challenges, failures and trying times. The simple truth is, we can release the past, no matter the circumstance, and rise up and begin again. We can literally re-create ourselves and start a "new life." Just like the ancient mythology of the phoenix, we rise out of the ashes and experience a fresh start.

Remember that wonderful phrase of hope, *And Still I Rise!* I am willing to release beliefs and attitudes that no longer serve me. I make room for new growth. *And Still I Rise!*

Many church members, recovery groups, cancer survivors, burn victims, foster children and educational communities have shared thousands of these wonderful little medallions. (See Resources page 329) The original design was inspired by a dear friend, James Dillet Freeman, a great inspirational writer whose poems have literally been carried to the moon and left there by astronauts. Since one side of the medallion is blank, I like to encourage people to write some word or phrase on that side with a permanent marker. That word or phrase is to describe what their life is rising into. What word describes the vision you are holding for your life? Perhaps it is "peace," "love," "forgiveness," "happiness," "success," "life," "power" (especially since we are working with our Twelve Powers).

DEACTIVATING NEGATIVE BEHAVIORS

The power of release is an important part of the visioning processes. We have to be willing to let go of all the mental "garbage" that keeps "recycling" in our lives. By becoming conscious of it, we can redirect it, release it and create a space for new attitudes and life.

Sometimes we have learned "adaptive behaviors," which are behaviors or actions that have helped us to survive past difficulties, abuse, neglect or trauma. If we continue to use these behaviors, they may become "maladaptive" and manipulative behaviors. We need to shed these behaviors and replace them in order to fully self-actualize, be authentically ourselves and allow ourselves to really be available to people. We must examine these adaptive behaviors, such as shutting down, being tough, being emotionally unavailable, discounting or judging others, dominating others out of our fear of being dominated, being passive and then lashing out in anger or aggression.

All of these behaviors may have helped us to get by at one time, but as our lives change and improve, these behaviors must be released and transformed. It is like living in a rough neighborhood and adapting to that environment, then moving to a more peaceful neighborhood but still acting "on guard" or "defensive" or "ready for fight or flight." The behavior is no longer appropriate for the new environment or circumstance, and it needs to be understood, released and replaced. Then new behaviors may be internalized.

All of us have family patterns that have been unconsciously ingrained in us. We must discern for ourselves what these patterns or imprints are. Once we see and understand them, we can then decide whether these behaviors are still useful and appropriate. What old behaviors do you continue to hang on to? What are some of the behaviors that may have served you in the past but are no longer helpful and may even be hurting you now?

One courageous woman wrote a letter that she did not

send to her mother, but that clearly addressed some of these
behaviors for herself:

Dear Mom,

*I want you to know that I have had difficulty
believing in my capabilities because of the messages I
got from you as a child—that I would not amount to
much; that I didn't need an education; that the most
I could expect was to get married. I had a lot of negative messages programmed at a young age, which
contributed to my making poor choices in my relationships in my adult life. I followed a pattern of self-
destruction, not knowing it was a subconscious
pattern. I felt I didn't deserve better, I guess.*

*I have struggled for the last ten or more years to
overcome these feelings of self-doubt and to realize
you did not deliberately want me to fail—you were
just full of your own anger and resentment, and you
had no other way to express them. You gave up and
figured we should resign ourselves to the reality that
we were born to fail. You lost yourself in your "illnesses and medications." I have chosen to deal with
my demons, to face the consequences of my actions
and to change my life.*

*Now I am at a crossroads because when I choose to
take responsibility for my life, I can't lose myself anymore in codependent behavior or drugs or denial.
Only faith, the hard work of facing the obstacles,
working through the fears, and being stronger and
more self-confident can nourish and sustain me as I
make the positive changes I am looking for.*

*I love you, Mom, and I'm so sorry you were not able
to live up to the potentials I know you have. I am
choosing to live up to mine.*

Often when you begin to release these behaviors, you also release a great deal of stress and tension that went along with them. Resenting your past is not productive. Resentment keeps you emotionally, mentally and physically blocked, and bound to the past. Make a wise choice today to do what you can to live more fully and freely by understanding your past and recognizing how it has brought you to this moment. No matter how difficult the past, you can overcome it as long as you are willing, like this brave soul, to face it without denial and to use every experience as a stepping stone. You have survived, you are alive and you will thrive.

It is not necessary to go through life with a thousand pounds of guilt, remorse, shame and pain on your back. Let it go! You can release the old ways of struggle and make the shift from "fretting" to "letting" a new way of life. You can let it rise from within you. Remember the phrase, *And Still I Rise!*

FIRE OF TRANSMUTATION

When you feel hurt or upset with someone, how do you let it go? Can you let it go or do you keep dwelling on the incident or conversation, replaying it over and over in your mind? I know that I tend to do this at times—we all do—but how can we move on? It isn't easy and people around us may even say, "Just let it go, forget about it." Sometimes we can do this. And then other times, the hurt is deep and takes time and care to heal.

Karen had gone through a painful separation and divorce from her husband. She had been in counseling for a while, processing through the mistakes that had happened in communication and the trust issues that each of them had brought to the marriage. She continued to grow, even though it was painful. She persisted in releasing old behaviors and unloving ways. She did everything she could to change and improve herself.

At the time she called me, she had reached a point where she was desirous of a special ceremony to complete this passage in her life. I gave her a few suggestions and we joined together at her home to have the healing ceremony. She began by reading a goodbye letter she had written to her former husband acknowledging the good times and the bad times they had had together. Then she took the letter with a picture of the two of them and burned them, as a rite of release, in her fireplace. Of course, sadness filled her heart as she acknowledged this. Afterwards, she took the ashes from the fireplace and put them in the ground and planted a new tree on top of them.

With this ritual she said symbolically, "Out of the ashes of what has been springs new life." And literally, those ashes nourished that tree. Every time she came home, she would see the tree growing and branching out just as she was doing in her life. This simple symbolic experience helped her to heal, release the past, honor the relationship and in a wiser way, continue to grow. Instead of staying stuck, she marked the passage with a ceremony of release and moved forward in her life.

It took time. It took a lot of processing. Eventually new, happier, healthier relationships came into her life.

What is holding you back? What can you release today that could help you to be free and happier? Let it go and experience that freedom now.

COLON OR LARGE INTESTINE

Dr. Robert. Could it be any more clear or obvious that the power of release-elimination expresses physically via the colon? Just as we use the power of release to let go of unhealthy and outmoded thoughts, feelings and memories, so does the colon eliminate physical wastes, toxins and unneeded substances from the body.

When we eat, is all of our food assimilated by our digestive system? No. Some of it, like roughage or fiber, cannot be broken down, so it passes through the digestive tract into the colon, which eventually eliminates it from the body. Moreover, even when we are careful about eating only healthy foods, we may inadvertently ingest harmful, toxic items in addition to vital nutrients. So, again, the body needs a way to remove these toxic substances.

The colon is also known as the large intestine, because its average diameter of two and one-half inches is larger than the small intestine. However, the colon is shorter in length, being about five to six feet long. The colon consists of the cecum, the ascending colon, the transverse colon, the descending colon, the sigmoid colon and the rectum. Projecting from the cecum is a finger-shaped organ, the appendix, which averages three to four inches in length. It contains a large amount of lymphoid tissue. (See Figure 11A.)

Undigested food (including fiber), water, mineral salts, pigments and some toxic items move into the colon through the ileocecal valve. This valve is located between the end of the ileum—the last section of the small intestine—and the first part of the colon, which is called the cecum. Most of the water and the minerals moving through the colon are reabsorbed in the ascending colon and the first half of the transverse colon. This leads to the solidification of the waste matter or feces, which are stored in the second half of the transverse colon, the descending colon and the sigmoid colon. During defecation, the feces are removed via the rectum and out the anus.

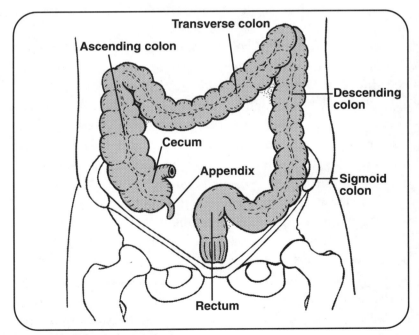

Figure 11A. Colon or large intestine

Isn't it interesting that, as part of the eliminatory process, the colon first reabsorbs water and essential mineral salts? It doesn't just release and remove everything that flows into it. Rather, it first retains and reabsorbs that which is still needed by the body, and then removes the rest.

We can take a lesson from this wisdom of our body. Sometimes, in our zeal to shed old habits and remove unhealthy ways of thinking and feeling, we end up eliminating the good as well as the bad. As the saying goes, "We throw out the baby with the bathwater." Even in the mistakes we have made or the adaptive patterns that we have repeated time and again, often there is a kernel of truth or a lesson we must learn before we can fully release the past. So, we need to have compassion for ourselves, to be wise and patient, not to force or push or unduly emphasize our power of elimination-release.

What happens when people do give excessive attention to their power of release, or they try to change everything about themselves all at once? This may lead to problems with the colon, such as repeated episodes of diarrhea, a spastic colon (irritable bowel syndrome), ulcerative colitis or Crohn's colitis.

What happens when individuals refuse to change, to let go, to release the old, unhealthy or worn-out ways of thinking and feeling, when they hang onto their anger or fear or resentment? They may experience constipation, develop tumors in their colon, or have other diseases of their colon. Imbalances in the power of release also may cause or contribute to appendicitis.

Jerry had irritable bowel syndrome, a mixture of pain, diarrhea, constipation, nausea and occasional vomiting. Like many people with this syndrome, he had nagging concerns about family problems, difficulties at work and financial challenges. He could not let his worries go. He was highly critical of others, focusing on and speaking bluntly about what he thought were their faults.

One day his boss pointed out his critical nature and challenged him to change. Initially, the stress of this revelation led to a worsening of his colon problems—more pain, cramping and loose stools. Then as Jerry took a serious look at and modified the way he thought about and treated others, his symptoms diminished. Instead of moderating his critical responses, however, he went to the other extreme and tried not to say anything negative about anyone, to not even point out obvious conditions that needed correction for the good of all involved. Once again, his bowel symptoms returned and worsened. Finally, he readjusted and found a middle way— he recognized his critical behavior and released it, but he also spoke clearly about his insights and feelings towards others without putting them down. His colon distress subsided. He brought balance into his releasing, both in his relationships and in his body.

URINARY SYSTEM

The power of release-elimination also expresses via the urinary system, which includes the kidneys, ureters, bladder and urethra. Every cell in the body produces metabolic by-products that diffuse into the blood, which carries them to the two kidneys. The kidneys are located lateral to the spinal column and against the back wall of the abdominal cavity. (See Figure 11B.) The primary function of the kidneys is to filter the blood. Excess water and minerals, wastes such as urea and uric acid from protein metabolism, bacterial toxins, degraded hormones, toxic chemicals and other unneeded substances are removed from the blood by the kidneys. However, red blood cells, white blood cells, platelets, needed minerals and other nutrients are retained in the blood.

Here again, we see that in the eliminatory process—in the body as well as the mind—we are to retain all that is good, vital, healthy and life-promoting, even as we release that which is in excess, unhealthy, toxic and no longer needed.

In the kidneys, the filtering of the blood produces urine, which is about 95 percent water and five percent solutes. Urine travels from the kidneys down the ureters to the bladder, which is a muscular sac capable of extension. During urination, the urinary sphincters open and the bladder muscles contract, thereby expelling urine through the urethra to outside the body.

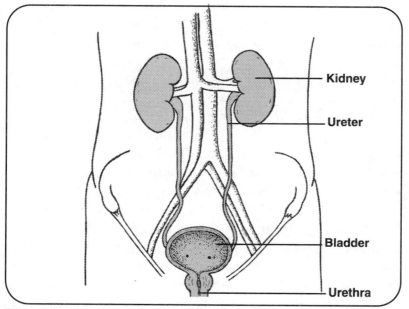

Figure 11B. Urinary system (male)

One quarter of the blood pumped by the heart down the aorta travels through the renal arteries to the kidneys. This shows just how vital our kidneys are to our health, how important it is that the kidneys continually filter the blood and remove unneeded substances. In like manner, we are wise when we give sufficient daily attention and energy to our power of release, when we mentally filter all that comes into our mind and soul. We are always changing, growing, adapting and letting go of the old to make way for the new. This should be a natural, joyous, integral part of our life, not something that we resist, neglect or block. Change is life, and life is change.

What happens if we do resist and refuse to let go of the old, unneeded, unhealthy parts of ourselves? This may lead to infections of the urethra, bladder or kidneys. There may be cysts or tumors (benign or malignant) of the kidneys or bladder, or kidney stones. If these conditions occur, get the best professional healthcare. At the same time, focus on your power of release to rebalance your urinary system.

Sheila was having one bladder infection after another. In counseling, she initially seemed to be easygoing and pleasant, but beneath the surface we discovered that she was filled with anger and hostility that had bothered her for years. She was really "pissed off" about a lot of old stuff and was blocked in her ability to find resolution. Of course, I suggested she continue to treat the bladder infections with proper medical care. However, I also asked her to visualize with each glass of water she drank that she was flushing out the old hurts that kept her so irritated and inflamed. We worked on ways to address her anger and her split way of being "nice" on the surface and "seething" underneath. She made the needed changes over a period of many months, and the bladder infections diminished along with her anger.

Some people refer to the skin as being an organ of

elimination. Indeed, when we sweat we do release a small amount of toxins. However, the skin removes less than 1 percent of the body's total toxins. The principal function of the skin is to provide a covering and boundary for the whole body. That is why the skin expresses primarily the power of order and organization.

Actually, all cells and organs in the body have some part of their function devoted to elimination of debris and toxic material. Thus, the liver, spleen and lymphatic system purify the blood. The lungs have fine hair cells, called cilia, lining their airways to catch dust particles, which then can be swept upward and coughed out of the system. However, the colon and the urinary system actually remove most of the wastes and toxins from the body. That is why they are the principal organs of elimination.

CONTINUOUS CYCLE OF LIFE AND DEATH

Have you ever continued to hold onto your pain and suffering, even when you knew intellectually that it would be far better to let them go? Most of us have had this experience at one time or another.

So, what is behind this inability and unwillingness to release the past, the worn-out, the error in our life? At the most basic level, it may be the fear of death, which often is misinterpreted to mean oblivion and total destruction. We may be afraid that when we let something go, nothing will take its place, and especially not something that is better than what we have been hanging on to so tightly. We often fear the unknown and cling to that which is familiar. We may be afraid that death of the physical body is the end of life, rather than knowing that life continues after our transition to new dimensions on the inner, invisible planes of life.

As I have shared previously, when I was about seven, my baby sister, Rosalie, suddenly died. I clearly remember going with my parents to the funeral home to view her body. When I touched it, it was cold, so I asked my mom what this meant. Mom bravely replied that Rosalie's soul had gone to heaven, and then Mom broke down in tears. Even as a young child, I knew that she did not really believe or understand what she was saying. I felt her pain, anguish and confusion.

Mom tried counseling with her minister, but his advice to have faith in God did not assuage her sorrow nor answer her questions. In those days, ministers were not trained to do grief counseling and did not believe in reincarnation. (Even if Mom had accepted this belief, Rosalie's death still would have been deeply traumatic.) There were no antidepressant medications. Rather, Mom entered the psychiatric hospital where she received electroshock therapy. She was never quite the same afterwards.

I grew up with a certain morbid curiosity and a deep fear of death. What was the point of living, of doing good, of growing and changing, if you only ended up dying? Going to heaven or hell did not make much sense either. Not until I discovered the law of karma and reincarnation did I begin my journey of letting go of the fear of death and of fully embracing the love of life.

And yet, just because we come to the initial realization that we are an eternal being who lives and evolves in different dimensions does not mean that we instantly release our fear of death and the unknown. It takes time to let go of this fear, to welcome change and the unknown, to have faith in a better tomorrow if we make the necessary changes today.

My early childhood experience with Mom came full circle

in 1990, when she died from complications of Parkinson's disease. For the previous ten years, her body and mind had slowly deteriorated. As her son and a physician, this was especially painful to watch, as there was little I could do to help her. Reawakened within me were all my fears and feelings of abandonment. I had lost her once before and now it felt like I was losing her again.

Only this time, I had a higher way to deal with her disease and impending death. I did not shut down emotionally, but rather I continued to open my heart to love her. I knew in the depths of my being that she was not just a dying body, but that her spirit would survive and grow and continue to evolve. I saw her illness and impending transition as an opportunity to heal the many residual wounds and imbalances in myself and all my family. Not that all of this was free of pain. To the contrary, sometimes it still hurt deeply, but I could feel and acknowledge and flow with the pain, and then release it and transform it with love.

A week before she passed on, I dreamt that her father (who had been "dead" for twenty years) had come to take her "home." A few days later, we placed her in a hospice, where she received the most loving care imaginable. A couple days after that, she was gone. The night after her death, I dreamt that she was in a type of "hospital" on the inner planes, where she was healing and adjusting to her new life. Countless dreams followed in which I followed her growth. In one particularly moving dream, a group of wise men said that in my next life, we would be together again.

Death was not the end of our evolving relationship. Rather it was just the beginning of a new chapter in our eternal life!

Sit comfortably and begin to relax as you breathe slowly and deeply. Each time you breathe out, let go of any worries, tensions or concerns from your daily activities. Let go and let God.

Then visualize in front of you a bright flame or fire of light. The flame is not hot but comfortable. It is an all-consuming flame, a fire that burns and transforms all that enters into it. You may see it as a violet flame, for some people think of this color as representing transmutation. Or it may appear as another color or just as fiery light. You may not see it but rather simply "feel" it in front of you or "sense" it as a higher vibration or energy.

Envision yourself stepping into this flame, so that it envelops your whole physical body and extends a foot or two away from your physical form into your whole auric field. You are now aflame with fiery light, which is all around and within you, and which will help you to release and eliminate and transmute anything in your thoughts, feelings, memories or physical body.

Ask yourself: What needs to be released now? What is no longer essential, healthy, nourishing or life-enhancing? Whatever it is, simply let it go. Let it be released into the flame of light so that it may be consumed in the fire of transmutation. Maybe it is some condition at work. Perhaps it is a relationship. Maybe it is some pain from your past that now can be released.

If you are having any difficulty with your colon or urinary system, imagine the fiery light invigorating and transmuting your organs of elimination. See the light in your kidneys, ureters, bladder, urethra and all parts of your large intestine.

Stay with this visualization until you feel cleansed and purified, until nothing more comes to your conscious awareness that you need to release in this session, until a sense of peace and rest wells up within you. Then, come out of your meditation, ready to begin anew.

1. I release all things to God-the-Good.
2. I do not hold onto that which holds me back. I release it and I am free to progress and prosper.
3. I now let go of a belief, constriction, set of values, bad habit, or worn-out way of thinking or doing things.
4. I release myself to experience greater life by freely forgiving myself and others.
5. I surrender my dreams, aspirations, goals and longing to God, so that my good can come forth in the most miraculous ways.
6. At the right time, I let go of my children so they can be strong, independent and free to find themselves.
7. My body is being renewed by replacing old cells and growing new ones.
8. All impurities, abnormal cells and congestion now are flushed out of my body.
9. I do mental housecleaning periodically as I clear out messy, restrictive, outmoded thoughts and beliefs.
10. I let go of a worn-out belief just as I would remove a burned-out light bulb and replace it with one that works.
11. I have the power to free myself and others.
12. "I am free, I am unlimited. There are no chains that bind me." (Janet Manning)
13. I let go of tension, stress and strain. I relax and trust God.
14. I do not resent anyone's good fortune. Their success shows the abundance available to me and everyone.

15. I release beliefs and attitudes that no longer serve a constructive purpose for me. I make room for growth.
16. I release loved ones who have made their transition into God's care and the pathway of ongoing life.
17. I am alive. I will survive and thrive.
18. What I now feel I will release and heal.
19. I am a mistake maker, but I am also a mistake breaker.
20. I let go of concepts of God that are cruel, fearsome, restrictive, judgmental, distant, dualistic, sexist and playing favorites.
21. I let go of "toxic" ways of thinking and behaving. I am now free to be more peaceful, healthy and successful.
22. I am fearless in facing and admitting where I need to change and grow. I do not deny or hide from myself.
23. I let go of addictions that keep my soul imprisoned in pain and emptiness.
24. I release worry and concern, and I take positive steps to support the ones I love.
25. Like the phoenix, I rise out of the past into new life and rebirth.
26. I face my challenges with courage and say, "And still I rise!"
27. I recognize old patterns and behaviors that hold me back and I joyously let them go.
28. New growth now comes from the "ashes" of my past mistakes to fertilize the garden of my life.
29. I release with care and gentleness, and my body responds with radiant health.
30. I let go and let God.

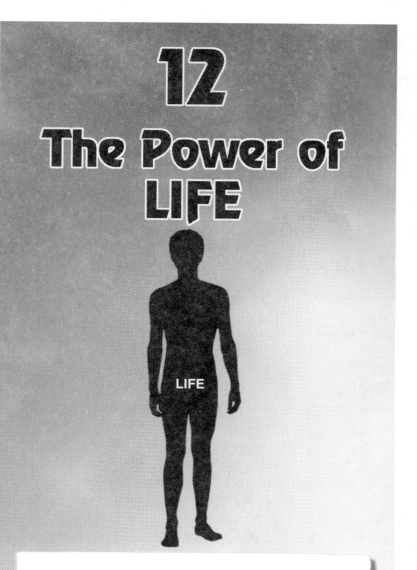

12
The Power of
LIFE

LIFE is my power to restore, heal, mend, procreate, regenerate, vitalize and energize. My life power is always present within me. It does not grow old, wither or pass away. I celebrate life. I honor my sexuality as a sacred and positive life expression. The power of life externalizes in my physical body through my male or female reproductive system.

Spirit

LIFE IS FOREVER UNFOLDING

David. We have the power of life. Life evolves in its many stages and expressions. Even in our conception and development in the womb, we go through all the stages of the evolution of humanity from simple cells to a complex human being. The forms of life continue to change for us. We don't have the same life expression (body) that we had when we were born or when we were five years old. The life power itself is ageless, formless, forever unfolding.

Our body is an expression of the life power. Life seems to come from our body but it doesn't. We often speak of life as if it "comes and goes." Life doesn't "begin" with birth or "end" with death. We talk about "new life arriving" and a person's life as being "over" and being "buried." However, we believe life is continuous, unfolding, renewing itself constantly.

This perspective is deeply held in the human race. The two most prominent festivals in Christianity are Christmas and Easter. Christmas is about the birth of the Divine in humanity, and Easter is about death and resurrection (rebirth) into new life. Both have a relationship to Earth/Sun cycles that relate to the return of spring, symbolizing rebirth and new life.

The Christian churches capitalized on Roman and

European celebrations by making the birthday of Jesus and the name "Easter" follow popular Earth celebrations of people the church wanted to become followers. This doesn't discount the meaning of such celebrations, but reinforces the universality of new life expression as Carl Jung, Joseph Campbell and other collectors of archetypes and sacred myths have shown. They confirm the celebration of life as being of greatest spiritual importance to us.

The only people who are disturbed by such correlations are those who want to have exclusive ownership of truth or who think truth was only revealed once and is not a perennial philosophy. The power of life is celebrated again and again, by culture after culture, ancient and modern, as pervasive as Easter eggs and the Christmas tree.

A HOLISTIC SPIRITUALITY

So, you and I are alive. What does that mean? I believe we are co-creators with God. We are also procreators of manifest human "life." We have a mysterious part in the soul's journey into a physical incarnation that develops, being assisted by the mating of a male sperm and a female egg in a woman's fallopian tube.

The Hebrew tradition teaches that sex, conception, birth, a body of flesh and bone are all causes for celebration and spiritual wonderment. In other religious traditions this part of our existence often is rejected—called "carnal," "sinful," "sense consciousness," "mortal," "animal," "error," "unreal," "maya" and "lower." Isn't it interesting that there are probably more negative names for the body in many religions than celebrations of our bodies as "good"?

A holistic spirituality embraces our spirit, soul and body as one energy—like steam, liquid and ice are all water—all the same, but in different forms of expression. Steam is not "good" and ice "bad." Likewise, we are whole beings.

"Carnal" means flesh. Jesus is seen by many as the "incarnation" of God. That means, "God in the flesh." Other religions see other avatars, saints, bodhisatvas or saviors as incarnations of God. I believe we are all incarnations of God in our own way. The carnal is to be affirmed, honored and celebrated as God appearing in ourselves.

Here is what Walt Whitman wrote in the poem "Song of Myself" in his book, *Leaves of Grass*:

> *Why should I wish to see God better than this day?*
> *I see something of God each hour of the twenty-four, and each moment then,*
> *In the faces of men and women I see God, and in my own face in the glass,*
> *I find letters from God dropt in the street, and every one is sign'd by God's name,*
> *And I leave them where they are, for I know that wheresoe'er I go,*
> *Others will punctually come for ever and ever.*

We are to revere and be thankful for the gift of God in and as our carnal expression—brain, eyes, ears, hands, feet, nose, lungs, heart, skin, stomach, kidneys, hair, nerves, bones and reproductive organs—all the many wonderful parts of our body temple. No part of us is evil or sinful or lower. Our body is not all we are, but it is certainly a miraculous expression of life. The body, sex, the "natural" world and the planet are not something to be overcome, subjugated, put down or ignored. We are to have reverence for our body and all other bodies.

LIFE GOES ON

We develop in our mother's womb for nine months and then we are born out into the opportunity for greater development and expression. The life experience in the womb ends, but it leads naturally to other possibilities. Development in the womb is followed by increased life opportunities. This is the way the Creator (creative life process) works.

In this lifetime, I am actually born again and again as I pass through various developmental stages and experiences. I see that although I change dramatically in many ways, I am still "me." When I graduate out of this body, I trust there is further life expression, development and work to do.

I remember driving down the highway and seeing a sign that said, "Where will you spend eternity?"

Where is "eternity"? When does "eternal life" begin? Does it start at physical death?

I believe that life is abundant and limitless. We are immortal beings, living in the midst of eternal life right now. The question then for me is not, "Where will I spend eternity?" but, "Am I living fully in the eternal now?"

SALUTATION TO THE DAWN

Look to this day,
for it is Life,
Within its brief span,
lie all the Verities,
and realities
of your existence.
The Bliss of Growth.
The Glory of Action.
The Splendor or Beauty.
For yesterday is but a Dream

> *and tomorrow is but a Vision*
> *but today well lived*
> *makes every Yesterday*
> *a dream of happiness*
> *and every tomorrow*
> *a vision of Hope.*
> *Look well therefore*
> *to this day.*
>
> The Sanskrit

The important realization for me is that life is not meas-
ured in terms of length but of quality. "Eternal life" refers to
the quality not the quantity of life. It is not just how long we
live but how well. Oliver Wendell Holmes said, "To be seventy years young is sometimes more cheerful and hopeful
than to be forty years old."

Our life is ageless, forever unfolding. Here is a powerful
statement of the life power based on Samuel Ullman's famous
"Youth." (Note how it manages to refer to many of the other
qualities we have called our Twelve Powers.)

> *Youth is not a time of life, it is a state of mind; it is*
> *not a matter of rosy cheeks, red lips and supple knees;*
> *it is a matter of the will, a quality of the imagination,*
> *a vigor of the emotions; it is the freshness of the deep*
> *springs of life.*
>
> *Youth means the predominance of courage over*
> *timidity, of adventure over the love of ease. This often*
> *exists in a man of sixty more than a boy of twenty.*
> *Nobody grows old merely by a number of years. We*
> *grow old by deserting our ideals.*
>
> *Years may wrinkle the skin, but to give up enthusi-*
> *asm wrinkles the soul. Worry, doubt, self-distrust, fear*

and despair—these bow the heart and turn the spirit back to dust.

Whether sixty or sixteen, there is in every human being's heart the love of wonder, the sweet amazement at the stars and the starlike things, the undaunted challenge of events, the unfailing childlike appetite for what-next, and the joy of the game of living.

You are as young as your faith, as old as your doubt; as young as your self-confidence, as old as your fear; as young as your hope, as old as your despair.

We can be more fully alive, alert and enthusiastic about life and living no matter what our chronological age may be. As George Bernard Shaw wrote,

I rejoice in life for its own sake. Life is no brief candle to me. It is a sort of splendid torch which I have got hold of for the moment, and I want to make it burn as brightly as possible before handing it on to future generations.

IMMORTAL JOURNEY

Gay Lynn. We often see our lives as beginning with birth and ending with death, as if these two events are bookends for our lives. In the larger scheme of things, at a soul level, this is not necessarily so. Our soul is on an immortal journey.

The English poet, William Wordsworth, captured this journey of the soul in *Ode on Intimations of Immortality, Section V:*

> *Our birth is but a sleep and a forgetting:*
> *The soul that rises with us, our life's star,*
> *Hath had elsewhere its setting,*
> *and cometh from afar:*
> *Not in entire forgetfulness,*
> *And not in utter nakedness,*
> *But trailing clouds of glory do we come*
> *From God, who is our home:*
> *Heaven lies about us in our infancy!*

And so, in the greater sense, life has no beginning and no end. You and I are always connected to life, and we are always connected to one another. We may say a person has died, but they remain alive inside of us, in our hearts, and in the immortal journey of their soul's life.

A loving couple named Sadie and John showed me this

beautiful thread of life and connectedness with one another. After forty years of marriage and being together, working side by side, John had a massive stroke.

David and I went to the hospital to see John, and there was his beautiful Sadie standing by his side, holding his hand and stroking his brow, as he lay motionless in a deep coma. We all joined hands and held John's hands and prayed together. As we prayed, a vivid image came into my mind of John standing in the middle of a tunnel. I could see the look of concern on his face, as he seemed to telepathically communicate with me that he could not come out of the tunnel, nor could he go through the tunnel. I did not say anything to Sadie but needed to tell David what I had seen. I was deeply concerned that John was unable to return, and he was not able to move on either. I wondered if we should say anything to Sadie. We decided to wait and see what happened over the next few days.

We spoke daily to Sadie, and about a week later she called to tell us that John had died. She said, "Right before the hospital called, I was at home doing some laundry. I felt John's presence close by me. I imagined that my wonderful husband was standing right in front of me, and I put my hands on his shoulders and said, 'It's okay if you need to go, John. I will be all right.'"

Sadie wept softly. I listened to Sadie and I too was filled with emotions as I remembered the tunnel. I could almost see John walking through it and waving goodbye. Sadie said, "It wasn't more than an hour later that the hospital called and said that I should come. I knew right away that John had died."

Beyond coma and unconsciousness, even beyond that passage that we call death, our lives and the power of life keep us eternally connected. The power of life is that golden thread that binds us together beyond space and time, within and yet beyond our physical bodies. The nature of this thread is formless, and you and I have the opportunity to give it shape and direction, and steadily stay in the flow of this life stream.

I can regenerate the life force in my own physical body, and be more energetically connected to my own life power and the power of life in those I love. It is a very common experience to have some intimation or flashes of concern when a loved one has had an accident or becomes ill or injured. You just "know" something has happened. In this experience I believe you and I are aware of the flow of the life power in the lives of our loved ones. This was so intimately illustrated by Sadie and John. They communicated life force to life force, and Sadie reassured John that he could leave her physically but that they would always be connected by their love and life power.

You can reflect daily on the power of life and being alive and vibrantly connected to all life. All people, even the planet, are alive. The ancient Greeks saw the planet as a living organism, Gaia. The native peoples of many cultures have had a personal relationship with Earth Mother and saw her as a precious living being.

Let us wake up to the life power more each day. My favorite Hebrew word is *L'chaim*—to life!

I sing the words of a chant to myself, often.

> *I am in the flow of life,*
> *I am in the flow of life,*
> *I am, I am, I am, I am,*
> *I am in the flow of life!*

SACRED SEXUALITY

A woman sat before me in counseling with great sadness at having been molested as a child. She had felt helpless and vulnerable and filled with shame and confusion around her sexuality. Now, years later, she was having trouble setting healthy boundaries with men and was sexually attracted to men who were abusive and emotionally unavailable.

Another man I counseled was confused and in pain as he tried to sort through being "emotionally incested" and abused by his mother. At an emotional level, he had been made to play the role of his mother's surrogate spouse. Now, he is sexually attracted to women who "need" him and have been hurt by other men. He has a desire to show them that he is different, that he can help them. The relationships end bitterly and yet he obsessively repeats the pattern. Really "nice" women seem sexually boring and unattractive.

A common theme in these stories, which I have heard for years in counseling, is that there is a feeling of sexual arousal and a desire to act it out with the people who continue the patterns of abuse and pain. How can this be? How can intelligent, educated, mature, sophisticated, spiritually aware people keep repeating these patterns?

It is so important to recognize that the body has a very strong and demanding voice. It can urge us in the wrong direction. The voice of the body can sometimes dictate our actions and override other parts of ourselves in any given moment.

The power of life-regeneration and particularly of our sexuality is one of the most potent of all our powers. We all face important decisions with how we use this power. We also have a great responsibility to help our children understand about healthy sexuality and to keep them safe in every way. This open dialogue is a critical key to changing the sexual abuse and misuse that still exist and are acted out inappropriately today.

Unfortunately, sexual abuse and sexually transmitted diseases are a huge problem of epidemic proportions in our society. When a person is violated or molested or is a victim of incest, rape or of obsessive attention being given to his (her) genitals, the messages in the mind, body and spirit are distorted. In these cases, counseling is suggested to recognize the unhealthy patterns. Some people do not even realize that the model they have had for sexuality has been distorted and is dysfunctional.

We need to talk about and understand both the functional and dysfunctional behaviors that exist, so that people are not vulnerable because they are uninformed. We must go beyond the biology of sexual function and address more traumatic issues like "date rape." Sexual maturity and changes are happening earlier in children, who also are deeply influenced by TV programs, movies and the Internet. Our children are sexually aware and active at increasingly younger ages. Our ability to share in open dialogue is the best way to keep our children safe, healthy, and confident in handling their own sexuality and the sexual impulses of others.

In order to help our children and to help us as adults, we need to create and develop a model of healthy, caring, sexually intimate relationships, which are clear in their overall focus and yet leave openness for each individual expression. In developing an open dialogue, we can gain knowledge that leads to new levels of self-esteem and self-respect. We can make new choices in sharing this precious part of ourselves in meaningful and mutually satisfying ways. Enjoyed wisely, in the right time, with a loving person in a committed and long-term relationship, our sexual energy can heal, energize and uplift us with a passion for life and living.

Used unwisely and out of balance, our sexual energy can be destructive, de-energizing and lead to emptiness and maybe disease with the advent of AIDS and other communicable viruses. Perhaps the onset of these sexually transmitted diseases has made us more open and conscious of our sexuality and the impact that it has on all our lives. We cannot avoid talking about this power. To deny our sexuality is to deny a vital part of our life energy and flow. But how can we elevate our awareness of this great power in a vacuum of silence? We must be open to many appropriate ways to have caring conversations with our loved ones, children and each other, so we all carry illumination rather than shame and embarrassment around the subject of sex.

The most important thing to keep in mind as you explore your own sexual life and experiences is that the longing for union with another is normal and natural. Remember, that which we are ultimately longing for is union with the Divine. I am sure as you keep this desire foremost in your thoughts and prayers, you will be guided to a satisfying and loving relationship.

Our purpose in all things that we do is to find a greater union with the Divine. No matter what it is we may be searching for, the goal is union with our Higher Self. Finding this, we experience an ecstasy because we are truly uniting with our deep self, the Divine, that same expression of the Divine within another human being.

Keeping sacredness around our sexuality immediately elevates it and the whole experience to a higher vibrational level. Clearly, sexuality is a joyful part of our existence and can be celebrated as a sacred act of love and shared union with all of creation.

REBIRTH AND RENEWAL

In the Scriptures, Romans 8:22, Paul puts forth the image of giving birth: "From the beginning till now the entire creation, as we know, has been groaning in one act of giving birth; and not only creation, but all of us who possess the first fruits of the Spirit, we too groan inwardly as we wait for our bodies to be set free—ready and able to deliver the first fruits of the Spirit."

The "fruits" refer to the creative impulses of the universe pouring through you and me. Our part is to lovingly cooperate and give birth to the Divine: Creating music, raising a family, writing a book, creating a life work, whatever that "fruit of the Spirit" is for me and you. We are all pregnant with the Divine. It does not matter if you are a man or a woman, if you are ten years old or 100—all of us conceive, gestate and deliver the creations or fruits of the Spirit. Our understanding of the Motherhood of God can help us to go "full term" and deliver with ease all that each of us is called to imagine and birth. The Mothering aspect of the Divine is nurturing, patient, in tune with the rhythms and stages of development.

Your contribution is essential. There are things you are to imagine and birth that can only come through you! What are some of those things? Dreams often show pregnancy or a baby, indicating new life and fresh possibilities. Imagine that you are pregnant, or that you have a newborn. What is it that you are birthing? What is calling you? What quality would you like to bring into the world?

Perhaps you are a peacemaker and you begin by creating peace in your home. Maybe you are an inventor and new ideas spring forth from within you. Perhaps you are wise and you help to teach and inspire people. Maybe you are kind and you give service with care and consideration. Or maybe you are a healer and your talents bring comfort and health to many.

What life expressions or creative ideas want to be expressed by you? These are your "babies" and you give them life! What can you do to help birth this baby today?

What you can conceive and believe, you can achieve!

REPRODUCTIVE SYSTEM

Dr. Robert. Our power of life-regeneration expresses in our physical body through our male or female reproductive system. With these organs, man and woman may procreate, bringing forth a precious son or daughter. Let's always remember, however, that we are not so much creators as we are co-creators with the Divine. For it is Spirit that breathes life into each child, who is first and foremost a child of God.

In the physical body, the male reproductive organs include the testes, epididymis, seminal duct, prostate gland and penis. (See Figure 12A.) The female reproductive organs include the ovaries, vagina, uterus, fallopian tubes and breasts. (See Figure 12B.)

In the male, sperm or reproductive cells are produced in the testes. Each sperm carries twenty-three chromosomes containing genes or hereditary factors that are transmitted from one generation to the next. With ejaculation during sexual intercourse, a duct system carries sperm through the erect penis into the woman's vagina. Accessory glands, including the prostate gland, form seminal fluid that is added to the sperm coming from the testes. Together, sperm and seminal fluid are called *semen*, from the Latin word for seed.

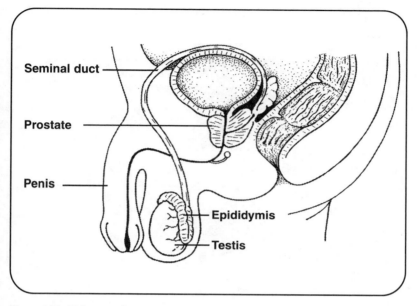

Figure 12A. Male reproductive system

In the female, the two ovaries contain a combined 500,000 ova or eggs, each of which has twenty-three chromosomes. During each menstrual cycle of approximately twenty-eight to thirty-two days, one ovum is released at about mid-cycle and is swept into one of the two fallopian tubes that are attached to the pear-shaped uterus or womb. If one sperm does not fertilize the egg, then the ovum disintegrates. In about fourteen days, the lining of the uterus, which has grown in preparation for a possible pregnancy, is shed, causing normal menstrual bleeding of about three to five days.

However, if sperm have traveled from the vagina up into the uterus and fallopian tubes, then a single sperm may join with the ovum. Now the combined forty-six chromosomes of the sperm and ovum begin directing the growth of an embryo,

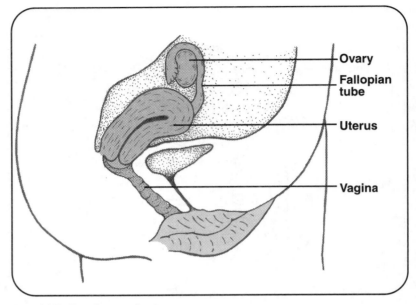

Figure 12B. Female reproductive system

which is embedded in the lining of the uterus. There it
becomes a fetus that grows for approximately nine months.
At birth, contractions of the uterus propel the baby through
the vagina and out of the mother's body. Ideally, milk produced by the mother's breasts or mammary glands provides
nourishment for the newborn infant.

CREATIVE LIFE FORCE

When I was about ten years old, our next-door neighbors,
Tom and Joyce, a couple in their early thirties, dearly wanted
to begin a family. Of course, I was too young to realize this,
but I do remember my parents talking about it in a general
way. Apparently, Tom and Joyce tried to conceive for the
next six to eight years, but they were unsuccessful. They

went to numerous doctors for tests and further advice. The tests showed that Tom's sperm count was normal, and Joyce had no disease of her reproductive organs.

Finally, they decided to adopt. The whole neighborhood was excited when they brought home their beautiful new son. I can remember them bringing him over to our house. And then less than a year later, guess what happened—Joyce became pregnant!

You probably know someone who has had a similar experience, since it is relatively common, even in these days of advanced medical technology. In these instances, the woman may try too hard, may feel anxious about becoming a mother, or may think of herself as being infertile. Then, once she adopts and becomes a mother, she may relax and let go of her fears, false judgments and apprehensions. In response, her body's reproductive organs change so that she can now conceive. How marvelous, mysterious and yet profoundly simple and direct is the interaction between our creative life force and our reproductive system!

Thus, when we use our power of life-regeneration in a loving, wise and balanced fashion, our reproductive system generally is healthy and vibrant. If we have a healthy, balanced, loving attitude about our sexuality, this too contributes to the vitality of our reproductive organs and functions.

However, when we misuse or abuse our power of creative life force, then we may develop physical diseases or dysfunctions of our reproductive system. In males, these may include inflammation of the epididymis and testes; inflammation, enlargement and cancer of the prostate gland; impotence; and lowered sperm count. Female reproductive disorders include vaginal infections; pelvic inflammatory disease; uterine fibroids; ovarian cysts; irregular, painful or heavy menstrual periods; infertility; cysts, infections and benign growths of the breasts; and cancer of the uterus, ovaries or breasts. (In the United States, the largest number of new cancer cases involves the reproductive organs: cancer of the prostate in men and breast cancer in women.) Both men and women may contract sexually transmitted diseases such as gonorrhea, syphilis, chlamydial infections, genital herpes and AIDS.

When disease does develop, always see your healthcare provider. Take whatever medications or undergo whatever treatments are therapeutic. However, always remember to focus on your power of creative life force, since this power has a direct influence on your reproductive system. Bring this power of life into a positive state of balance and harmony, which then will reflect into your reproductive organs.

KUNDALINI: THE FIRE OF LIFE

In the East, in teachings like yoga, Hinduism and Buddhism, our power of life—our creative life force—is said to be located at the base of our spine, in the area near our regenerative chakra and organs. This power is called *kundalini*, which means "serpent power" or the "fire of life." This is our power of regeneration, renewal, re-creation and rebirth.

As we grow and evolve, the kundalini fire is said to rise up our spine and to open all our other chakras or spiritual centers, until the creative life force reaches and opens our crown chakra at the top of our head.

This symbolic description of the rising kundalini means that we are to use our creative life force in ways that uplift, inspire and heal ourselves and others. To do this, we also must use all of our other Twelve Powers. These include the power of release that expresses through the sacral chakra; strength that correlates with the spine; order at the solar plexus chakra; love which flows through the heart chakra;

will and power which express at the throat chakra; imagination and good judgment and enthusiasm that function through our third eye; understanding which externalizes through our five physical senses; and faith that is centered in the crown chakra.

In other words, we are to use our life power in conjunction with all our other powers in order to create good, whether that good involves our sexual exchanges, our work, our artistic endeavors, our family, friends or environment. When we create good works, good projects, good services and loving relationships, we bring about regeneration, rehabilitation, reformation and rebirth.

What happens when people use their creative life force in a misguided, unhealthy, selfish way, without the proper infusion of their other powers? They create disorder, disease and dysfunction.

So, when it comes to our creative life force, we have the power to bring about regeneration or degeneration. We can have healthy, balanced, committed, loving sexual relations that are an integral and sacred part of our life; or we can misuse or abuse our sexual, creative energies.

Therefore, let's be sure that we always think and act in ways that create regeneration, which truly serve the highest good of all people involved. By creating good, by helping others, by bringing about healing, balance and upliftment, we continually reinvigorate and revitalize our mind, soul and body. We help to reform and renew all life on our beloved planet Earth.

Sit quietly in meditation and begin to focus on the base of your spine, where the kundalini or fire of life is said to initially dwell. This is the general area of your regenerative chakra, which is the center for the creative life force, the power of regeneration that is eternally within you.

Now imagine the creative life energy beginning to rise up your spine, up from the areas of the sacral and regenerative chakras. The kundalini power or fire of life moves up the spine to the solar plexus chakra, the heart chakra, the throat chakra, the third eye chakra and finally to the crown chakra at the top of the head. As the kundalini rises into each chakra or power center, you feel and see that chakra and the corresponding body organs being empowered with new, vitalizing, creative energy.

When the life force reaches the crown chakra and brain, it continues to rise up a couple feet over your head. Then, it showers down upon you, flowing down around your body, spilling out into your auric field that extends a foot or two from your physical form, flowing down your spine and into all other parts of your body. In particular, direct this regenerative energy to any part of your body that needs rebalancing, rejuvenation and renewal. If you are having difficulty with your reproductive system, then focus your creative life force in this region.

In time, you feel like you have been filled to overflowing with the power of the creative life force. Your mind, body and soul are renewed, recharged, revitalized and regenerated.

Now you are filled to the brim with light. You have become a body of light. You birth your light body.

1. I am alive!
2. I love life and life loves me.
3. I value and love my body, and I always speak positive words about my body.
4. God is the unending Source of my life.
5. My life is a miracle in the making.
6. I speak words of life and energy to each organ and cell of my body.
7. I have reverence for life.
8. I give myself permission to enjoy life and to live fully.
9. I am grateful for my life and for every opportunity to learn and grow.
10. Today is the first day of the rest of my life.
11. I live life abundantly.
12. I am the ever-renewing, ever-unfolding expression of infinite life.
13. I take time in my busy life to be renewed in spirit, mind and body.
14. I am leaving a legacy in this world, which attests to a life well lived by me.
15. I am connected to the infinite thread of life, which is ongoing.
16. Death is but a door to another phase of life.
17. I am free from the fear of death and the death wish. I live today with meaning and passion.
18. I communicate in love with those who have "passed on" from this life into the next.

19. I travel the eternal highway of continuous life improvement and opportunity.
20. I give birth to the good within me.
21. I am regenerated and renewed in the light, love and life of my I Am Self.
22. I carefully and lovingly use my life energy, always doing that which helps, heals, uplifts and prospers myself and others.
23. I am reborn daily.
24. I am born again and again and again and again in the light.
25. In all the desires of my mind, body and spirit, I am seeking union with the Divine.
26. My sexuality is a sacred part of my spirituality.
27. I wisely balance my sexual desires with wisdom and understanding and all my other Powers.
28. The urge of life is vibrant within my body. Every cell tingles and pulsates and is alive.
29. The kundalini or fire of life rises within me as I create good in all parts of my life.
30. All that I think, feel and do regenerates my whole being.

APPENDIX A:

CORRELATION OF DISCIPLES AND POWERS

C harles Fillmore was an avid student and teacher of a metaphysical interpretation of the Bible. He spent much of his meditation and study seeking what were, for him, meaningful correlations between Bible names and the qualities they represent in every person. He correlated each of the Twelve Powers with one of the twelve disciples of Jesus. We find these correlations interesting as metaphors for the serious student to consider, but have not included them extensively in our book because they are somewhat speculative and not essential to working with your Powers.

Following is a list of how Mr. Fillmore correlated the Twelve Powers with the twelve disciples:

POWER	DISCIPLE
Faith	Peter
Love	John
Strength	Andrew
Wisdom	James Zebedee
Power	Philip
Imagination	Bartholomew
Understanding	Thomas
Will	Matthew
Order	James Alphaeus
Enthusiasm	Simon the Zealot
Release	Thaddeus
Life	Judas Iscariot

For further study on these correlations, see *The Twelve Powers* by Charles Fillmore, *Metaphysical Bible Dictionary* by Unity School, and *Birth of the Light Body* by Nada-Yolanda and Robert Knapp, M.D.

APPENDIX B:

CORRELATIONS WITH BODY CENTERS

Many books on the Twelve Powers refer to the body-center locations postulated by Charles Fillmore in *The Twelve Powers of Man*, originally published in 1930. We have suggested a modern medical updating of these body locations as carefully researched and used by a medical doctor—a help that none of the other writers has had, including Mr. Fillmore. Dr. Robert Knapp confirms most of the locations or energy centers as theorized by Charles Fillmore and expands our understanding of our Powers in the light of modern-day scientific knowledge. No doubt, science will continue to make amazing discoveries, and these should be added to our awareness of how our Powers function in our bodies and in our lives.

The following chart shows the Twelve Powers, along with Mr. Fillmore's and Dr. Knapp's correlating physical centers:

POWER	FILLMORE	KNAPP
Faith	Pineal gland	Cerebrum of brain
Love	Back of heart	Heart, liver, spleen
Strength	Low back/loins	Spine & nerves
Wisdom	Pit of stomach	Pituitary & endocrines
Power	Root of tongue	Larynx, muscles & limbs
Imagination	Between the eyes	Thalamus of brain
Understanding	Front brain	Five physical senses
Will	Center front brain	Respiratory system

POWER	FILLMORE	KNAPP
Order	Navel	Digestive system, skin, bones
Enthusiasm	Medulla oblongata	Hypothalamus & medulla oblongata
Release	Lower abdomen	Colon & urinary system
Life	Generative organs	Reproductive system

A MODERN UPDATE

Dr. Knapp offers the following comments about the reasons for his confirmation and updating of the correlating body centers that were proposed by Charles Fillmore:

In his writings, Mr. Fillmore said that when he focused on a particular Power, he would feel a corresponding stimulation, activation, quickening or tingling in a specific part of his body. He often referred to these locations as "nerve centers" because he felt it was the nerves that were being stimulated. Then, given what he knew of anatomy and physiology, he also correlated the Powers with particular organs of the body. A majority of his insights and correlations were brilliant, decades ahead of what scientists and researchers have begun to understand about the interconnection between the spirit, mind, emotions and body.

However, Mr. Fillmore was not a physician or scientist. Moreover, in the 1920s when he formulated his correlations, the functions of many body organs were not known. Therefore, it appears that some of his correlations need further elucidation and updating. In some instances, it appears that he had the right general location but not the best correlation with a particular organ.

FAITH—CEREBRUM OF BRAIN. Mr. Fillmore located the faith faculty in the pineal gland, in the upper central portion of the brain, between the two cerebral hemispheres. (See Figure 4, p. 88.) I (Dr. Knapp) have positioned the faith power in the same general location, but have placed it primarily in the cerebrum of the brain. (See Figure 1, p. 15.) Fillmore wrote that faith is the "perceiving power of the mind." In the physical body, this ability to perceive takes place in the cerebrum. The cerebrum contains the key cells and centers that serve as the computer circuitry for anchoring and experiencing our thoughts, feelings and memories; and for coming into communion with our spiritual Self.

In Fillmore's time, the pineal was commonly referred to as being the seat of the soul. In esoteric anatomy, the pineal is the endocrine gland that corresponds to the crown chakra at the top of the head. Moreover, we now know that the pineal secretes the hormone melatonin, which helps to regulate whether the cerebrum is in its awake or sleep mode. Thus, for all of these reasons, it is understandable why Mr. Fillmore would have designated the pineal as being the faith center.

LOVE—HEART AND CIRCULATORY SYSTEM. Fillmore placed the power of love at the back of the heart. This correlation of love with the heart is commonly accepted today. To it, I have added all the other organs that are involved in the circulation of the blood. These include the liver, spleen, blood vessels and lymphatic system (See Figure 2, page 41). Anything having to do primarily with the blood correlates with love.

STRENGTH—SPINE AND NERVES. Fillmore placed the power of strength in the low-back region, in what he called the loins which is the area between the lowest ribs and the hipbones, including the lower part of the spine. (The word "loins" also may be used to refer to the genital or pubic area.) One interpretation of this placement has been that it refers to the muscles of the low back. However, it seems that strength correlates more specifically with the spinal cord and nerves, which innervate the low-back muscles and the muscles throughout the body (See Figure 3, page 62).

The spinal cord passes from the base of the skull down through the spinal vertebrae, which make up the spinal column or backbone, to the low back area. Many nerves branch out from the base of the spinal cord to innervate the low back and the entire lower body. When people have problems with strength-stability-steadfastness, they commonly feel pain or discomfort in their low back region.

Thus, it would seem that what Mr. Fillmore was sensing in his low back when he focused on the power of strength-stability-steadfastness was primarily his spinal cord and nerves. Moreover, it is the steady and stable functioning of the spinal cord and nerves that confers strength to our whole body.

WISDOM—ENDOCRINE GLANDS. Fillmore placed this power at the pit of the stomach. I have placed it at the pituitary gland and the rest of the endocrine glands, including the pancreas which is located behind the stomach (See Figure 4, page 88). The pancreas serves as a wise judge that regulates blood sugar by releasing two hormones, insulin and glucagon. Perhaps Mr. Fillmore was sensing the functioning of the pancreas when he focused on the power of wisdom-judgment.

Of all the body organs, the pituitary and other endocrine glands most closely portray the aspect of judgment. They carefully weigh and evaluate the level of circulating hormones, then secrete just the right amount of their hormones to bring a wise balance and harmony to the whole body.

Fillmore did not correlate any of the Twelve Powers with the pituitary and other endocrine glands (other than the pineal gland). The functions of many of these glands were not known in the 1920s.

Two of the apostles, who represent the Twelve Powers, were named James: James Zebedee and James Alphaeus. Fillmore postulated that James Zebedee represented the power of wisdom-judgment whereas James Alphaeus portrayed the power of order. He placed both of these powers in the same general location: wisdom-judgment in the pit of the stomach, and order at the navel. Rather than both of them being in the same general area, it is more in keeping with the actual functioning of the body that James Zebedee-wisdom-judgment correlates with the endocrine glands, whereas James Alphaeus-order correlates with the digestive system in the area in back of the navel (See further description below about order-digestive system.)

POWER—LARYNX, MUSCLES AND LIMBS. Fillmore correlated the faculty of power with the throat (which includes the larynx or voicebox) and the root of the tongue (See Figures 5A and 5B, page 114). I certainly agree with his ideas on this. Eastern teachings likewise speak of the throat chakra as being the center for power.

In addition to Fillmore's correlations, I have added the muscles and the limbs: arms and legs (See Figure 5C, page 118). The muscles are the only organs that can change shape. When the muscles contract and relax, they move the bones to which they are attached. This movement brings power and dominion on the physical level, which is expressed especially by the arms and legs.

IMAGINATION—THALAMUS. Fillmore placed the imagination faculty between the eyes. Indeed, when we receive or create new images, we may feel activity in the forehead region, including between the eyes. In addition to this general area, I have correlated imagination with the thalamus in the center of the brain (See Figure 6A, page 140).

In Fillmore's day, little was known about the functioning of the thalamus. Even today, it is considered primarily as an integration center for information gathered by the five senses as this data travels to the cerebrum. However, the thalamus also serves as an integration center or way station for the use of our imagination faculty. Psychic impressions or images register first in the third-eye screen in the forehead area, and then anchor into the physical body at the thalamus, which relays the images to the cerebrum.

UNDERSTANDING—FIVE PHYSICAL SENSES. Fillmore positioned this power in the front brain. I have correlated understanding with the five physical senses that gather a vast amount of data from the physical dimension (See Figures 7A and 7B, pages 174 and 175). Without this data, we cannot understand our place and function in the physical world. Fillmore did not correlate any of the Powers with the five senses.

When we gather information via our physical senses, we also need to analyze, comprehend and understand it. This takes place in several different parts of the cerebrum. Some of our higher understanding capabilities are now known to occur in the frontal lobes of the cerebrum, in other words in the front brain. According to the latest scientific studies, this area of the brain is essential for abstract thinking, conceptual planning, foresight and mature judgment. Perhaps this is why Fillmore felt activation of his front brain when he focused on his power of understanding.

WILL—RESPIRATORY SYSTEM. Fillmore correlated this power with the central front brain. I have placed it in the respiratory system: nose, sinuses, trachea, bronchi and lungs (See Figure 8, page 196). Fillmore made no correlation of any Power with this major system in the body.

Here again, as with understanding, when Fillmore focused on the power of will, he may have been sensing the higher will functions that do involve the frontal lobes of the cerebrum. According to medical studies, individuals with lesions (such as tumors) of their frontal lobes have difficulties with initiative and volition. Volition means "the act of willing, choosing or resolving; the exercise of will."

ORDER—DIGESTIVE SYSTEM, SKIN AND BONES. Fillmore located the power of order at the general area of the navel. Obviously, the navel itself has no function. Rather, it would seem that Fillmore was focusing on a general region, which I have correlated specifically with the digestive system (See Figure 9, page 226). The major parts of the digestive system include the stomach and small intestine, which are located in the area behind the navel. In regards to the power of order, I have also added the bones that give the body its solid internal framework, and the skin that serves as its external covering and boundary.

ENTHUSIASM—MEDULLA OBLONGATA AND HYPOTHALAMUS. Fillmore related this power to the base of the brain, and particularly to the medulla oblongata. To this I have added the hypothalamus and the entire brainstem, of which the medulla oblongata is a part (See Figure 10, page 251). Scientists knew little about the function of the hypothalamus in the 1920s. Its close interaction with the pituitary gland, and its regulation of the body's metabolic rate and energy level, were not discovered until the late 1960s. Centers in the midbrain that help to regulate our mood— from elation to depression—were not delineated until the 1970s. Yet, Fillmore somehow correctly "knew" that this area at the base of the brain expressed the power of zeal-enthusiasm.

RELEASE—COLON AND URINARY SYSTEM. Fillmore wisely gave the general location as the abdominal region and wrote specifically of the colon (See Figure 11A, page 278).

This interconnection between release-elimination and the colon seems obvious. To this I have added the urinary system—kidneys, ureters, bladder and urethra—which eliminate excess fluid, minerals and wastes from the body (See Figure 11B, page 282).

LIFE—REPRODUCTIVE SYSTEM. Fillmore correlated the power of life-regeneration with the generative function and organs. These are also called the reproductive organs (See Figures 12A and 12B, pages 307 and 308). I fully concur with this correlation, which is another one that seems obvious and apparent.

APPENDIX C:
COLOR CORRELATIONS

Some of the books and courses on the Twelve Powers refer to a correlation of a color with each of the Powers. Charles Fillmore made no color correlations. These were originally formulated in Unity Church by Joel Baehr, a Unity minister who has a master's degree from the Cranbrook Academy of Art in Bloomfield Hills, Michigan. Dr. Knapp has also used other color correlations that were received inspirationally by Nada-Yolanda, as given in her and Dr. Knapp's book, *Birth of the Light Body*.

We have not made an issue of the colors in this book because they are fairly subjective. They are interesting to experiment with, but they are not essential to your ability to understand and work with your Powers.

For your information and comparison, however, we list here the two most popular color correlation systems:

POWER	JOEL BAEHR	*BIRTH* BOOK
Faith	True blue	Royal blue
Love	Pink	White
Strength	Spring green	Lemon yellow
Wisdom	Yellow	Green
Power	Purple	Aqua
Imagination	Light blue	Crystal clear
Understanding	Gold	Cream yellow
Will	Silver	Sky blue
Order	Olive green	Mustard yellow
Enthusiasm	Orange	Pink
Release	Russet	Violet
Life	Red	Red

RESOURCES

Blue Ribbons. "Who I Am Makes a Difference" ribbons are available from Helice Bridges, Difference Makers International, P.O. Box 2115, Del Mar, CA 92014. Phone: 800-887-8422. California residents call: 760-634-1851. E-Mail: *ablueribbon@aol.com*; Web site: *www.blueribbons.com*

The Traveler by James Dillet Freeman is available in a small folder for "he" or "she" from Unity School, 1901 NW Blue Parkway, Unity Village, MO 64065, or from any local Unity chapter.

Phoenix Medallions. These come in packages of 60 for $15. The explanation for using these is found in the Williamsons' book *Transformative Rituals*. The Transformative Center, 2750 Van Buren Street, Hollywood, FL 33020. Phone: 954-922-5521 Fax: 954-922-2762

Home Blessing Decal. "This House Is Protected By God" decal was created as a visual affirmation and reminder that God is our source of divine protection. Using the six colors of the rainbow, it is a dazzling piece of art that illuminates any window or door in your home (size 3¼" by 3¼"). The decal is available from Things To Be Done, 20001 Greenfield Road, Detroit, MI 48235. Price: $3.50, plus postage. Quantity discounts available. Phone: 313-835-5059

Twelve Powers in You: 52 Weekly Lessons by David Williamson. These are the originating lessons on which the "Spirit" sections of the book *Twelve Powers in You* are based. These lessons come in a notebook form and are designed for a year-long weekly program of study. They are available from The Transformative Center, 2750 Van Buren Street, Hollywood, FL 33020. Phone: 954-922-5521. $25.

I Am Golden Light music/song tape. This forty-minute cassette has one original, lyrical, uplifting song for each of the Twelve Powers. Songs were written and performed by Deborah Jacobs and Janet Thiemermann, longtime students of the Twelve Powers. Available from The Transformative Center, phone: 954-922-5521, and from Mark-Age, Inc., phone: 423-784-3269. $12.

Birth of the Light Body. The metaphysical sections of this treatise on the Twelve Powers were inspirationally received and written by Nada-Yolanda, executive director of Mark-Age, Inc. Robert Knapp, M.D. researched and wrote the medical-physical sections, which are the primary source for the "Body" sections in the book *Twelve Powers in You*. This text and a free introductory catalog are available from Mark-Age, Inc., P.O. Box 10, Pioneer, TN 37847. Phone: 423-784-3269. E-mail: *iamnation@aol.com*. $17.

Amnesia Video—Irv Rudley. Irv produced the fourteen-part TV/video series that is also titled *Twelve Powers In You*, which is the companion to the book *Twelve Powers In You*. Many of the photos in this book come from these videos. For your own consultation or video project, contact him in Hollywood, FL at: 954-927-2040.

NOTES

Chapter 2: The Power of Love

p. 45 "In one study, Harvard students" McClelland, D.C. and C. Kirshnit. "The effect of motivational arousal through films on salivary immunoglobulin A." *Psychology and Health,* 1988, 2:31-52.

p. 45 "In another study, researchers" Cohen, S., W. J. Doyle, D. P. Skoner, et al. "Social ties and susceptibility to the common cold." *Journal of the American Medical Association,* 1997, 277:1940-44.

p. 45 "Another study revealed that people" Thomas, C. B., and K. R. Dusynski. "Closeness to parents and the family constellation in a prospective study of five disease states: suicide, mental illness, malignant tumor, hypertension, and coronary heart disease." *Johns Hopkins Medical Journal,* 1974, 134:251.

p. 45 "A different study of 1,100 men" Graves, P. L., C. B. Thomas, and L. A. Mead. "Familial and psychological predictors of cancer." *Cancer Detection & Prevention,* 1991, 15(1):59-64.

p. 46 "In a review of forty-five" Miller, T. Q., T. W. Smith, C. W. Turner, et al. "A meta-analytic review of research on hostility and physical health." *Psychological Bulletin,* 1996, 119:322-48.

p. 46 "Researchers have discovered" Seeman, T. E., and S.

L. Syme. "Social networks and coronary artery disease: a comparison of the structure and function of social relations as predictors of disease." *Psychosomatic Medicine,* 1987, 49(4):341-54

Chapter 8: The Power of Will

p. 197 "In one classic study" K. Purcell et al. "Effects on asthma in children of experimental separation from the family." *Psychosomatic Medicine,* 1969, 31:144.

p. 197 "In another compelling" S. Locke and D. Collagen, *The Healer Within: The New Medicine of Mind and Body* (New York: E. P. Dutton, 1986), 141.

BIBLIOGRAPHY

Alcoholics Anonymous. New York: Alcoholics Anonymous World Services, Inc., 1939.

Allan, James. *As a Man Thinketh.* New York: Barnes & Noble, 1992.

Angelou, Maya. *The Complete Collected Poems of Maya Angelou.* New York: Random House, 1994.

Artess, Lauren. *Walking a Sacred Path: Rediscovering the Labyrinth as a Spiritual Tool.* New York: Riverhead Books, 1995.

Benson, Herbert. *Timeless Healing: The Power and Biology of Belief.* New York: Scribner, 1996.

Bradshaw, John. *Bradshaw On: The Family: A Revolutionary Way of Self-Discovery.* Deerfield Beach, Fla.: Health Communications, Inc., 1988.

Butterworth, Eric. *Spiritual Economics: The Prosperity Process.* Unity Village, Mo.: Unity Books, 1983.

———. *The Concentric Perspective: What's in It from Me!* Unity Village, Mo.: Unity Books, 1989.

Campbell, Joseph. *The Power of Myth.* New York: Bantam, Doubleday, Dell Publishing Group, 1991.

Canfield, Jack and Mark Victor Hansen. *Chicken Soup for the Soul.* Deerfield Beach, Fla.: Health Communications, Inc., 1994.

Chotzinoff, Samuel. *Toscanini: An Intimate Portrait.* New York: Alfred A. Knopf, 1956.

Clissold, Stephen. *St. Teresa of Avila.* London: Sheldon Press, 1979.

Colgrove, Melba, Harold Bloomfield, and Peter McWilliams. *How to Survive the Loss of a Love.* Los Angeles: Prelude Press, 1993.

Lama, Dalai. *The Art of Happiness*. New York: Riverhead Books, 1998.

Drummond, Henry. *Love: The Greatest Thing in the World*. Uhrichville, Ohio: Barbour & Co., 1994.

Eikerenkoetter, Frederick (Reverend Ike). *The Disciples: Your Twelvefold Divine Power* cassette album. Thinkonomics, P.O. Box 15725, Boston, MA 02215.

Eisler, Riane. *Sacred Pleasure*. New York: HarperCollins, 1995.

Faraday, Ann. *Dream Power: Learn to Use the Vital Self-Knowledge That Lies Stored in Your Dreams*. New York: Berkley Books, 1972.

Fillmore, Charles. *The Twelve Powers of Man*. Unity Village, Mo.: Unity Books, 1930 (republished in 1999 as *The Twelve Powers with Christ Enthroned in Man* by Cora Dedrick Fillmore).

Fillmore, Charles. *Christian Healing*. Unity Village, Mo.: Unity Books, 1920.

Fox, Matthew. *Meditations with Meister Eckhart*. Santa Fe, N.M.: Bear & Company, Inc., 1983.

Freeman, James Dillet. *The Story of Unity*. Unity Village, Mo.: Unity Books, 1954.

————. *Be!* Unity Village, Mo.: Unity Books, 1957.

————. *Of Time and Eternity*. Unity Village, Mo.: Unity Books, 1981.

Friedman, Meyer, and Ray H. Rosenman. *Type A Behavior and Your Heart*. New York: Alfred A. Knopf, 1974.

Gaither, James, compiled with commentary. *The Essential Charles Fillmore*. Unity Village, Mo.: Unity Books, 1999.

Gandhi, Mohandas K. *An Autobiography or The Story of My Experiments with Truth*. Ahmadabad, India: Navajivan Publishing House, 1949.

Garfield, Charles A. *Peak Performance: Mental Training*

Techniques of the World's Greatest Athletes. Los Angeles: Jeremy P. Tarcher, Inc., 1984.

Gibran, Kahlil. *Jesus: The Son of Man.* New York: Alfred A. Knopf, 1928.

———. *The Prophet.* New York: Alfred A. Knopf, 1923.

Gray, John. *What You Feel You Can Heal.* Mill Valley, Calif.: Heart Publishing, 1994.

Green, Elmer, and Alyce Green. *Beyond Biofeedback.* New York: Dell Publishing Co., 1977.

Hafen, Brent, et al. *Mind/Body Health.* Needham Heights, Mass.: Allyn & Bacon, 1996.

Hanh, Thich Nhat. *Living Buddha, Living Christ.* New York: Riverhead Books, 1995.

———. *The Long Road Turns to Joy: A Guide to Walking Meditation.* Berkeley, Calif.: Parallax Press, 1996.

———. *Peace Is Every Step.* New York: Bantam Books, 1991.

Hausmann, Winifred Wilkinson. *Your God-Given Potential: Unfolding the Twelve Spiritual Powers.* Unity Village, Mo.: Unity House, 1978.

Keirsey, David, and Marilyn Bates. *Please Understand Me: Character and Temperament Types.* Del Mar, Calif.: Prometheus Nemesis Book Company, 1984.

King, Martin Luther Jr. *Strength to Love.* Minneapolis: Augsburg Fortress Publishing, 1989.

Lewis, Jim. *The Twelve Thrones.* Denver: Unity Church, 1983. 3021 S. University Blvd., Denver, CO 80210.

Jackson, Phil, and Hugh Delehanty. *Sacred Hoops, Spiritual Lessons of a Hardwood Warrior.* New York: Hyperion Publishing, 1995.

Jacobs, Deborah, and Janet Thiemermann. *I Am Golden Light* Twelve Powers song tape. Hollywood, Fla.: The Transformative Center, 1999.

Jenkins, Peggy D. *A Child of God: Activities for Teaching*

Spiritual Values to Children of All Ages. Englewood Cliffs, N.J.: Prentice-Hall, Inc., 1984.

Jones, Laurie Beth. *Jesus C.E.O., Using Ancient Wisdom for Visionary Leadership.* New York: Hyperion Publishing, 1992.

Jung, Carl. *Man and His Symbols.* Garden City, N.Y.: Doubleday & Co., 1964.

Maday, Michael, ed. *New Thought for a New Millennium: Twelve Powers for the 21st Century.* Unity Village, Mo.: Unity Books, 1998.

Millman, Dan. *Everyday Enlightenment: The Twelve Gateways to Personal Growth.* New York: Warner Books, Inc., 1998.

Nada-Yolanda, and Robert Knapp, M.D. *Birth of the Light Body.* Kingsport, Tenn.: Quebecor Printing, Inc., 1995.

The New Jerusalem Bible. New York: Doubleday, 1985.

Ornish, Dean. *Love & Survival: The Scientific Basis for the Healing Power of Intimacy.* New York: HarperCollins, 1998.

————. *Dr. Dean Ornish's Program for Reversing Heart Disease.* New York: Ballantine Books, 1990.

Paulson, J. Sig. *Your Power to Be.* New York: Doubleday & Co., 1969.

Pietsch, William V. *Human Be-ing.* Available from Aztec Shops, San Diego State University, San Diego, CA 92182.

Ponder, Catherine. *The Healing Secret of the Ages.* West Nyack, N.Y.: Parker Publishing Co., Inc., 1966.

Progoff, Ira. *At a Journal Workshop: The Basic Text and Guide for Using the Intensive Journal Process.* New York: Dialogue House, 1975.

Rabel, Ed. *The Twelve Powers of Man* (cassette album currently not available). Unity Village, Mo.: Unity Cassettes.

Reeve, Christopher. *Still Me.* New York: Ballantine Books, 1998.

Reilly, Patricia Lynn. *A God Who Looks Like Me: Discovering a Woman-Affirming Spirituality.* New York: Ballantine Books, 1995.

Richardson, Marilyn K. *The Twelve Gifts from God: The Children's Material.* Lee's Summit, Missouri.

Roth, Charles. *A Twelve-Power Meditation Exercise.* Unity Village, Mo.: Unity Books, 1989.

Siegel, Bernie S. *Love, Medicine & Miracles.* New York: Harper & Row, 1986.

————. *Prescriptions for Living: Inspirational Lessons for a Joyful, Loving Life.* New York: HarperCollins, 1998.

Smith, Louis. *Twelve Powers Prayer/Self-Hypnosis Treatment* cassette. 600 N. Old Woodward, Suite 303, Birmingham, MI 48009.

Starbird, Margaret. *The Goddess in the Gospels: Reclaiming the Sacred Feminine.* Santa Fe, N.M.: Bear & Company, 1998.

————. *The Woman with the Alabaster Jar: Mary Magdalen and the Holy Grail.* Santa Fe, N.M.: Bear & Company, 1993.

Taylor, Jeremy. *Dream Work: Techniques for Discovering the Creative Power in Dreams.* New York: Paulist Press, 1983.

Vahle, Neal. *Torch-Bearer to Light the Way: The Life of Myrtle Fillmore.* Mill Valley, Calif.: Open View Press, 1996.

Warch, William. *How to Use Your Twelve Gifts from God.* Anaheim, Calif.: Christian Living Publishing, 1976.

Weatherhead, Leslie. *The Will of God.* Nashville, Tenn.: Abingdon Press, 1987.

Whitfield, Charles L. *Healing the Child Within.* Deerfield Beach, Fla.: Health Communications, Inc., 1987.

Williamson, David. *Twelve Powers in You: 52 Weekly*

Lessons (notebook with 52 study sheets). Hollywood, Fla.: The Transformative Center, 1999.

Williamson, Gay Lynn, and David Williamson. *God's Will for Me Is Good* (2 cassettes). Hollywood, Fla.: Unity of Hollywood, 1998.

———. *Transformative Rituals: Celebrations for Personal Growth.* Deerfield Beach, Fla.: Health Communications, Inc., 1994.

———. *Golden Eggs: Spiritual Wisdom for Birthing Our Lives.* Deerfield Beach, Fla.: Health Communications, Inc., 1996.

Witherspoon, Thomas E. *Myrtle Fillmore: Mother of Unity.* Unity Village, Mo.: Unity Books, 1977.